Milton's Wisdom

Christ and the Six Days of Creation. From Josephus's *The Antiquities of the Jews*. Bibliothèque Nationale. Latin 5047. Reprinted by permission.

Milton's Wisdom

Nature and Scripture in *Paradise Lost*

John Reichert

Ann Arbor

THE UNIVERSITY OF MICHIGAN PRESS

Copyright © by the University of Michigan 1992
All rights reserved
Published in the United States of America by
The University of Michigan Press
Manufactured in the United States of America

1995　1994　1993　1992　4　3　2　1

Library of Congress Cataloging-in-Publication Data

Reichert, John, 1935–
  Milton's wisdom : nature and scripture in Paradise lost / John Reichert.
    p.   cm.
  Includes bibliographical references and index.
  ISBN 0-472-10324-5 (alk. paper)
  1. Milton, John, 1608–1674. Paradise lost.   2. Bible in literature.   3. Wisdom in literature.   4. Nature in literature.   I. Title.
PR3562.R37   1992
821'.4—dc20   92-20087
                                                             CIP

For Judy

"With thee conversing..."

Acknowledgments

When I consider how often my own understanding of *Paradise Lost* has been deepened or expanded by the arguments and discoveries of other readers, I find it difficult not to think of criticism as a collaborative adventure, a sociable and only partly quixotic meandering along paths that lead us over time, for all the detours and dead ends, somewhat closer to the truth. I want, therefore, to express my gratitude to all the Miltonists whose names appear in the endnotes to this volume—both those who persuaded me and those who (but only after provoking me to think and think again) did not. I owe a debt at least as great to friends who have read various parts of this study in its earlier stages, shared their wisdom with me, and saved me from many a piece of foolishness: Charles Huttar of Hope College, Scott Elledge of Cornell, Peter Berek of Mount Holyoke College, and, at Williams, Ilona and Robert Bell, Stephen Fix, and Clara Park. The late John Stambaugh, a gifted classicist, linguist, and teacher, gently corrected and patiently augmented my small latin and less greek. John Knott, of the University of Michigan, read the entire manuscript in something like its present form, and I cherish the advice and encouragement he has given me over the years.

I am grateful to the President and Trustees of Williams College for their generous and continuing support of my research, and to the National Endowment for the Humanities for a Fellowship during the year in which this study began to take shape. Much of chapter 6 appeared in *ELH* 48 (1981) and is reprinted here with the permission of the Johns Hopkins University Press.

Contents

Introduction 1

Chapter

1. Milton's Wisdom and Spenser's 9

2. The Books of Wisdom 19

3. Nature, Scripture, and the Architecture of
   Paradise Lost 51

4. Meditating on the Creatures, Part 1:
   The Case of Satan 69

5. Meditating on the Creatures, Part 2:
   Milton, Eve, Adam, Raphael 99

6. The Arts of Conversation 133

7. Meditating on the Word 169

8. Wisdom and the Loss of Paradise 205

9. The Sum of Wisdom 231

Appendixes

A. The Prologues to Books 3 and 7 261

B. Augustine, the Creatures, and the Love of God 267

Notes 271

Index 293

Introduction

> The end then of learning is to repair the ruins of our first parents by regaining to know God aright, and out of that knowledge to love him, to imitate him, to be like him, as we may the nearest by possessing our souls of true vertue, which being united to the heavenly grace of faith makes up the highest perfection. But because our understanding cannot in this body found it selfe but on sensible things, nor arrive so cleerly to the knowledge of God and things invisible as by orderly conning over the visible and inferior creature, the same method is necessarily to be followed in all discreet teaching.
> —*Of Education* (1644)

Milton's terse description of the aim of learning and the method by which it can be achieved is suggestive in several ways, not least in the indication it gives that he was persuaded at the time that the ruins of our first parents *can* be repaired, and that the preferred way of gaining access to things invisible to mortal sight and thus "regaining to know God aright" is to con over "the visible and inferior creature," otherwise known as the book of nature, or the book of God's works. Neither of these claims was universally accepted during the Reformation, and the question of whether Milton accepted either of them when he came to write *Paradise Lost* has exercised a good many minds.

The pedagogical method Milton recommends is likewise of interest because the recommendation is underwritten by another book—Scripture, or the book of God's Word—which gives authority to it. In his Letter to the Romans Paul asserts that "the invisible things of [God] from the creation are clearly seen, being understood by the things that are made, even his eternal power and Godhead" (Rom. 1:20–21). Scripture is likewise inscribed, needless to say, in the poetry of *Paradise Lost*. Consider, to cite an obvious example, the way one of

Moses' many curses on those who do not serve the Lord ("And among these nations shalt thou find no ease, neither shall the sole of thy foot have rest" [Deut. 28:65]) reappears, when we read of Satan making his painful way over the fiery and lava-like "land" in hell, in Milton's wryly understated and sarcastic comment: "Such resting found the sole / Of unblessed feet" (1.237–38).[1]

Whether Milton's little treatise would leave the students much time for the conning over of the creatures, given the extraordinary number of authors whose own books will be assigned readings in the Miltonic curriculum, is an open question. What is not at question is that much of *Paradise Lost* is concerned with the instruction given to Adam and Eve in how to interpret the two books, nature and Scripture, in which the wisdom of God was thought to be expressed. Sometimes it is Raphael, Michael, or the Son who attempts to teach them to know God aright; sometimes they learn on their own. Raphael teaches them, in Adam's words, about "the scale of nature," and how "in contemplation of created things / By steps [they] may ascend to God" (5.509–12). Eve, on the other hand, is clearly drawing on her own experience of "created things" when she calms Adam's anxiety at Raphael's arrival by reminding him that "small store will serve, where store, / All seasons, ripe for use hangs on the stalk; / Save what by frugal storing firmness gains / To nourish, and superfluous moist consumes" (5.322–25). Or again, Adam is trying hard to "read" Scripture as he struggles, with modest though incomplete success, to understand the meaning of God's warning, "the day thou eat'st thereof...inevitably thou shalt die" (8.329–30). He requires us, Adam says, to keep

> This one, this easy charge, of all the trees
> In Paradise that bear delicious fruit
> So various, not to taste that only tree
> Of knowledge, planted by the tree of life,
> So near grows death to life, whate'er death is,
> Some dreadful thing no doubt; for well thou know'st
> God hath pronounced it death to taste that tree,
> The only sign of our obedience left....
>
> (4.421–28)

I am persuaded that, though much good work has been done on the general subject of Milton's attitudes toward nature and Scripture,[2] the two books permeate the narrative and organize the rhythms of *Paradise Lost* in ways that have gone largely unnoticed, as have the many guises in which Urania's sister "eternal Wisdom," from whom nature and Scripture may be said to emanate, appears in the epic. In the pages that follow I invite the reader to take a close look at the poem through the perspective provided by the pairing of the two books.

The first chapter is devoted to Milton's critique in *Paradise Lost* of Spenser's treatment of nature, or the visible world of the creatures, in his "Hymne of Heavenly Love" and "Hymne of Heavenly Beautie." The contrast between the epic and the two hymns highlights the celebration, in *Paradise Lost,* not only of the creaturely glories of Eden, but also of the natural world into which we have fallen and in which we live. By wrenching the ideas and language of the hymns out of their original contexts and putting them in the mouths of unlikely characters in unlikely situations, Milton undermines Spenser's mysticism and the radical division he makes between the earthly and heavenly spheres. In so doing he also points up the distinction between Spenser's Sapience—a woman to be adored from afar—and his own far more affable and accessible Wisdom.

The notion that God's wisdom is expressed in the books of nature and Scripture would have been a familiar one to Milton's readers. In the second chapter I survey several of the most influential texts in this tradition in order, first, to give a sense of the variety of ways in which earlier writers had figured and conceptualized the two books, and second, to sketch the background of the epistemological controversies that arose in the Reformation over the relative value of the two books. My reading of the poem, both in this chapter and elsewhere, parts company with those which have tried to ally Milton with the Puritans' insistence on fallen man's inability to profit from the book of nature, their exclusive reliance on the Word. On the one hand, Milton had his own grave doubts about our ability to ground our interpretations of Scripture on sure foundations, and on the other, he invokes the law of nature in his prose with considerable frequency. *Paradise Lost* provides compelling evidence, furthermore, of his belief in the enduring capacity of the creatures to instruct and delight: Adam and Eve's distillation of the language of both the Roman (Sarum) and Protestant forms of worship in the "natural" liturgy they fashion on the basis of their own experience of the creatures;

the fallen Adam's remarkable success in learning to read the sights of woe and the visible signs of God's intentions that Michael reveals to him in Book 11; and the poem's frequent lyrical "tributes," as Louis Martz has called them, "to the beauty of the earth, as tended now by fallen man and woman."[3] Though Scripture may have remained the last word for Milton, he was closer, in these as well as in other respects, to the Anglican Hooker than to Calvin.[4]

In the prologue to Book 3 Milton presents himself, in his blindness, as having been denied access to "the book of knowledge fair," presented in its stead "with a universal blank / Of nature's works to [him] expunged and razed, / And wisdom at one entrance quite shut out" (3.47–50). In the prologue to Book 7, at which point "half yet remains unsung," he is concerned not with vision and the sight of nature's works, but with his need for Urania's "voice divine" to sustain his own "mortal voice" and "still govern [his] song," and his need as well for a "fit audience" (7.2–30). This turn from the reading of the visible world to the hearing and transmitting of the "voice divine" parallels the turn from the pedagogical method Michael employs in Book 11, where he instructs Adam to "behold" the effects of his "original crime" (11.423–24), and the method he employs in Book 12, where he instructs Adam, whose "mortal sight" is failing, to "give due audience, and attend" (12.9–12). Building on these turnings, I explore in the third chapter the possibility that nature and Scripture may have provided Milton with a thematic principle of symmetry for the ordering of the twelve books of *Paradise Lost,* with Books 1, 3–6, and 11 focusing on beholding the creatures, and 2, 7–10, and 12 focusing on listening to the Word.

When Satan beholds the creatures and meditates upon them in soliloquy, he characteristically responds with feelings of wonder, incipient love, appreciation, or well-grounded self-blame. They inevitably give way, however, to feelings of envy and resentment, or to a determination, the futility of which he almost always acknowledges, to destroy. The fourth chapter explores these meditations, noting in them his surprisingly full though always ineffectual understanding of God's design. These aspects of his habits of mind and feeling are so inconsonant with the standard view of the Satan of Books 1 and 2 as to suggest that that view is fundamentally mistaken and needs to be revised.[5] The chapter concludes with an attempt to provide the revision.

In the fifth chapter I consider several readings of the book of nature concentrated in Books 4 and 5, the readers including the poet, Adam and Eve, Raphael, and, yet once more, Satan. The poet's descriptive or "visual" passages are designed, I argue, to dislocate the reader, providing something analogous to the experience of losing one's way and standing in need of guidance. The garden thus takes on the appearance of a perfect place where the possibilities of getting lost or being tempted are always near at hand. A similar effect is created as we listen to Eve, Adam, Satan, and Raphael offering their own very different perspectives on nature as it appears at night, all of them revisions and expansions of the brief passage from the prologue to Book 3 in which Milton describes the world he can no longer see. The descriptions become increasingly sensuous as we are led along toward the stories of Satan's rebellion and the war in heaven. Raphael's description of the activities and pleasures of the angels on the evening prior to the uprising parallel those in which Eve and Adam engage in Eden, suggesting, as the poem so often suggests, the continuities between heaven and earth, the angelic and the human. The story of the war in heaven is also a story of the prototypical rape and destruction of nature's works, and as such, from my point of view, it brings to a close a thematic development that began, in Book 3, with the Father bending down his eye "his own works and their works at once to view" (59). The destruction prepares us for the new beginning manifested in Book 7 by the power of the "omnific Word" as it exacts obedience from the creatures waiting for the command to *be,* and from Chaos itself.

There is a tradition dating back at least as far as Dr. Johnson according to which Milton was regarded either as neither suited for nor interested in the dramatist's calling, and as incapable of creating characters possessed of what we would now call interiority. Johnson wrote that Milton "would not have excelled in dramatick writing" because "he knew human nature only in the gross, and had never studied the shades of character, nor the combinations of concurring or the perplexity of contending passions." In T. S. Eliot's more nastily dismissive view, Milton "had little interest in, or understanding of, individual human beings," and he lacked "that understanding which comes from an affectionate observation of men and women."[6] Nothing in Milton's writings save, perhaps, his portrayal of Satan more forcefully calls these judgments into question than his dramatization of the Fall, and of the conversations that lead up to and away from it. Those conversations are the subject of the sixth chapter. The Fall involves, of course, disobedience, a failure to heed the Word or a hearkening to the wrong voice, a disregard for God's "sole command." But both Eve's sin and Adam's also involve misreadings of the book of nature, the subversion or denial of the hierarchical order of the creatures. Eve is misled into elevating the brute to the level of the human. Adam exalts the woman above the man. Both, in Paul's words, "serve the creature more than the Creator" (Rom. 1:25). Both indulge in idol worship, which was traditionally regarded as the prime sin against the order of nature. The odd thing about them, though, is the uncanny intuition of God's plan, the faith in his wisdom and mercy, that each of them reveals at the most perilous moments— Eve in her arguments for working apart from Adam, and Adam in the reasons he gives for "submitting to what seemed remediless." These moments of insight and trust not only suggest why Adam and Eve are worth saving; they look beyond the Fall to their subsequent efforts, with God's help, to work out their own salvation.

If Adam and Eve in Book 9 fall away from the Word, in Book 10 they rediscover and remember it, gradually constructing from God's seemingly unrelated pronouncements a purpose and a means of achieving it. Adam's despairing soliloquy is an exemplary Puritan meditation on the Word, the words in this case being those God had spoken directly to him, i.e., "increase and multiply," and "for dust thou art, and shalt to dust return." During their subsequent conversations, as together they extend the meditative process, Adam and Eve reinterpret these words in the light of that other biblical "passage" that Eve recalls—the curse placed on the serpent—in a way that permits them to find grounds for overcoming despair and for turning to God in prayer. Their efforts bear fruit. Death is deferred, and they are given "many days" of grace wherein they may "repent" and cover "one bad act with many deeds well done" (11.254–58).

With the exception of Virginia R. Mollenkott's *Milton and the Apocrypha,* which lists many allusions in *Paradise Lost* to The Wisdom of Solomon and Ecclesiasticus,[7] very little notice has been taken of Milton's appropriation in the epic of the biblical Wisdom literature—an appropriation that I attempt to demonstrate in chapter 8. Those two apocryphal works, taken together with the canonical Job, Proverbs, and Ecclesiastes, in fact provide an intriguing if secondary perspective on several aspects of the poem, such as Adam's fervent desire to learn from Raphael as much as he can about the heavens, the earth, and himself; the nature of what he learns; and the relevance of the pursuit of wisdom to the Fall. Furthermore, both the Hebraic and classical Wisdom traditions held out the possibility of social intercourse and friendship between human beings and the gods, and the Hebraic tradition in particular pictures that intercourse in ways that ally it with the strong delight Adam takes in conversing with God and the archangels and they with him.

Like Ecclesiasticus and The Wisdom of Solomon, *Paradise Lost* concludes with a history of God's chosen people. Michael's initial purpose is to provide Adam with some recompense for his loss of the visible, audible presence of God and his angels. His primary aim—the subject of my concluding chapter—is to give him the knowledge and wisdom needed to face the not very brave new world he and Eve are about to enter. In Book 11, as many readers have noted, Michael attempts to "turn his pupil," as David Loewenstein has put it, "into a kind of semiologist, training him in the art of reading and interpreting God's signs in fallen history."[8] In the process, and in a way that accords with Milton's views on the emotive power of the genre of history, Michael subjects Adam to a vivid and emotion-fraught but ultimately purgative reawakening of those feelings he experienced in his despairing soliloquy in Book 10. In Book 12, in the course of a long discussion that returns again and again to the instability and corruptibility of language, the archangel instructs Adam in the reading of Scripture.[9] As the student responds to his catechist, we can hear him thinking and speaking in an increasingly scriptural idiom on his own, suggesting that the Spirit is working within him and that the law is written in his heart. Eve, too, has had a Scripture lesson, and she is given the last and most important word, the Word Adam had been at such pains to understand: "By me the promised seed shall all restore." As the couple leaves Paradise, therefore, they have within them, if nothing like an assurance, at least the makings, of a paradise within them happier far.

CHAPTER 1

Milton's Wisdom and Spenser's

Milton's Eve, as every reader of *Paradise Lost* knows, tastes a piece of fruit that is, she is sure, "of operation blest / To sapience" (9.796–97). When she describes to Adam the effect the fruit has on her, she says she feels "not death, but life /Augmented, opened eyes, new hopes, new joys, / Taste so divine, *that what of sweet before / Hath touched my sense, flat seems to this, and harsh*" (9.984–87).[1] Spenser, Milton's "better teacher" and his "original,"[2] described a woman the sight of whose face so fills one with inward "joy and pleasure" that "*all that earst seemd sweet, seemes now offense, / And all that pleased erst, now seemes to paine*" (269–70).[3] The woman whose aspect produces this effect is none other than Sapience herself, the eternal wisdom of God, his "soveraine dearling," a glimpse of whose "celestiall face" is the reward offered in Spenser's "An Hymne of Heavenly Beautie" to those happy few whose "high flying mynd[s]" can "mount up aloft through heavenly contemplation" to the very heaven of heavens.

The two italicized passages point to an important nexus between the "better teacher" and his student. Why was Milton at pains to identify Eve's joy upon tasting the forbidden fruit with the holy joy of Spenser's visionaries? We recognize of course that Eve's experience is in some sense illusory, even if she is accurately reporting how things *feel* or *seem* to her at the moment, while Spenser is describing the real thing, the transcendent experience of divine wisdom. But it is not enough to say—indeed it may not be accurate to say—that Eve's experience is a blasphemous parody of what Milton would have regarded as the real thing. There is evidence in *Paradise Lost* to suggest that Milton distrusted the kind of experience Spenser celebrates in the "Hymne of Heavenly Beautie," and in the "Hymne of Heavenly Love" as well, where the vision attained is a vision of Christ. Milton, I will argue, is applying considerable pressure to his original.

At the beginning of the "Hymne of Heavenly Beautie" the poet's thoughts have already been "ravisht" by the "contemplation of those goodly sights, / And glorious images in heaven wrought" (*HHB* 1–3), and it is his ambition to share the experience with others. The first step for those who wish so to be ravished is to "feed" their "gazefull eyes" on the sight of the "frame of this wyde universe." The next is to move from the earth through the skies, on to the invisible heavens, and finally to "that Highest farre beyond all telling, / Fairer than all the rest which there appeare, / Though all their beauties joyned together were," for a view of the "celestial face" of Sapience, the "soveraigne" queen. To do this, Spenser tells the reader, one must gather "plumes of perfect speculation / To impe the wings of thy high flying mynd [and] mount up aloft through heavenly contemplation."

This comes very close to the process that Satan claims to have followed as he describes to Eve the effect on him of the forbidden fruit. And his guise at this point in the temptation is not that of courtly lover but of the "philosophic" Spenser, the successful Platonic searcher after heavenly beauty. Before eating the fruit Satan had been a creature "of abject thoughts and low" (9.572). But afterwards, having gained the powers of reason and speech:

> Thenceforth to speculations high or deep
> I turned my thoughts, and with capacious mind
> Considered all things visible in heaven,
> Or earth, or middle, all things fair and good;
> But all that fair and good in thy divine
> Semblance, and in thy beauty's heavenly ray
> United I beheld; no fair to thine
> Equivalent or second, which compelled
> Me thus, though importune perhaps, to come
> And gaze, and worship thee of right declared
> Sovereign of creatures, universal dame.
>
>   (9.602–12)

Satan's praise for Eve is Spenserian (and Neoplatonic). Satan's "Beauty's heavenly ray" is Spenser's "celestiall beauties blaze" (*HHL* 277), the "pure beams" from which "al perfect beauty springs" (*HHB* 296). Satan tells Eve that all that is "fair and good" he sees "united" in her "divine semblance," and it is Divinity itself whom Spenser calls "fairer than all the rest which there appeare, / Though all their beauties joyned together were" (*HHB* 102–3). Satan addresses Eve, in short, as Spenser's "sovereign" queen, as his Goddess, as Sapience.

Milton would have found in Spenser's hymns little distinction between the psychology of a man's sexual love for a woman and his love for Christ or Sapience, and he rejected that psychology. He did find, however, a strong assertion, in the second pair of hymns, of the greater value of heavenly love and beauty. To those who become "ravisht with devouring great desire / Of [Christ's] deare selfe" Spenser says:

> Thenceforth all worlds desire will in thee dye,
> And all earthes glorie on which men do gaze,
> Seeme durt and drosse in thy pure sighted eye,
> Compared to that celestiall beauties blaze....
>
> (*HHL* 274–77)

To nothing in the hymns did Milton object so strongly as he did to the rejection of the world endorsed in these lines—lines which return us to the two passages with which we began: to Eve's "what of sweet before / Hath touched my sense, flat seems to this, and harsh," and to Spenser's "all that earst seemd sweet, seemes now offense, /And all that pleased earst, now seemes to paine." Eve's response to what she calls the fruit's "sciential sap" (9.837), like Spenser's response to the sight of Sapience, is to dismiss all former sweetness. Spenser's philosophy of love is a philosophy of renunciation, and it is this in the hymns that Milton most sought to subvert. When a man loves a woman, for Spenser, "thereon his mind affixed wholly is," and "all other blisse seemes vaine" (*An Hymne in Honour of Love* 204, 208). If you are to love Christ, "all other loves... thou must renounce, and utterly displace." Then "in no earthly thing thou shalt delight" (*HHL* 262–64, 272).

As for the lovers who behold eternal wisdom:

> Their joy, their comfort, their desire, their gaine,
> Is fixed all on that which now they see,
> All other sights but fayned shadowes bee.
> And that faire lampe, which useth to enflame
> The hearts of men with selfe consuming fyre,

Thenceforth seemes fowle, and full of sinfull blame.

(*HHB* 271–76)

In the two sacred hymns heavenly love *is* heavenly, i.e., unearthly, even though the imagery through which it is conveyed remains heavily, painfully sensuous. It is heavenly, in other words, only in the sense that earth's beauties and pleasures are rejected. Spenser offers us the visible world, the book of nature's works, as the first object lesson on the road to heavenly contemplation, but it is no sooner seen and read than it is rejected and denounced:

> The meanes therefore which unto us is lent,
> Him to behold, is on his workes to looke,
> Which he hath made in beauty excellent,
> And in the same, as in a brasen booke,
> To reade enregistred in every nooke
> His goodnesse, which his beautie doth declare,
> For all thats good, is beautifull and faire.
>
> Thence gathering plumes of perfect speculation,
> To impe the wings of thy high flying mynd,
> Mount up aloft through heavenly contemplation,
> From this darke world, whose damps the soule do blynd,
> And like the native brood of Eagles kynd,
> On that bright Sunne of glorie fixe thine eyes,
> Cleared from grosse mists of fraile infirmities.

(*HHB* 127–40)

Milton rejects the division Spenser makes between the two worlds, and he rejects the isolation of any single pleasure or beauty or love at the expense of all others. How, he must have wondered, can a world of darkness, damps (i.e., noxious fogs), and the "grosse mists of fraile infirmities" declare the Creator's goodness and beauty?

Such renunciation is a natural but sinful temptation in *Paradise Lost.* Indeed Adam is "fondly overcome with female charm" because, for a space, to borrow Spenser's phrase, "his mind affixed wholly is" on Eve. Eve's reaction to the forbidden fruit—her reappraisal of what had seemed sweet as "flat" and "harsh"—is the fourth and last in a series of closely related passages, clustered in the eighth and ninth books, all of which dramatize what Arnold Stein has called "the surprise of a new experience not yet understood."⁴ The first two occur during Adam's recounting of his own history to Raphael. He describes his first moment of consciousness when, "as new waked from soundest sleep," he turns his "wondering eyes" toward heaven, and then toward the lovely landscape, "so fresh and gay," and the living, moving creatures that surround him, causing his heart to overflow "with joy." In answer to his call to the "great maker" whose existence he immediately infers, God causes him to sleep and leads him upward into "the garden of bliss":

> A circuit wide, enclosed, with goodliest trees
> Planted, with walks, and bowers, *that what I saw*
> *Of earth before scarce pleasant seemed.* Each tree
> Loaden with fairest fruit that hung to the eye
> Tempting, stirred in me sudden appetite
> To pluck and eat. . . .
>
> (8.304–9)

What Adam expresses in the italicized lines is, to draw on Stein once more, a "disparagement, a kind of turning away, perhaps rejection," of what he had seen before.⁵ But transport is no guarantee of wisdom. Adam's immediate reaction is a sudden and undiscriminating appetite, prompted by each tree's tempting fruit. Without a guide he would be lost, but the guide appears and at once teaches him the necessity of cautious discrimination. "Of every tree that in the garden grows / Eat freely with glad heart. . . . But of the tree whose operation brings / Knowledge of good and ill . . . shun to taste" (8.321–27).

In the second passage, as Adam recalls his very first reaction to the sight of Eve, both his need for a guide and his developing capacity for self-guidance are dramatized as he tempers his own expressions, revising retrospectively as he proceeds:

> Under his forming hands a creature grew,
> Manlike, but different sex, so lovely fair,
> That *what seemed fair in all the world, seemed now*
> *Mean, or in her summed up, in her contained*
> *And in her looks,* which from that time infused
> Sweetness into my heart, unfelt before,
> *And into all things from her air inspired*
> *The spirit of love and amorous delight.*
>
> (8.470–77)

Adam moves from a renunciation of the world he had previously cherished, to a recognition of its presence in Eve, to an enhanced appreciation of it. He qualifies his disparaging contrast ("what seemed fair... seemed now / Mean") and then inverts it, declaring that all things in her presence become even fairer, inspired with "the spirit of love and amorous delight." Adam has come to see Eve, in the words of Castiglione's Peter Bembo, as "in suche wise beawtifull, that all other beawtifull thinges, be beawtifull, bicause they be partners of the beawtie of [her]."[6] Love calls us, as Richard Wilbur has said, to the things of this world.

The potential danger, these passages imply, lies in dismissing what is fair or good for the sake of what seems, or even for what is, fairer or better—the danger of getting carried away, transported. Those who look upon Spenser's Sapience conceive "such wondrous pleasures... And sweet contentment, that it doth bereave / Their soule of sense... And them transport from flesh into the spright" (*HHB* 256–59). For Adam the danger lies in being transported to a height from which he may fall, a ravishment that leaves him unable to discriminate. Adam shares with Raphael his nervousness about Eve's effect on him:

> Transported I behold,
> Transported touch; here passion first I felt,
> Commotion strange, in all enjoyments else
> Superior and unmoved, here only weak
> Against the charm of beauty's powerful glance.
>
> (8.529–33)

Each of these passages from *Paradise Lost* dramatizes or describes the effects of the "creatures," whether the trees and bowers and tempting fruits of Eden, or the angelic form of Eve, on those who experience them. All are associated with images of ascent, the leaving of a lower realm of sensory experience for a higher realm. In *Paradise Lost* upward flight, transport, is always fraught with risk and ought to be accompanied with a prayer for safe return. Spenser's "Hymne of Heavenly Beauty" moves upward, through transport, toward "the love of God, which *loathing* brings / Of this vile world" (298–99). In like fashion Adam and Eve, when together they taste the fruit, "fancy that they feel / Divinity within them breeding wings / Wherewith to scorn the earth" (9.1009–11). The key word here is not *fancy*, which merely suggests that they are as wingless as ever. It is *scorn*. The earth Adam and Eve would scorn is, as we will have several occasions to observe, an "earth...like heaven, a seat where gods might dwell" (7.328–29), a world to which the gods descend. It is not an earth divinity would loath or scorn.

Spenser's Sapience, though "ravishing," is aloof and remote—a figure to behold and contemplate in isolated transport. Milton's Wisdom, embodied in the Son, Raphael, and Michael (see chapter 8), is accessible and sociable. "She" condescends to Adam and Eve for conversation and in friendship, just as Urania, who is Milton's muse and Wisdom's sister, descends from heaven nightly to visit the poet. The prelapsarian values and pleasures that Milton most persuasively dramatizes, and that most define what makes a place a paradise, are those associated on the one hand with the beauty and fecundity of nature, and on the other with the pleasures of human society as they are portrayed through Adam and Eve's conversations with each other and with the gods: the value and pleasure of love, of sharing one's experiences with someone who wants to listen, of welcoming an honored guest, of working or worshiping together, of being instructed. Adam may claim, in the heat of argument, that "solitude sometimes is best society" (9.249), but one would be hard put to find evidence for it in the poem. It is his fear of the loss of "best society"—Eve's "sweet converse and love"—that leads him to disobey God, and it is the impending loss of the company of the gods, and of the sight of God's face, the sound of his voice, that most grieves him when he learns he must depart from Eden.

Adam and Eve's flight of fancy, which leads to their scorning of the earth, of course runs counter to the wisdom of Milton's poem. Raphael advises Adam to be *lowly* wise (8.173). Even at his most Spenserian moment, when he holds out to Adam and Eve the prospect of a time when their bodies "may at last turn all to spirit,... and winged ascend / Ethereal," Raphael is careful to add that they may choose, if they wish, to remain in their present, earthly Paradise, the heavenliness of which he never tires of declaring. When Michael imparts to Adam the "sum of wisdom" he will need in order to build a paradise within, all the emphasis is on strong faith and good works, not on mounting aloft through heavenly contemplation. And if, in the hymns of heavenly love and beauty, the love of God seems to go hand in hand with contempt of the world, for Milton it is absolutely inseparable from a love of the world and of the creatures which inhabit it. Adam and Eve enact their love of God by extolling his works and by loving each other. Nor are they alone in magnifying the creation. Satan, who has seen some majesty and should know, praises the earth as a "terrestrial heaven" (9.103), and the angelic choir jubilantly exclaims, on the Sabbath following the creation: "Witness this new-made world, another heaven" (7.617).

As in our world, there is change and contrast in Eden, and in heaven too—"change delectable," Raphael calls it—and there is dissension and disobedience. There is, indeed, warfare in heaven. No place in *Paradise Lost*—not even hell itself—lacks at least fleeting moments of "change delectable." No place guarantees change for the better or is exempt from the possibility of change for the worse. In Michael's words, "God attributes to place / No sanctity, if none be thither brought / By men" (11.836–38). In Satan's, "The mind is its own place, and in itself / Can make a heaven of hell, a hell of heaven" (1.254–55). This is so because for Milton, that prototypical liberal,[7] there is simply no higher good than freedom—that condition without which such concepts as responsibility, obedience, loyalty and love, would lose all meaning.[8] And a world in which there is freedom is a world in which change and contrast, good and evil, creation and destruction, will exist side by side. Even in this poem, which presents so vividly in its concluding books the tragic effects of the Fall on human history, we can hear throughout a steady undertone celebrating the world we live in. Consider, for example, the following two similes, which Milton uses to communicate the sense of sudden joy or wonder. The first is used to express the fallen angels' turn from dread to joy at Satan's volunteering to embark on his journey earthward, the second to catch Satan's own bedazzled admiration for Eve:

> As when from mountain tops the dusky clouds
> Ascending, while the north wind sleeps, o'erspread
> Heaven's cheerful face, the louring element
> Scowls o'er the darkened landscape snow, or shower;
> If chance the radiant sun with farewell sweet
> Extend his evening beam, the fields revive,
> The birds their notes renew, and bleating herds
> Attest their joy, that hill and valley rings.
>
> (2.488–95)

> As one who long in populous city pent,
> Where houses thick and sewers annoy the air,
> Forth issuing on a summer's morn to breathe
> Among the pleasant villages and farms
> Adjoined, from each thing met conceives delight,
> The smell of grain, or tedded grass, or kine,
> Or dairy, each rural sight, each rural sound;
> If chance with nymph-like step fair virgin pass,
> *What pleasing seemed, for her now pleases more,*
> *She most, and in her looks sums all delight.*
> *Such pleasure took the serpent....*
>
> (9.445–55)

Both similes are drawn from Milton's memory of our own fallen world, and of the fallen literature of that world. Both describe sudden change and contrast, from darkened landscape to the evening beam of the radiant sun, from the close stench of the populous city to the clear air of a morning in the countryside. Louis Martz's comment on the second passages applies, in principle, to the first as well. It is a "tribute to the beauty of the earth, as tended and inhabited now by fallen man and woman.... The comparison suggests that Satan's design will not be wholly successful. He has not utterly destroyed God's Paradise of Delight, since the poet here still delights in these manmade scenes of farm and village, and in feminine beauty, almost as much as he delights in this imagined garden and in Eve herself."[9] Both passages stress the renewing power of the creatures—the sun, rural sights and sounds, fair virgins—on those who behold them. The first is aimed at suggesting that the "spirits damned" have not lost "all their virtue," the second at showing how Eve's "heavenly form / Angelic" has "overawed" Satan's malicious intent. The second, we should also note, concludes with an echo of Adam's evolving and carefully wrought praise of Eve—his assertion that "what seemed fair in all the world, seemed now...in her summed up," and his reference to her inspiring "into all things...the spirit of love and amorous delight." Though Satan is in every respect the adversary, he is also, time and time again, an extraordinary witness to the beauty and goodness of heaven and earth alike.

CHAPTER 2

The Books of Wisdom

Having caught, from a rather special perspective, a glimpse of Milton's down-to-earth conception of wisdom, and of his deep respect for what Spenser, echoing Sidney's *Defense of Poesie*,[1] calls the "brasen" book of God's "workes," let us set that book alongside its companion volume. As the judicious Richard Hooker warms up to the task of constructing his case against the Calvinists' conviction that "Scripture is the only rule of all things which in this life may be done by men," he invokes a cluster of ideas to which we will return frequently in our consideration of *Paradise Lost:*

> Whatsoever either men on earth or the Angels of heaven do know, it is as a drop of that unemptiable fountain of wisdom; which wisdom hath diversely imparted her treasures unto the world. As her ways are of sundry kinds, so her manner of teaching is not merely one and the same. Some things she openeth by the sacred books of Scripture; some things by the glorious works of nature: with some things she inspireth them from above by spiritual influence; in some things she leadeth and traineth them only by worldly experience and practice. We may not so in any one special kind admire her, that we disgrace her in any other; but let all her ways be according unto their place and degree adored.[2]

The first notion that figures prominently in the passage is that of wisdom, which flows from an "unemptiable fountain," and who, personified, instructs us both through creation, or "the glorious works of nature," and through the Word, or the sacred books of Scripture. She is that woman whose praises are sung, and who sings her own praises, in the biblical Wisdom literature—in Proverbs, The Wisdom of Solomon, and Ecclesiasticus (or The Wisdom of Jesus the Son of

Sirach). In these writings, and in many of the Psalms, she is closely associated with the creation, as she is in *Paradise Lost* in Uriel's account of the "wisdom infinite" that brought forth the works of God "but hid their causes deep" (3.706–7), as well as in the invocation to Book 7, where, as Urania's sister, she is pictured as having been with the almighty Father "before the hills appeared or fountain flowed." In Ecclesiasticus we read that God created Wisdom "before all things," and "poured her out upon all his works" (1:4, 9). When the psalmist sings the praises of God's works, he exclaims, "O Lord, how manifold are thy works! in wisdom hast thou made them all" (Ps. 104:24). "O give thanks unto the Lord ... that by wisdom made the heavens" (Ps. 136:1–5). This traditional view of Wisdom's role in the creation of the world is illustrated by an illumination in a twelfth-century manuscript in the Bibliothèque Nationale which contains Josephus's *Antiquities of the Jews*. The illumination (see frontispiece) shows Christ standing between two rows of medallions that depict the works of the six days of the creation. In the seventh medallion, and at the center, sits Wisdom, who is looking up to the Creator as if awaiting his comment.[3]

Solomon (we shall call him Solomon for convenience, though there is no reason to believe that he wrote the book that bears his name), in his famous prayer for wisdom, asks:

> O God of my fathers, and Lord of mercy, who hast made all things with thy word, and ordained man through thy wisdom ... : Give me wisdom, that sitteth by thy throne.... And wisdom was with thee: which knoweth thy works, and was present when thou madest the world, and knew what was acceptable in thy sight, and right in thy commandments. (Wisd. 9:1–9)

Here as elsewhere Wisdom is associated especially with the creation of man. Both Milton and the editors of the Geneva Bible make something of the fact that only in his creating of man did God call upon a second party: "Let *us* make man in our image, after our likeness." Milton has the "Eternal Father" address these words "audibly" to the Son, who *is* his "wisdom" (3.170), because man is to be "chief / Of all his works" (7.515–18). The Geneva gloss informs us that God "taketh counsell with his wisdome and virtue, purposing to make an excellent worke above all the rest of his creation."

Wisdom is associated, however, not only with the creation but also with the Word, with speech, the law, prophecy, and the interpretation of language. "The word of God most high is the fountain of wisdom," and indeed Wisdom says of herself, in language that alludes to the opening chapters of Genesis, "I came out of the mouth of the most High, and covered the earth as a cloud" (Ecclus. 1:5; 24:3). Her teachings are identified with "the book of the covenant of the most high God, even the law which Moses commanded" (Ecclus. 24:23). After the Israelites' successful passage through the Red Sea, it is claimed, Wisdom "opened the mouth of the dumb, and made the tongues of them that cannot speak eloquent" (Wisd. 10:21). "She knoweth the subtilties of speeches, and can expound dark sentences" (Wisd. 8:8). And in "all ages entering into holy souls, she maketh them friends of God, and prophets" (Wisd. 7:27). Hence Wisdom, or Sophia, was sometimes portrayed in medieval gospel illuminations as a muse inspiring and directing the work of one of the evangelists as he bent over his book or scroll. Figure 1, from a mid-fourteenth-century illuminated gospel in the monastery of Chilandari on Mount Athos, represents Luke sharpening his pen as he works on his gospel. The muse figure standing behind him with her left hand on his right arm is identified as Wisdom by the inscription (in Serbian Church Slavic) over her head.[4] And the so-called "author page" in the Paris Psalter (fig. 2) shows David holding a psalter open to Psalm 71 (72 in the King James Version), the last psalm traditionally attributed to him. Sophia and Prophetia stand slightly behind him on his right and left respectively.[5] In a related tradition that identified Wisdom with the Blessed Virgin (a tradition with which Milton would have had little sympathy) an Armenian Gospel miniature of 1323 presents Sophia suckling the apostles Peter and Paul.[6]

The pairing of Scripture and the works of nature as the prime books in whose pages we may read God's ways was, by the end of the sixteenth century, altogether commonplace, and not among the theologians only.[7] As Francis Bacon puts it in *The Advancement of Learning*, "our Savior" laid before us "two books or volumes to study . . . first the Scripture, revealing the will of God, and then the creatures expressing his power."[8] And Sir Thomas Browne, in celebrating God's wisdom as "His most beauteous Attribute," speaks of the same two volumes, the "written one of God" and the other "of his servant Nature, that universal and publick Manuscript, that lies expans'd unto the Eyes of all."[9]

Saint Luke the Evangelist accompanied by Divine Wisdom. Gospel book. Mount Athos: Monastery of Chiliandari, 13 (m). fol. 155r. Reprinted, by permission, from *The Treasures of Mount Athos* (Athens, 1974).

The Exaltation of David. The Paris Psalter MS Gr. 139, fol. 7v.
Reprinted, by permission of the author, from Hugo Buchthal,
Miniatures of the Paris Psalter (London, 1938).

A good deal can depend on the "place and degree," to borrow Hooker's phrase, that one assigns to each of wisdom's manners of teaching. Hooker puts "the glorious works of nature" on more or less equal footing with "the sacred books of Scripture" in order to make room in his argument for appeals to tradition, "worldly experience and practice," reason, and the laws of nature—both the nature we see around us and human nature. Bacon and Browne, perhaps, devoted more of their intellectual energy to the book of creatures than to Scripture. For Bacon, indeed, the volume of the creatures is "a key" to Scripture, "not only opening our understanding to conceive the true sense of the scriptures, by the general notions of reason and rules of speech; but chiefly by opening our belief, in drawing us into a due meditation of the omnipotency of God, which is chiefly signed and engraven upon his works."[10] For Calvin, on the other hand, as for the Puritans Hooker hoped to persuade, "the evidence of God in creation does not profit us." Calvin is effusive in his celebration of the order, beauty, and wisdom of the visible creation. He argues, nevertheless, that "although the Lord represents both himself and his everlasting kingdom in the mirror of his works with very great clarity, such is our stupidity that we grow increasingly dull toward so manifest testimonies, and they flow away without profiting us." "How horrible is the blindness of the human mind," he goes on to say. "It is therefore vain that so many burning lamps shine for us in the workmanship of the universe to show forth the glory of its Author. Although they bathe themselves wholly in their radiance, yet they can of themselves in no way lead us unto the right path."[11]

The two books have an ancient, curious, and complex history, whether taken separately or in conjunction. The importance of Scripture as a source of knowledge is perhaps obvious enough. It is authenticated in the Scriptures themselves, whether as the Word which, in the beginning, was *with* God and *was* God (John 1:1), or as the words God actually speaks ("Man doth not live by bread only, but by every word that proceedeth out of the mouth of the Lord" [Deut. 8:3]), or as the divinely inspired reading required for salvation: "From a child thou hast known the holy scriptures, which are able to make thee wise unto salvation through faith which is in Christ Jesus. All scripture is given by inspiration of God, and is profitable for doctrine, for reproof, for correction, for instruction in righteousness:

that the man of God may be perfect, throughly furnished unto all good works" (2 Tim. 3:15–17).

Within the Christian tradition the notion of nature, or the creatures, as evidence of God's existence and nature is founded most centrally on the first two chapters of Paul's Letter to the Romans. Paul argues there that all men, whether Jew or Gentile, whether or not they had ever been exposed to Scripture, or the law of Moses, had sufficient knowledge of God to render them blameworthy when they failed to glorify him: "For the wrath of God is revealed from heaven against all ungodliness and unrighteousness of men, who hold the truth in unrighteousness; because that which may be known of God is manifest in them; for God hath shewed it unto them. For the invisible things of him from the creation of the world are clearly seen, being understood by the things that are made, even his eternal power and Godhead; so that they are without excuse" (1:18–20). Paul is concerned to show, in John Coolidge's pithy phrase, that "man's natural reason will do to be damned by."[12] It is the creatures, "the things that are made," along with "the law written in their hearts" (2:15), that provide all men with sufficient knowledge of God to be held responsible for their unrighteousness.

Origen, writing in the third century, was, if not the first, one of the earliest of the church fathers to expand on Paul's notion, and in doing so to Platonize it, by seeing it as offering directions for a form of spiritual exercise whereby we may "ascend" to divinity. Having set up a parallel between the categories of being and becoming and those of the intelligible and the visible, he writes:

> It is in this way also that the disciples of Jesus look at the things that are becoming, so that they use them as steps to the contemplation of the nature of intelligible things. "For the invisible things of God," that is, the intelligible things, "are understood by the things that are made" and "from the creation of the world are clearly seen" by the process of thought. And when they have ascended from the created things of the world to the invisible things of God they do not stop there. But after exercising their minds sufficiently among them and understanding them, they ascend to the eternal power of God, and, in a word, to His Divinity.... But some of those who by God's providence have ascended to the knowledge of such

profound truths do not behave worthily of the knowledge, and are impious, and hold down the truth in unrighteousness. And because of their knowledge of these profound truths, they are not able to have any further opportunity for an excuse before God.[13]

Milton's Adam is not far from Origen when he says to Raphael:

Well hast thou taught the way that might direct
Our knowledge, and the scale of nature set
From centre to circumference, whereon
In contemplation of created things
By steps we may ascend to God.

(5.508–12)

Though Origen, so far as I know, never spoke of the book of nature, he clearly coupled nature and Scripture as providing us not only with knowledge of God, but also with certain hermeneutical problems not unlike those we shall see Milton facing. Commenting on how the wisdom of God is manifest in the subtlest details of Scripture, just as the art of God is manifest in each and every creature and in its parts, he acknowledges that the difficulty of understanding many aspects of the creation parallels those difficulties that arise in attempting to understand Scripture. "He who has once accepted these Scriptures as the work of Him who created the world, must be convinced that whatever difficulties in regard to creation confront those who strive to understand its system, will occur also in regard to the Scriptures." We must refer the knowledge of such matters to the one God, he says, who will open them to us at a later time if we are judged worthy.[14]

Neither Paul's justification of God's wrath against the unwashed unrighteous, however, nor Origen's emphasis on exercising the mind in contemplating the creatures, is specifically Christian. Both have an important antecedent in the earlier biblical Wisdom literature. The author of the apocryphal Wisdom of Solomon wrote:

Surely vain are all men by nature, who are ignorant of God, and could not out of the good things that are seen know him that is: neither by considering the works did they acknowledge the workmaster; But deemed either fire, or wind, or the swift air, or the circle of the stars, or the violent water, or the lights of heaven, to be the gods which govern the world. With whose beauty if they being delighted took them to be gods; let them know how much better the Lord of them is: for the first author of beauty hath created them. But if they were astonished at their power and virtue, let them understand by them, how much mightier he is that made them. For by the greatness and beauty of the creatures proportionably the maker of them is seen. But yet for this they are the less to be blamed: for they peradventure err, seeking God, and desirous to find him. For being conversant in his works they search him diligently, and believe their sight: because the things are beautiful that are seen. Howbeit neither are they to be pardoned. For if they were able to know so much, that they could aim at the world; how did they not sooner find out the Lord thereof? (Wisd. 13:1–9)

This passage introduces a lengthy diatribe against the making of idols of wood or stone, of clay or precious metal, for the "devising of idols," whether in "the image of man" or of "some vile beast," is "the beginning of spiritual fornication" (Wisd. 13–15 passim). So it is for Paul. Those who knew God but "glorified him not as God... changed the glory of the uncorruptible God into an image made like to corruptible man, and to birds, and fourfooted beasts, and creeping things... and worshipped and served the creature more than the Creator" (Rom. 1:21–25).

Hugh of Saint Victor, writing in the early twelfth century, made explicit the book metaphor implied by Origen's discussion of the difficulties nature and Scripture pose for the interpreter. "It is," he wrote, "as if the entire sensible world were a book written by the finger of God... in order to make manifest the wisdom of the invisible things of God." Or again: "There are three books.... The second is the work of God, which never ceases to be, in which visible work the wisdom of the invisible things of God is visibly written."[15] It was not until the thirteenth century, however, that the two books—nature and Scripture—were brought together and related to the destiny of Adam and his fallen progeny. Bonaventure saw God as making himself known through both books, or rather as making a different aspect of himself known in each book:

The first principle renders itself knowable to us both through *Scripture* and through the *creation;* it manifests itself through the book of the *creatures* as the *effective* principle, and through the book of *Scripture* as the *restorative* [*reparativum*] principle, and since the *restorative* principle cannot be known unless the *effective* principle is known, therefore sacred Scripture, though it treats principally of the works of *restoration,* it must nevertheless treat of the works of *creation,* insofar as it leads to knowledge of the first principles both efficient and restorative [*reficientis*]; and therefore this knowledge is both *sublime* and *saving* [*salutaris*]: *sublime* because it is knowledge of the effective principle, which is God the creator; *saving,* because it is knowledge of Christ the savior and mediator.[16]

Bonaventure's two sets of terms, the one having to do with God's efficiency or creative power, the other with remaking, renewing, and saving, point to the temporal and functional relationship between the two books. He says elsewhere that

> the testimonial of the *book of nature* was efficacious in the state of created nature, when the book itself was not obscured, nor the eye of man darkened. But through sin the eye of man grew clouded, and that mirror [*speculum*] was made enigmatic and obscure, and the ear of the inner intelligence became deaf to the hearing of its testimony. And therefore divine providence generously provided the testimony of the second book, namely the *book of Scripture,* which was produced [*editus*] according to divine revelation, which has never failed nor will fail from the beginning of the world until the end.[17]

The Fall, in other words, corrupted both nature itself and our ability to read it aright, and consequently divine providence supplied man with the Scripture, with its laws, commandments, and its promise of salvation to all who believe. In the crisper words of Richard Greenham, one of the most popular of the Elizabethan Puritans, "our father *Adam* had nothing to leade him by, but the great booke of the creatures, which when by sinne it was blotted, the Lord supplied this want by the word."[18] For Bonaventure, however, and, as we shall see, for Milton, regenerated man, aided by the Scriptures, is still able to apprehend God in and through the creatures, for in them, as Bonaventure says, the highest power, wisdom, and benevolence of the Creator continue to shine forth.[19]

Bonaventure's favorite figure signifying the relation of the creatures to the Creator is that of the *vestigium* (trace, track, footstep), a figure that makes its way into a postlapsarian exchange between Adam and Michael that we shall consider shortly. But Bonaventure was extraordinarily prolific with his figures. He thought of the whole sensible world not only as a book, but also as a mirror or reflecting surface (*speculum*). He thought of the creatures as, among many other things, mirrors, shadows (*umbrae*), echoes, and, in the case of human beings, as images and likenesses of God.[20] By Milton's day these terms, though occasionally controversial, were as commonplace as the idea of the book of nature itself. They take us straight to Eve's first glimpse of that book when she looks into "the clear / Smooth lake," earlier referred to as a "crystal mirror" (4.263), and sees her image, which echoes her looks with "answering" looks. In one sense she truly sees an image or reflection of one who was made in God's image—one in whose "looks divine / The image of [her] glorious maker shone" (4.291–92)—and the beauty of the image inspires appropriate feelings of sympathy, love, and desire. Or, more precisely, Eve's face reflects her mind by expressing those feelings, while the reflection mirrors only her face. Or, in yet another sense, what she sees is a "shadow" (4.470), which the OED defines both as a "reflected image" and also as an "unreal appearance; a delusive semblance or image; a vain and unsubstantial object of pursuit."

Eve's love affair with herself, as many readers have recognized, would have proven vain and unsubstantial. Just as the voice of God is needed to rein in Adam's indiscriminate appetite for the tempting fruits of Paradise, so is it needed to distract and rescue Eve from her potentially fatal self-absorption, and to reply to her initial questions by telling her what is expected of her and what she will be called.[21] For Bonaventure, as for Milton, the right making of images is a kind of procreation. "If, therefore, all things that can be known generate a likeness of themselves," he argued, "they manifestly proclaim that in them as in mirrors we can see the eternal generation of the Word, the Image and Son, eternally emanating from God the Father."[22] And with a similar thought in mind the voice divine instructs Eve:

> But follow me,
> And I will bring thee where no shadow stays
> Thy coming, and thy soft embraces, he

> Whose image thou art, him thou shall enjoy
> Inseparably thine, to him shalt bear
> Multitudes like thyself, and then be called
> Mother of human race.
>
> (4.469–75)

We read the book of nature with our eyes, the book of Scripture with our ears. The one is visible, the other audible. Nature, in *Paradise Lost,* has many faces, and Scripture many voices—the voices of God and his emissaries when they speak, and the voice of God sounding in the reader's ear when it picks up on one of the hundreds of biblical allusions in the poem. The prototype of both face and voice is the creating and redeeming Logos, the Word itself, for, as Milton wrote in *Christian Doctrine,* "the Word is both Son and *Christ,* ... and as he is the image, as it were, by which God becomes visible, so he is the word by which God is audible."[23] As such, and like Wisdom, the Word mediates between divinity and humanity.

Faces are met with everywhere in *Paradise Lost*—the faces of the creation itself and of the individual creatures—and they are telling. It is primarily the faces that Milton gives to nature that make it legible, though only to those capable of reading it. As the Son of God is preparing to cast the rebel angels into hell, the hills that had been uprooted in the battle hear his command and return "each to his place," and thus "heaven his wonted face renewed / And with fresh flowerets hill and valley smiled." But though the rebels see the change, they are unable to read it and act on its meaning. "To convince the proud," Raphael asks, "what signs avail, / Or wonders move the obdurate to relent?" (6.780–90). When Adam, on the contrary, first awakens to life he notes that "all things smiled," and he responds with wonder, joy, curiosity, and a desire to know and adore his maker (8.257–83).

It is G. K. Hunter's view, which I strongly share, that "in almost everything Milton wrote he felt a deep need to assert the likeness of the divine and the human," and that in *Paradise Lost* he "tends to stress the continuity ... of life before the Fall and life after the Fall, just as he stresses the continuity between life on earth and life in heaven."[24] The likenesses and continuities are nowhere more tersely and cogently expressed than in Milton's reference, in the invocation to Book 3, to the "human face divine"—the culminating element in the brief elegy the poet sings for the world of nature's works that he can no longer see, the book he can no longer read. In that seeming oxymoron, we are brought up against one of those striking conjunctions of the personal and the theological, of the divine and human spheres, and of the poet's fate and Adam's, that lend such power to the prologues. The phrase refers, of course, to the faces of actual human beings, Milton's living contemporaries, still divine even though "defaced" and "discountenanced" by the Fall. It links fallen man not only with Adam and Eve, in whose "looks divine / The image of their glorious maker shone" (4.291–92), but also, as a proleptic pun, with the Son of God:

> Beyond compare the Son of God was seen
> Most glorious, in him all his Father shone
> Substantially expressed, and in his face
> Divine compassion visibly appeared,
> Love without end, and without measure grace....
>
> (3.138–42)

The Father's face is invisible to all but the Son, but the substance of the Father is expressed visibly in or through the Son's face, which is to say that, in heaven as on earth, the Son is the incarnation of the Father, a human face divine. (See also 3.384–89; 6.680–82, 719–21.) The Son's countenance, and hence God's,[25] is "conspicuous" (3.385)—that is, easily seen—a fact that takes on considerable importance when the fallen Adam draws on his memory of that countenance, and in so doing interprets it, in his struggle against despair:

> Undoubtedly he will relent and turn
> From his displeasure; in whose look serene,
> When angry most he seemed and most severe,
> What else but favour, grace, and mercy shone?
>
> (10.1093–96)

If the Father's human face is invisible to all but the Son, it is nevertheless of crucial significance in Milton's story. Those who claim to hear fatherly anger in the Father's *voice* as he contemplates his offspring's imminent transgression ("ingrate, he had of me / All he could have; I made him just and right" [3.97–98]) are surely hearing what is there, for, as Michael Lieb has pointed out, the Son's redemptive sacrifice is motivated precisely by the sight of such emotions writ upon his father's *face*.[26] Addressing the Father, the Son assures him that, following his triumph:

> Thou at the sight
> Pleased, out of heaven shalt look down and smile,
> While by thee raised I ruin all my foes,
> Death last, and with his carcass glut the grave:
> Then with the multitude of my redeemed
> Shall enter heaven long absent, and return,
> Father, to see thy face, wherein no cloud
> Of anger shall remain, but peace assured,
> And reconcilement; wrath shall be no more
> Thenceforth, but in thy presence joy entire.
>
> (3.256–65)

The Son, then, acts less out of "immortal love / To mortal men" than out of "filial obedience." Milton wants to insist on this fact, and on the centrality of the Father's angrily human face divine moving the Son to act. In the words that the angelic chorus sings to the Father, "He to appease thy wrath, and end the strife / Of mercy and justice in thy face discerned . . . offered himself to die / For man's offence" (3.406–10).

The faces of the creatures in *Paradise Lost* are extraordinarily expressive. They move others to act, and sometimes they give us away. Satan's address to the sun is glossed thus by the narrator:

> Thus while he spake, each passion dimmed his face
> Thrice changed with pale, ire, envy and despair,
> Which marred his borrowed visage, and betrayed
> Him counterfeit, if any eye beheld.
>
> (4.114–17)

Though he attempts to smooth "each perturbation" of his face "with outward calm," Uriel "saw him disfigured, more than could befall / Spirit of happy sort" (4.127–28). In like fashion, when the newly fallen Eve approaches Adam, she tries, but fails, to put a good face on her words: "Thus Eve with countenance blithe her story told; / But in her cheek distemper flushing glowed" (9.886–87), and Adam has no difficulty seeing that she has been "defaced" (9.901). Faces and voices, those twin metonymies of presence, are sometimes one, and faces themselves can speak. Eve's face puts on a dumbshow that says she is guilty before she utters words: "In her face excuse / Came prologue, and apology to prompt" (9.853–54).

The divine voices Adam and Eve hear—God's, Raphael's, Michael's—are also human voices, for their speech itself is, as Raphael explains to Adam, an accommodation to "human ears" and "earthly notion[s]" (7.176–79). These voices take on for them an almost embodied reality, a potentially lasting resonance in the inner ear of memory. When Raphael concludes his account of the creation of the world, "the angel ended, and in Adam's ear / So charming left his voice, that he awhile / Thought him still speaking, still stood fixed to hear" (8.1–3). And Adam later tells Raphael how "sternly [God] pronounced / The rigid interdiction, which resounds / Yet dreadful in mine ear" (8.333–35).

Adam and Eve need only keep that interdiction in their ears, that one command which Eve nicely personifies as "sole daughter of [God's] voice" (9.653). That voice, which Adam and Eve are free to remember or to forget, is the equivalent of conscience, which the Father himself describes as a "guide" placed within them: "My umpire conscience, whom if they will hear, / Light after light well used they shall attain" (3.193–95). Conscience, the voice of God within us, is, then, the aural counterpart of inner illumination. Disobedience, etymologically, is a failure of hearing, a hearkening to the wrong voice, or the crowding out of one voice by another. Eve's dream enacted potential disobedience through a mistaking of Satan's voice for Adam's. Her actual disobedience involves not only wonder at the serpent's ability to speak with human voice, but, more crucially, the physical entrance into her of the wrong words: "Into the heart of Eve his words made way ... and his words replete with guile / Into her heart too easy entrance won ... and in her ears the sound / Yet rung of his persuasive words" (9.550, 733–37). Adam's sin, too, is an aural sin. "Was she thy God," the Son asks, "that her thou didst obey / Before his voice? ... Because thou hast hearkened to the voice of thy wife...." (10.145–46, 198).

Such a treatment of sin is at least consistent with the Puritans' radical scripturalism, what U. Milo Kaufmann calls their "aural orientation toward the Word, with the Scripture a voice for the inner ear."

Kaufmann argues that "Puritanism gave priority to the sense of hearing," citing Calvin's conviction that "true acquaintance with God is made more by the ears than by the eyes."[27]

For Milton too, whether in the unfallen or in the fallen world, it is probably the case that "true acquaintance with God is made more by the ears than by the eyes." In *Paradise Lost* the Word often guides Adam and Eve toward a truer understanding of what they have seen in nature or provides them with information that the visible creation simply cannot yield, whether to unfallen man or angel. This movement from nature to Scripture, from the visual to the aural, is recreated in *Paradise Lost* at many moments. Much of Books 4 and 5 prior to Raphael's arrival is devoted to Adam and Eve's responses to the sight of the creatures, but the angel is sent to supplement their understanding by underscoring the central importance of the verbal caution God had given to Adam (5.519–23) and by revealing to them what they need to know, but could not otherwise learn, about the enemy who plots their fall. In Book 8, as if in preparation for the crucial test to come, we are presented with no fewer than five occasions when Adam presents his own reflections on the creatures, or his doubts about nature's or his creator's wisdom, only to receive verbal guidance or corrective instruction from Raphael or God.

To what extent did Milton dismiss the book of the creatures as a source of divine knowledge? How close was his position to Calvin's? The basic issue is the extent to which the righteousness, free will, and capacity for understanding that were lost in the Fall have been restored by grace. One would therefore expect Milton's attitude toward our ability to profit from the book of nature to differ from Calvin's in roughly the same proportion that his more-or-less Arminian stance differed from Calvin's view that "the mind of man has been so completely estranged from God's righteousness that it conceives, desires, and undertakes, only that which is impious, perverted, foul, impure, and infamous. The heart is so steeped in the poison of sin, that it can breathe out nothing but a loathsome stench."[28] Milton rejected Calvin's doctrine of predestination and believed that God held out the possibility of salvation to all people. Indeed he seems to place virtually no limit on the extent to which recovery is possible. In *Christian Doctrine* he writes: "The unwritten law is the law of nature given to the first man. A kind of gleam or glimmering of it still remains in the hearts of all mankind. In the regenerate this is daily brought nearer to a renewal of its original perfection by the operation of the Holy Spirit."[29]

Throughout his public career, furthermore, Milton invoked the law of nature in his discussion of almost every controversial subject he touched upon. In 1644 in *The Doctrine and Discipline of Divorce,* using a phrase that nicely elides the law of nature and the book of nature, he asks:

> What can be a fouler incongruity, a greater violence to the reverend secret of nature, then to force a mixture of minds that cannot unite, & to sowe the furrow of mans nativity with seed of two incoherent and uncombining dispositions.... If the noysomnesse or disfigurement of body can soon destroy the sympathy of mind to wedlock duties, much more will annoyance and trouble of mind infuse it self into all the faculties and acts of the body, to render them invalid, unkindly, and even unholy against the *fundamental law book of nature;* which *Moses* never thwarts, but reverences: therfore he commands us to force nothing against sympathy or naturall order no not upon the most abject creatures; to shew that such an indignity cannot be offer'd to man without an impious crime.[30]

Or again, in 1651 he tells Salmasius that "the law of God does most closely agree with the law of nature" and that "there is nothing more in accord with the laws of nature than the punishment of tyrants."[31] He expresses his pleasure, in 1660, that parliament is "not bound by any statute of preceding Parlaments, but by the law of nature only, which is the only law of laws truly and properly to all mankinde fundamental; the beginning and the end of all Government; to which no Parlament or people that will throughly reforme, but may and must have recourse; as they had and must yet have in church reformation (if they throughly intend it) to evangelic rules."[32]

Milton's views on Scripture itself, and the certainty it affords, are complicated, first by the fact that Scripture constitutes an accommodation of God's nature to human understanding, and second by his profound skepticism with regard to the possibility of knowing with certainty what the Scriptures have to say. Milton begins the second chapter of *Christian Doctrine,* entitled "Of God," with the bold assertion that God "has left so many signs of himself in the human mind, so many traces of his presence through the whole of nature, that no sane person can fail to realise that he exists.... It is indisputable that all the things which exist in the world, created in perfection of beauty and order for some definite purpose, and that a good one, provide proof that a supreme creative being existed before the world, and had a definite purpose of his own in all created things."[33] Yet without pausing to provide a transition, he declares that "no one ... can form correct ideas about God guided by nature or reason alone, without the word or message of God."[34] Correct ideas, for Milton, were more than ideas of God's existence, his purposiveness, and his creative power, all of which are manifest in the creation. They meant, for example, the attributes, such as his eternalness, his immutability, his omnipresence, for which Milton proceeds to muster proof texts from Scripture. Even with the aid of Scripture, however, "God, *as he really is,* is far beyond man's imagination, let alone his understanding."[35] All that Scripture itself offers us is "such a mental image of him as he... wishes us to form." If he really is as he presents himself in Scripture, "why should we think otherwise?" If he is not, "on what authority do we contradict [him]?"[36]

When Milton turns in *Christian Doctrine* to the subject of "Holy Scripture" itself (Book 1, chapter 30), what begins as a reassuringly straightforward declaration of its transparency and clarity becomes increasingly unreassuring. In *The Sword of the Spirit: Puritan Responses to the Bible,* John Knott traces Milton's evolving attitude toward Scripture, starting with his earlier prose, in which he expresses his "overwhelming confidence" in its power "to impress its truth upon the understanding." "His primary intellectual weapon was the idea of the pure, simple, and powerful Word of God, accessible to every individual." As time went on, however, truth, including the truth of Scripture, came to seem more elusive, its attainment laborious, methodical, and gradual. Increasingly "the struggle of truth and error proved to be more complex than it had seemed when he first mounted the chariot of zeal, and he found himself having to deal with the process by which men found the truth."[37]

Milton's argument in *Christian Doctrine* seems to recapitulate that twenty-five year history. After a brief explanation of why the apocryphal books lack the authority of the canonical, and within the context of an equally brief testimony to the educative value of the Scriptures, Milton testifies that "the scriptures are, both in themselves and through God's illumination absolutely clear. If studied carefully and regularly they are an ideal instrument for educating even unlearned readers in those matters which have most to do with salvation." They are "plain and sufficient in themselves." He refers with considerable scorn to those who write "as if scripture did not contain the clearest of all lights in itself: as if it were not in itself sufficient, especially in matters of faith and holiness: as if the sense of the divine truth, itself absolutely plain, needed to be brought out more clearly or more fully, or otherwise explained...."[38]

At this point, however, recognizing that historically the meaning of the Scriptures—like it or not—simply *has* been the source of controversy, he introduces a critical distinction: "The scriptures are difficult or obscure, at any rate in matters where salvation is concerned, only to those who perish." We are then given a list of the requisites for reading the scriptures rightly, and though it is a good list, Milton apparently had difficulty bringing it to a close. It is daunting enough seriously to undercut all the prior claims of clarity and sufficiency:

> The requisites are linguistic ability, knowledge of the original sources, consideration of the overall intent, distinction between literal and figurative language, examination of the causes and circumstances, and of what comes before and after the passage in question, and comparison of one text with another. It must always be asked, too, how far the interpretation is in agreement with faith. *Finally,* one often has to take into account the anomalies of syntax.... *Lastly,* no inferences should be made from the text, unless they follow necessarily from what is written.[39]

What Milton is illustrating is that special version of the hermeneutic circle shared by those reformers who rejected the Church as the authoritative interpreter. (How can we hold our interpretation of the Scriptures up to the standard of faith if they themselves afford "the clearest of all lights" with regard to "matters of faith?") What Milton turns to in place of the Church is the Spirit, and in doing so he reintroduces the distinction between those who perish (the unbelievers) and those who do not: "Every believer is entitled to interpret the scriptures; and by that I mean interpret them for himself. He has the Spirit, who guides truth, and he has the mind of Christ. Indeed, no one else can usefully interpret them for him, unless that person's interpretation coincides with the one he makes for himself and his own conscience." And what use, we must ask, is another person's interpretation if it coincides with one's own?

If we add to this skepticism Milton's keen awareness that the reader of the Bible is confronted, particularly in the case of the New Testament, with unreliable, corrupt texts,[40] it is no wonder that Milton found himself increasingly caught up in the subjectivist dilemma. What distinguishes him from so many of his predecessors is the clarity with which he perceives the dilemma and the way the dilemma moves him toward tolerance and, by implication, a recognition (like Origen's) of the need for long-enduring patience: "If there is disagreement about the sense of scripture among apparent believers, they should tolerate each other until God reveals the truth to all."[41] Or again, from *A Treatise of Civil Power:*

> It cannot be deni'd, being the main foundation of our protestant religion, that we of these ages, having no other divine rule or autoritie from without us warrantable to one another as a common ground but the holy scripture, and no other within us but the illumination of the Holy Spirit so interpreting that scripture as warrantable only to our selves and to such whose consciences we can so perswade, can have no other ground in matters of religion but only from the scriptures. And these being not possible to be understood without this divine illumination which no man can know at all times to be in himself, much less to be at any time for certain in any other, it follows cleerly, that no man or body of men in these times can be the infallible judges or determiners in matters of religion to any other mens consciences but thir own.[42]

This is a powerfully unequivocal profession of our inability to be sure in matters of scriptural interpretation. I have emphasized Milton's skepticism not in order to show that he does not share, in some measure, the Puritans' "orientation" toward the Word, but merely to prevent oversimplifying his attitudes toward, or his poetical uses of, the two books. Though Scripture may speak of things about which nature must remain silent, it is no more transparent in its speech, and no less in need of supplementing. Words are necessary not only to help Adam read the book of nature. They are likewise needed to explain the Word, and sometimes to explain the explanation. Think of Adam's question to Raphael, for example: "What meant that caution joined, *If ye be found / Obedient?*" (5.513–14; cf. Isa. 1:19), which prompts an answer—Raphael's account of Satan's rebellion and the war in heaven—which runs well over 1,200 lines. Or think of Adam misinterpreting Michael's interpretation of what it means to say that the woman's seed shall bruise the serpent's head, and of Michael's consequent need to offer a corrective *re*-interpretation (12.382–455).

There has been a strong tendency in recent scholarship, of which I would like to consider two instances, to exaggerate Milton's adherence to the Puritans' strict theology of the Word, with its concomitant devaluation of nature. In a discussion of the prologue to Book 3, with its references to Milton's having been "cut off" from the sight "of Nature's works," and from the wisdom contained in the "Book of knowledge," Herman Rapaport has argued that the blind Milton, because he "can no longer read the signs which God has written into the book of nature," "openly challenges" it. "Milton has only distrust for the notion of the onto-encyclopedic book, even if that book be nature herself." "We know from the *Prolusions*," he argues, "that Milton firmly rejected the books of the scholastics at an early age, and it should not surprise us that in *Paradise Lost* he once more attacks the book of knowledge fair, a concept dear to the medieval exegetes who had, after all, strong scholastic leanings."[43]

This strikes me as a peculiarly circuitous argument, justified neither by the prologue itself nor by the prolusions. The third prolusion, "Against Scholastic Philosophy," moves from its attack on the "useless and barren controversies of scholasticism" toward a concluding exhortation "to seek out and explore the nature of all living creatures," as well as the clouds, "the dews of morning," snow, hail, and the stars and sun, until "your mind ... at last attain the summit of human wisdom and at last know itself." This list of the creatures, like Adam and Eve's morning hymn (*PL* 5.153–208), is based on Psalm 148 and the *Benedicite omnia opera*. The seventh prolusion, "Learning Brings more Blessings to Men than Ignorance," contains a similar passage that begins: "The more deeply we delve into the wondrous wisdom, the marvellous skill, and the astounding variety of its creation ... the greater grows the wonder and awe we feel for its Creator and the louder the praises we offer Him."[44] Unless there is an irony in these passages that Rapaport neglected to mention, they both suggest that "at an early age" Milton the student, far from distrusting the book of nature, saw it as affording not only relief from the dry tedium of scholastic philosophy, but access to the Creator's wisdom as well.

Georgia Christopher's *Milton and the Science of the Saints* presents a more far-reaching and supple case for aligning Milton's views on the relationship between nature and Scripture with those of Calvin (and Luther), and hence her attempt to construe two crucial passages in *Paradise Lost* as supportive of that alignment may help demonstrate the problem I am referring to. The first passage—important because it involves fallen man—is the question that Adam, using Bonaventure's favorite figure, puts to Michael when the angel tells him he must leave Paradise: "In yonder nether world where shall I seek / His bright appearances, or footstep trace?" (11.328–29). Christopher finds Adam's question "quite wrongheaded," because, she writes, "the answer is no*where,* for 'God attributes to place / No sanctity' (11.836–37). Nor can anything important about God be discerned from the face of things now fallen, what with roses growing thorns, beasts turning predatory, and all the air darkening."[45] What Michael actually says, however, is that "God attributes to place / No sanctity, if none be thither brought / By men who there frequent, or therein dwell," which means, I take it, that if Adam and Eve bring sanctity to "their place of rest" (12.646), wherever it may be, God will sanctify it. Furthermore, Michael's answer to Adam's question suggests that it was not a wrongheaded but a very good question to ask:

> Adam, thou know'st heaven his, and all the earth.
> Not this rock only; his omnipresence fills
> Land, sea, and air, and every kind that lives....
> Yet doubt not but in valley and in plain
> God is as here, and will be found alike
> Present, and of his presence many a sign
> Still following thee, still compassing thee round
> With goodness and paternal love, his face
> Express, and of his steps the track divine.
>
> (11.335–54)

In short, nature, or the book of the creatures, will continue to signify, for those who can read it, just what it signified before the Fall: namely, the omnipresence, goodness, and love of the Creator. Indeed even the predatory beasts and the darkening air to which Christopher refers are legible. The fallen but regenerate Adam had already read them, correctly, as "mute signs in nature" of God's purpose, a warning of what lay in store for them (11.194–95).

The second passage is the story Adam tells of his very first encounter with the creatures and the Word:

> Thou sun, said I, fair light,
> And thou enlightened earth, so fresh and gay,
> Ye hills and dales, ye rivers, woods, and plains,
> And ye that live and move, fair creatures, tell,
> Tell, if ye saw, how came I thus, how here?
> Not of my self; by some great maker then,
> In goodness and in power pre-eminent;
> Tell me, how may I know him, how adore,
> From whom I have that thus I move and live,
> And feel that I am happier than I know.
> While thus I called, and strayed I knew not whither,
> From where I first drew air, and first beheld
> This happy light, when answer none returned, . . .
> . . . one came, methought, of shape divine,
> And said. . . .
>
> (8.273–96)

Christopher comments as follows:

> As if to demonstrate the inadequacy of natural theology, Adam's waking query of the world yields no important answers, no reply from Creation about who made it all. The answer comes from "A shape Divine," for even in Paradise God is "seen" and known as a guiding voice.... At the beginning of psychic life stands God's word.... Milton thereby suggests that man possesses... an innate knowledge of God impressed upon him by divine speech during his earliest hours in the Garden.[46]

Adam, however, does not, in fact, ask the question "Who made it all?" He asks a less general question, a question about himself: "How came I thus, how here?" And he answers it before the guiding voice speaks; answers it, apparently, by drawing inferences from the sight of the creatures, who fill his heart with joy, and by perusing that other creature, himself: "some great maker... in goodness and in power pre-eminent."

It is true that Adam would have strayed had not God appeared to him in a dream and carried him into Paradise, just as he would have there begun his "wandering" yet again had not God spoken to him. But he realizes before God speaks not only that he owes his being to "some great maker" worthy of adoration, but also that he is happy, i.e., fortunate. What is innate in Adam, what stands "at the beginning of psychic life," is a capacity to see, to read the face of things ("all things smiled"), and to reason ("Not of myself; by some great maker then"). The order of events suggests that nature, and "wondering eyes," are necessary, if not fully sufficient components of one's first lesson in theology. The question that the creatures cannot answer, at this point in the story, is how to know and adore that maker, and we may note that Milton's prose writings suggest that the creatures could not have provided Adam with religious (as distinct from theological) knowledge, i.e., the knowledge of how to adore or worship the Creator. On more than one occasion he expressed the conviction that "true Religion is the true Worship and Service of God, learnt and believed from the Word of God only. No Man or Angel can know how God would be worshipt and serv'd unless God reveal it."[47] Insofar as the Word provides the answer to Adam's question, it is contained in two straightforward instructions: first, "till and keep" the garden; second, "shun to taste" the forbidden fruit (8.320–27).

If in his prose, however, Milton makes a clear-cut distinction between what can be learned from nature (i.e., theological knowledge) and what only the Word can reveal (i.e., the forms of worship), the epistemological boundaries tend to fade in the poem. Adam's and Eve's earliest conversations, taken as a whole sequence, have a markedly liturgical flavor. They worship in ways they have not been taught, constructing a natural religion as well on their own. We follow them from their afternoon supper through their evening worship. We see them awaken as the birds sing their "matin song" (5.7). They begin their "orisons" (5.145) at "that sweet hour of prime" (5.170). The most memorable passages may be those in which Eve tells of her birth, of her love for Adam, or of her dream, but the couple's chief activity involves the expression of gratitude for what they have been given and of praise for the giver. The rhythms of their worship arise naturally from the cycles of their labor, nourishment, and repose.

In his earlier years Milton had shown great contempt for the Book of Common Prayer ("though Englisht, yet [it is] still the Mass-Book"), as indeed for all set forms of prayer, which "imprison and confine by force, into a Pin-fold of sett words, those two most unimprisonable things, our Prayers and that Divine Spirit of utterance that moves them."[48] And Adam and Eve do not follow set forms. Their "unmeditated" orisons are said or sung "in various style" (5.146–49). But those orisons are at least closely related to established liturgical forms. Milton's readers would have recognized their morning prayer as similar in both theme and structure to Psalm 148 and to the prayer book's ancient canticle for morning prayer, the *Benedicite omnia opera*. Either we can see Milton as alluding to those hymns of praise or, if Barbara Lewalski is correct, we can see Adam and Eve as the very creators of the genre.[49]

Milton was, after all, raised on the prayer book, and he was no doubt acquainted with John Knox's *Book of Common Order*, which was widely used by the Puritans from 1559 until the Westminister Directory appeared in 1644. There is evidence too that he was familiar with the "occasional forms of prayer," designed for daily use in the home, which were often appended to both Church of England and Puritan psalters and prayer books, as well as with the great traditional hymns of the Roman liturgy such as those set forth in the Sarum Breviary. It is clear that Milton wanted the words of Adam's and Eve's mouths and the meditations of their hearts to be both acceptable and familiar in the sight of his fit audience. His own apostrophe to holy Light at the beginning of Book 3, as well as his subsequent prayer for the light that shines within—both of them presented in the context of his blindness—would have been familiar liturgical gestures to his readers. Consider, for example, the beginning of the following "prayer conteining the duety of every true Christian," which appears in many sixteenth- and seventeenth-century editions of the Book of Common Prayer:

> Powre upon me (O Lord) thy holy Spirit of wisedome and grace ... and so lighten the naturall blindness and darknesse of my heart through thy grace, that I may dayly be renewed by the same spirit and grace.... Purge the grossenesse of my hearing and understanding, that I may profitably reade, heare, and understand thy worde and heavenly will.

Or consider the following rather livelier prayer for inner illumination, a "prayer to be said at our first waking":

> Much better is the light of the soul and insight of the mind [*oculus mentis*] than the light, or eyesight, of the body. The eyesight of the body every silly beast hath: but the sight of mind none hath but men, yea, none have it but wise men. Thou, therefore, O Lord Jesu Christ, which art the greatest of all lights, the only true light, the light whence springeth the light of the day, and the sun: thou light, which enlighteneth every man that cometh into the world. . . . thou mind and wisdom of the heavenly Father, enlighten my mind, that (being blind in all other things) I may see nothing, but that which belongeth to thee.[50]

The first words we hear Adam utter are spoken after their meal, and they are words of gratitude and praise. His language (with the key phrases here italicized) is not scriptural. It is the language not of the Bible but of daily Christian worship, the language of such prayers and thanksgivings as were said before and after eating, as in the following typical excerpts: "Glory, praise, and honour be unto thee most merciful and omnipotent Father, who of thine *infinite goodness* hast created man to thine own image and similitude, who also hast fed and daily feedest of thy most *bountiful* hand all living creatures." "*We do not present ourselves* here before thy Majesty *trusting in our own merits* or worthiness." "Sanctify these gifts which we receive of thy merciful *liberality*." "Let all the people rejoice in *praising and extolling* his great mercies. . . . We render thanks unto thee (O Lord God) for the *manifold* benefits which we continually receive at thy *bountiful* hand":[51]

> Sole partner and sole part of all these joys,
> Dearer thy self than all; needs must the power
> That made us, and for us this ample world
> Be *infinitely good,* and of his good
> As *liberal* and free as infinite,
> That raised us from the dust and placed us here
> In all this happiness, *who at his hand*
> *Have nothing merited,* nor can perform
> Aught whereof he hath need. . . .
> . . . Then let us not think hard

> One easy prohibition, who enjoy
> Free leave so large to all things else, and choice
> Unlimited of *manifold* delights:
> But *let us ever praise him, and extol*
> *His bounty....*
>
> (4.411–37)

Adam's speech differs from that of set prayer in at least one important respect, however. What he is doing is not offering praise or rendering thanks, but discovering that it behooves them to do so. In the passage just quoted we see him working not from axioms afforded him by his religion, but constructing a religion, and extending their natural theology as well, on the basis of his experience, letting his natural feelings impel him toward worship. Since we are so happy, so well provided for (he argues in effect), the "power that made us" must be infinitely good. The very use of the abstract phrase, *the power*, rather than a proper name, reinforces the sense that Adam is figuring things out rather than speaking out of developed habits or received ideas.

After their supper, and after the sun has set, Adam reminds Eve of the God-ordained rhythms of their life:

> fair consort, the hour
> Of night, and all things now retired to rest
> Mind us of like repose, since God hath set
> Labour and rest, as day and night to men
> Successive....
> Man hath his daily work of body or mind
> Appointed....
> Mean while, as nature wills, night bids us rest.
>
> (4.610–33)

The theme is repeated when

> Thus at their shady lodge arrived, both stood,
> Both turned, and under open sky adored
> The God that made both sky, air, earth, and heaven
> Which they beheld, the moon's resplendent globe
> And starry pole: Thou also madest the night,
> Maker omnipotent, and thou the day,

> Which we in our appointed work employed
> Have finished happy in our mutual help
> And mutual love, the crown of all our bliss
> Ordained by thee....
> But thou hast promised from us two a race
> To fill the earth, who shall with us extol
> Thy goodness infinite, both when we wake,
> And when we seek, as now, thy gift of sleep.
>
> (4.720–35)

These are among the standard gestures of evening prayers and hymns. One of the best-known evening prayers includes a passage that begins, "Forasmuch as it hath pleased Thee to make the night for man to rest in, as Thou hast ordained him the day to travail, grant, O dear Father, that we may so take our bodily rest." And a popular vesper hymn begins, "God creator of all things, ruler of the heavenly pole, clothing day with seemly light, night with the gift of sleep, So that rest may restore relaxed limbs from their accustomed labor...."

> (Deus Creator omnium,
> Polique Rector vestiens:
> Diem decoro lumine,
> Noctem soporis gratia;
> Artus solutos ut quies,
> Reddat laboris usui....)[52]

The couple sleeps, and Milton is at pains to affirm that Adam sleeps well. ("His sleep / Was airy light from pure digestion bred, / And temperate vapours bland" [5.3–5].) It is the sort of sleep one prayed for, as when the prayer and hymn just quoted proceed to ask "that our sleep be not excessive or overmuch after the unsatiable desires of the flesh" and that "faith may make temperate the vapor of sleep (*somni vaporem temperet*)."

Adam wakes, as the hymn set for Monday matins would have it, "with limbs refreshed by sleep."[53] Eve does not, but remains, until Adam awakens her, in "unquiet rest." The reader, after all, has been reminded more than once of Satan lurking in the background of their entire conversation, uttering threatening words of envy and hatred, approaching nearer "to view his prey" (4.399), stalking in the shape of a lion, couching close in the shape of a tiger, turning aside "for envy, yet with jealous leer malign" (4.503). And while the couple sleeps, he is discovered

> Squat like a toad, close at the ear of Eve;
> Assaying by his devilish art to reach
> The organs of her fancy, and with them forge
> Illusions as he list, phantasms and dreams,
> Or if, inspiring venom, he might taint
> The animal spirits that from pure blood arise....
>
> (4.800–805)

For Milton's devout reader the words describing this sinister assault would have been familiar indeed. No stronger fear was expressed in the standard devotions than the fear (to cite yet once more the evening prayer quoted above) that we may, in sleep, be overcome by "fantasies, dreams, or other tentations." In vesper hymns one prayed to God to "let the dreams and phantasms of night (*somnis et noctium phantasmata*) stand far off, and hold back our foe, lest our bodies be polluted."[54] One asked for protection against "the deceit of our envious foe."[55] In morning hymns one asked God to "blunt the teeth of the envious one" and to kindle one's faith to make it strong against "the venom of [his] fraud (*fraudis venena*),"[56] or to "let the phantasms of night disappear, the soul's guilt fall away, and whatever frightening thing of sin night has brought with its darkness come to an end."[57] Such fears are apparent even in the Roman marriage rite, which concluded with the priest's visit to the bride and groom on the wedding night, where he prayed over their bed that they be guarded "from all phantasies and illusions of devils."[58]

The dream that proceeds from Satan's devilish art gives Adam and Eve their first lesson in the mysterious workings of evil ("Yet evil whence? In thee can harbour none, / Created pure" [5.99–100]). It also instructs them, very gently, in the ritual of penance and absolution:

> So cheered he his fair spouse, and she was cheered,
> But silently a gentle tear let fall
> From either eye, and wiped them with her hair;
> Two other precious drops that ready stood,

> Each in their crystal sluice, he ere they fell
> Kissed as the gracious signs of sweet remorse
> And pious awe, that feared to have offended.
>
> (5.129–35)

But this is still a predominantly "pagan" expression of contrition. Eve maintains her composure and can hardly be said to weep. She *let fall* a tear from either eye. The language belongs as much to the tradition of secular love poetry as to that of Christian devotion, and she is as yet more a Venus than a Magdalene, as we may note by comparing it with a passage from Shakespeare's *Venus and Adonis:*

> She vail'd her eyelids, who like sluices stopp'd
> The crystal tide that from her two cheeks fair
> In the sweet channel of her bosom dropp'd....
> Whereat her tears began to turn their tide,
> Being prison'd in her eye, like pearls in glass,
> Yet sometimes falls an orient drop beside....
>
> (lines 956–58)

The absolution has its desired effect. "So all was clear, and to the field they haste" (136), but first, "lowly they bowed adoring, and began their orisons" (144–45). Once again, as with Adam's noontime expression of praise and gratitude of the previous day, Milton underscores their discovery of sacred song. While the canticle on which their hymn is partly based begins at once with the imperative "O all the works of the Lord, bless ye the Lord: praise him and magnify him forever," Adam and Eve's begins with a statement of fact leading to an inference:

> These are thy glorious works, parent of good,
> Almighty, thine this universal frame,
> Thus wondrous fair; thy self how wondrous then!
> Unspeakable, who sit'st above these heavens
> To us invisible or dimly seen
> In these thy lowest works, yet these declare
> Thy goodness beyond thought, and power divine:
> Speak ye who best can tell, ye sons of light,
> Angels, for ye behold him, and with songs
> And choral symphonies, day without night,

> Circle his throne rejoicing, ye in heaven,
> On earth join all ye creatures to extol
> Him first, him last, him midst, and without end.
>
> (5.153–65)

Basing their praise solely on their reading of the book of nature, the couple is acting out Paul's assertion that "the invisible things of [God] from the creation of the world are clearly seen, being understood by the things that are made" (Rom. 1:20). The hymn, because it is sung in unison, has the effect of temporarily canceling or overriding the differences between Adam and Eve. It reflects their shared understanding of God as they have derived it from their experience of Eden. They observe that the creatures "declare" God's goodness. Hence the invitation, "*speak* you who best can *tell*." The knowledge their song expresses, even in these opening lines, reaches considerably beyond the fact, which Adam had in the beginning so quickly surmised, that their maker is "in goodness and in power pre-eminent" (8.279), and it includes several of those attributes of God that Milton lists, in a dry and formal style, in *Christian Doctrine*. He is "wondrous," "unspeakable," and eternal ("Him first, him last, him midst, and without end" [5.165]). As these lines inform us, they have inferred the existence of angels, presumably from the "millions of spiritual creatures" Adam describes, who "with ceaseless praise [God's] works behold / Both day and night," and whom they have heard "singing their great creator" (4.677–84).

Prior to Eve's Satanic dream, Adam and Eve knew of nothing to pray for, their needs—or at least those needs they were cognizant of—being so amply satisfied. It is the dream, then, that initiates in them the act of prayer itself. Their morning hymn concludes with a brief prayer for safety or protection, and it is here that Milton first names their activity as prayer:

> Hail universal Lord, be bounteous still
> To give us only good; and if the night
> Have gathered aught of evil or concealed,
> Disperse it, as now light dispels the dark.
> So prayed they innocent, and to their thoughts
> Firm peace recovered soon and wonted calm.
>
> (5.205–10)

Their metaphors take us back to Milton's own prayer at the end of the invocation to Book 3 ("all mist from thence / Purge and disperse"), to the Book of Common Prayer itself ("Graciously hear us, that those evils, which the craft and subtilty of the devil or man worketh against us, be brought to nought, and by the providence of thy goodness, they may be dispersed"),[59] and, as Fowler has pointed out, to similar prayers embedded in the morning hymns: "Let the darkness yield to light, and night to the sun, so that any guilt which night has brought may give way to the workings of light."[60]

At this point, with firm peace and calm recovered, Adam and Eve set forth to work in the garden, as God, aware of the "stir" Satan has raised in Paradise, sends Raphael to warn them of the danger that threatens them. Except for a brief exchange in which they prepare for Raphael's visit we do not hear them conversing alone together until the morning of the Fall.

CHAPTER 3

Nature, Scripture, and the Architecture of *Paradise Lost*

When Milton built the grand Palladian temple that is *Paradise Lost*, to what extent did he have in mind as structural principles the pair of books that we have been exploring? I am persuaded that in fact he may have had them very much in mind. The structure that emerges, as will be clear, is not one that the reader is likely to be aware of while caught up in the process of reading the poem. It involves a symmetrical arrangement of the whole epic, an arrangement one can perceive only after stepping back from the text to reflect on how its parts are ordered. For the reader carried along by the ongoing movement of a phrase or sentence or episode, it remains as unnoticed as the regularity that governs that "mystical dance" in heaven: "mazes intricate, / Eccentric, intervolved, yet regular / Then most, when most irregular they seem" (5.620–24). One feels the intricacies, the intervolutions, as one reads. Yet the regularity is present, and its features coincide with the most familiar turning points of the poem, such as the prologues to Books 3 and 7, the poet's assertion that "half yet remains unsung" (7.21), and Michael's pausing "betwixt the world destroyed and world restored" at the beginning of Book 12.

Let me suggest, then, saving many of the details for subsequent chapters, that the central eight books of the poem, Books 3 through 10, would appear to turn, at their midpoint, and at the midpoint of the epic, from a preoccupation with nature to a preoccupation with the Word. The invocation to Book 3, which has at its core the fact that for the blind Milton the book of nature's works has been "expunged and razed," is addressed to "holy Light" and treats of eyes and "mortal sight," of physical blindness and inner vision. Here Milton is the poet as seer, and the invocation concludes with a prayer for the purgation and dispersal of "all mists" from his mind so that he may "see and tell / Of things invisible to mortal sight." In Book 3 the emphasis is on the Son as obedient to, and expressive of, God's face. He is the "radiant image" of his father (3.63). Books 3 through 6, in keeping with this beginning, have as their dominant motif the seeing and the reading of nature's works, concluding, in Book 6, with a scene depicting their destruction.

The invocation to Book 7, though strikingly similar in its structure to the invocation to Book 3 (see appendix A), has at its core not Milton's blindness and inner vision, but his profound dependence on Urania's "voice divine" to guide his song. It treats of Urania's and Wisdom's "celestial song," of the hoarseness and muteness which could silence the poet's own "mortal voice," and of the "evil tongues," "barbarous dissonance," and "savage clamor" that threaten to drown it out. Here Milton is the poet as singer, and he prays, "Still govern thou my song, / Urania, and fit audience find." In Book 7 the emphasis is on the Son as expressing not the face but the Word of God—his voice—and on the obedience of both Chaos and the creatures to that voice. Put differently, here Adam and Eve are not seeing and reading nature's works. They are listening to Raphael's voice and hearing in it also God's creating words. Recurring fourteen times through its pages, the refrain of Book 7 is the simple but powerful fiat, the creative performative "let there be" or "let the...." The dominant motif of Books 7 through 10 is the Word: first in its issuing forth to create the world; next in Adam's instruction under the tutelage of the Word; then in Satan's successful replacing of it with his own words; and finally, in Book 10, in Adam and Eve's collaborative and ultimately saving meditation on the Word that leads them to turn to God for forgiveness.

A similar movement from creatures to the Word, or from the visual to the audible, can be seen in Books 11 and 12, as Michael restores Adam's understanding, first by teaching him to see and interpret the misshapen creatures of the fallen world, and then by teaching him to listen to, to understand, and to speak, the words of Scripture. The sins or vices portrayed in Book 11 are directed against the creatures. They are sins of brute violence and gross, self-destructive intemperance: the murder of Abel; the hideous diseases of the lazar-house brought about by the perversion of "pure nature's healthful rules" (11.523); the godly-seeming men who, "unmindful of their maker... yield up all their virtue" to the "lustful appetance" of the "fair atheists" (11.611–25); the destruction of the creatures of the pastoral world as seen in the slaughter of cattle, oxen, ewes, and lambs, followed immediately by the destruction of a city and the massacre of its inhabitants (11.646–82); and finally, the luxury, riot, prostitution, rape, adultery, and "civil broils" (11.714–18) that lead God to repent himself "of man depraved" and bring on the Flood. Book 11 ends, at last, with the saving of the creatures as they enter Noah's ark in "sevens and pairs," and with the rainbow signaling God's intention to let his creation survive.

Book 12, on the other hand, is concerned almost entirely with the corruption and preservation of language as represented in both the spoken and written word. Michael tells Adam of Babel and Pentecost, of promises, covenants, and laws—of the preserving of the "records" of the covenant in the ark (12.252), of the "written records pure" left by Jesus' followers (12.513), of the Spirit engraving the law of faith in the hearts of believers. Above all, its subject is Michael's gradual unfolding of the proto-covenant, the Word pronounced against the serpent, the meaning of which Adam and Eve had earlier, with considerable though incomplete success, struggled to understand.[1]

The turn from Book 11 to Book 12 following the Flood parallels the transition from Book 6 to Book 7 following the picture of the destruction of the creatures in the war in heaven. Each picture of ruin is followed by a new beginning, the "world destroyed" followed by the "world restored" (12.3). Milton highlights the structural similarity. Metaphorically at the end of Book 6, and literally at the end of 11, evil is "soon / Driven back redounded as a flood on those / From whom it sprung" (7.56–58).

If one were to extrapolate from such evidence an overarching pattern, a schematic ordering of the twelve books of the poem, *Paradise Lost* would appear to be divided into three groups—Books 1 and 2, Books 3 through 10, and Books 11 and 12—with the first half of each group emphasizing nature, or the visual, and the second half Scripture, or the aural.

Of course such a notion seems absurd, given the fact that *Paradise Lost* first saw the light of day as "a poem in ten books," and the further fact that Milton's revision of the poem consisted simply in the dividing of the original Books 7 and 10 into two books each and the addition of scarcely more than a handful of lines. Nevertheless, I think there is sufficient evidence to warrant exploring the possibility that Milton was not merely rendering his epic Virgilian when he increased the number of books to twelve. And I take sustenance from Arthur Barker, who argued that "Milton's mind operated at ease only when he perceived in or imposed on his material a precise mathematical division of some sort." "Why," Barker asked, "did Milton in 1674 find himself dissatisfied with the composition and pattern implied by the division of the material of *Paradise Lost* into ten books? Is it possible that the simple division into twelve books... indicates... that subsequently he saw in it a pattern which the ten-book division tended to obscure?"[2] (Barker argued that the twelve books fall, according to three different principles of organization, into six groups of two books each, three groups of four books each, and two groups of six books each. Whether descriptions such as his or my own of the arrangements of the parts of *Paradise Lost* testify to the complexity of Milton's rage for order or to the intensity of the critic's is open to question.[3])

It is impossible, of course, to say with any certainty what patterns Milton saw in the first edition that led him to revise it, though we can begin by noting that the claim that "half yet remains unsung" (7.21) did not appear halfway through the ten-book edition but rather at the beginning of the seventh book. Furthermore, Book 7 begins, in both editions, with the prayer for Urania to "descend from heaven" (7.1), initiating a frequently noted series of falling actions that complements the predominating rising actions of the first six books.[4] Third, the hexameral subject matter of Book 7 relates what is quite literally a new beginning, both for God and, within his narrative, for Raphael. And finally, the entire second half of the later edition (Books 6 through 10 in the first edition) is scriptural in a sense in which the first half is not. From the moment Raphael undertakes to satisfy Adam's desire to know "how this world / Of heaven and earth conspicuous first began, / When and whereof created" (7.62–64), the events related and dramatized by Raphael and Milton, and later by Michael, are biblical events given in biblical order, from Genesis to Revelation, from Old Testament to New, filled in, or supplemented, with the story of Adam and Eve's gradual regeneration after the Fall. The first half of the poem, though it is equally furnished with biblical allusion, and its events are based on hints, however slight, from Scripture, decidedly does *not* follow the biblical order.

These facts serve, however, only to suggest the logic of seeing Book 7 as an appropriate starting point for the second half of the poem. If Milton needed a reason for dividing the original Book 10 where he did, one might regard Michael's words to Adam—"Thus thou hast seen one world begin and end; / And man as from a second stock proceed" (12.6–7)—as reason enough.[5]

Still, the more elaborate thematic pattern I have proposed must rest on the assumption that the alternations from the visual to the aural, or from the creatures to the Word, were present throughout the whole poem, and that Milton's revision, either by design or by accident, simply had the effect of making them fall into place. To make good the claim that the structure I have described is operative throughout, one would have to show a change from Book 1 to Book 2 analogous to the change from 11 to 12—a change, that is, from something like the creatures to something like the Word. There is a sense, however, in which the first two books are anomalous. Hell and chaos, as we shall see, stand in opposition to both nature and the Word. Only at the very end of Book 2 does Satan approach the point where "nature first begins / Her farthest verge, and Chaos to retire / As from her outmost works a broken foe" (2.1037–39). The military metaphor suggests a perpetual battle, as nature's works, God's self-expression, relentlessly subject Chaos to defeat. Chaos, furthermore, though he has very recently *heard* the word of God, nevertheless shows every sign of hostility to it, regarding it resentfully as having "encroached" on his own domain (2.998–1006).[6]

Nevertheless, it is certainly the case that Satan's situation is defined for us at the outset of Book 1 in visual terms, with an emphasis on what his eyes witness, in both senses of the word:

>Round he throws his baleful eyes
>That witnessed huge affliction and dismay
>Mixed with obdurate pride and steadfast hate:
>At once as far as angels' ken he views
>The dismal situation waste and wild,
>A dungeon horrible, on all sides round
>As one great furnace flamed, yet from those flames
>No light, but rather darkness visible
>Served only to discover sights of woe,
>Regions of sorrow, doleful shades ....
>
>   (1.56–65)

Hell is visible only by virtue of the eerie, chiaroscuro lighting produced by its strange fires. It is world of "utter darkness," a "fiery deluge, fed / With ever-burning sulphur" (1.68–72), a world "void of light, / Save what the glimmering of these lived flames / Casts pale and dreadful" (1.181–83). At the same time both the poet and Satan recall for us the very different "light of heaven" (1.73), "the happy realms of light," the "transcendent brightness" (1.85–86) from which the fallen angels have been driven. As we will note in the next chapter, the sight of the place itself exerts a powerful influence on the thought, feeling, and argument of every one of Satan's and Beelzebub's seven speeches.

The epic similes of Book 1 name the creatures of the natural world—whale, moon, Norwegian pine, autumnal leaves, locusts, bees—but they function less to help us visualize than to point to sizes beyond measure, multitudes beyond numbering. Satan himself, "prone on the flood, extended long and large / Lay floating many a rood, in bulk as huge / As whom the fables name of monstrous size, / Titanian, or Earth-born, that warred on Jove...or that sea-beast / Leviathan, which God of all his works / Created hugest that swim the ocean stream" (1.196–202). Or consider Satan's "ponderous shield...massy, large, and round....The broad circumference / Hung on his shoulders like the moon" (1.284–87); or his spear, "to equal which the tallest pine / Hewn on Norwegian hills, to be the mast / Of some great ammiral, were but a wand" (1.292–94); or his legions, "thick as autumnal leaves that strew the brooks / In Vallombrosa" (1.302–3), as "thick bestrewn" as the "floating carcasses and broken chariot wheels" of Pharoah's troops on the Red Sea coast (1.310–11). The legions are as numberless as "a pitchy cloud / Of locusts" (1.340–41), a "multitude, like which the populous north / Poured never from her frozen loins" (1.351–52). Throning numberless to enter Pandaemonium, they are as "thick swarmed" as "bees / In spring time" that "pour forth their populous youth about the hive / In clusters" (1.767–71).

Just as we do not know whether the peasant mentioned in the closing lines of Book 1 "sees / or dreams he sees" fairie elves reveling in the moonlight, so we cannot be certain of what we see. The images within the similes are disconcerting because they do not stand still, but rather "modulate," to use Geoffrey Hartman's term.[7] Satan's huge shield, first presented in a close-up, is gradually diminished, presented as the moon as it might be seen through "optic glass" (1.288). The references designed to convey Satan's vast size shift, first, from the fabulous ("Briareos or Typhon") to the biblical, and hence real but typological, Leviathan, and then to the historical, actual whale "with fixed anchor in his scaly rind" (1.206). In a single extended simile the legions of "angel forms" lying on the "inflamed sea" are compared first to "autumnal leaves," then to "scattered sedge" on the Red Sea coast, then to "floating carcasses / And broken chariot wheels" (1.301–13).

Furthermore, as Elizabeth Fuller has argued in her amplification of Hartman's essay, the images within the similes "do not reinforce their referents, but take the poem into qualitatively different worlds": "The warmth of the bees' activity in their almost human city and the flowery springtime, the cool and peaceful beauty of the midnight revels, and the feelings these arouse in the reader take the poem far away from the heated and painful conflicts of hell."[8] In like fashion the poignantly fleeting references to "the pleasant valley of Hinnom" (1.404), "the flowery dale of Sibma clad with vines" (1.410), and "fair Damascus, on the fertile banks / Of Abbana and Pharphar, lucid streams" (468–69) afford brief but eloquent glimpses of the alluring sights of the fallen but still beautiful world of nature as we know it, and of Eden.[9]

These glimpses, however, are perpetually in danger of being eclipsed by the disturbingly unnatural. The reader of Book 1, like the reader of Book 11, is assaulted with images of physical violence, brutality, and the destruction of God's creatures disfigured or deformed: Moloch, "horrid king besmeared with blood / Of human sacrifice, and parents' tears" (1.392–93); Dagon, "when the captive ark / Maimed his brute image, head and hands lopped off / In his own temple" (1.458–60); Satan, his face "intrenched" by "deep scars of thunder" (1.601). Images of the eruption or destruction of nature are presented in such a way as to suggest grotesque human wounding and pain, including the pain of forced childbirth. Mammon, whose "crew / Opened into the hill a spacious wound / And digged out ribs of gold," is also he who will first teach men "with impious hands" to "rifle . . . the bowels of their mother earth / For treasures better hid" (1.686–90). We hear, too, within a simile, of:

> the shattered side
> Of thundering Aetna, whose combustible
> And fuelled entrails thence conceiving fire,
> Sublimed with mineral fury, aid the winds,
> And leave a singed bottom all involved
> With stench and smoke.
>
> (1.232–37)

Other similes refer to nature in its corrupted state, anticipating the effects of the Fall on the creatures. Satan's form, which "had yet not lost / All her original brightness," is compared to the sun when "from behind the moon / In dim eclipse" it sheds "disastrous twilight ... on half the nations, and with fear of change / Perplexes monarchs" (1.589–99; cf. 10.412–13, 11.183–84). The "glory" of his followers has been "withered," "as when heaven's fire / Hath scathed the forest oaks, or mountain pines, / With singed top their stately growth though bare / Stands on the blasted heath" (1.612–15; see 10.1075–76).

Finally, Milton introduces the roll call of the fallen angels, whose subsequent deeds on earth he describes, with a clear allusion to Paul's account of how those who had come to know God through his works nevertheless fell into idol worship and "changed the glory of the uncorruptible God into an image made like to corruptible man, and to birds, and fourfooted beasts, and creeping things" (Rom. 1:23):

> By falsities and lies the greatest part
> Of mankind they corrupted to forsake
> God their creator, and the invisible
> Glory of him that made them, to transform
> Oft to the image of a brute....
>
> (1.367–71)

The sacrilegious worshiping of the creatures, whether kings, like Moloch, or man-made images of a brute, like the statue of Dagon, "sea monster, upward man / And downward fish" (1.462–63), is one of the major themes of Book 1. We read of the Israelites "bowing lowly down / To bestial gods" (1.434–35); of the Egyptians, "their wandering gods disguised in brutish forms" (1.481–82); of Jeroboam, "likening his maker to the grazed ox" (1.486). Another, closely related theme is that of the desecration or profanation of the sacred: the placing of heathen altars next to the altar of God, or of heathen shrines within his sanctuary; the violation of holy rites with "abominations" and "cursed things" (1.388–90) or with "wanton rites" and "lustful orgies" (1.414–15). Solomon builds his temple of idolatry "right against the temple of God" (1.401–2). Ahaz destroys "God's altar" and builds another of the "Syrian mode" in which to burn his "odious offerings" (1.472–75). Sion's daughters exhibit their "wanton passions in the sacred porch" (1.453–54); Ely's sons fill "with lust and violence the house of God" (1.495–96). Such profanation, such mixing of the holy with the unholy or impure, assaults the creation because for Milton one of the fundamental laws of nature is that like things should be united with like. As we are told in Book 7, God at the creation "downward purged / The black tartareous cold infernal dregs /Adverse to life," and "the loud misrule / Of Chaos far removed, lest fierce extremes / Contiguous might distemper the whole frame" (7.237–40, 271–73). It is that same law that necessitates the ejection of man from Paradise: "longer in that Paradise to dwell, / The law I gave to nature him forbids: / Those pure immortal elements that know / No gross, no unharmonious mixture foul, eject him tainted now" (11.49–52).[10]

To enter the hell of Book 2 is to enter a very different world. Its predominant imagery is not visual but auditory. It contains, both actually and proportionately, far more speech and dialogue than Book 1, and the emphasis in the first half is on the arguments made, the voices that speak, and the audible responses of the listeners. The sounds described are muffled, indistinct, hoarse, and above all they and their meanings are "hollow"—hollow either because they are secondhand, echoic sounds, emerging from hollow spaces, or because they are semantically empty, specious, lacking in substance. When Belial speaks, "All was false and hollow; though his tongue / Dropt manna." "His thoughts were low ... yet he pleased the ear" (2.112–17). He speaks "with words clothed in reason's garb" (2.226). When Mammon concludes his speech, the simile Milton uses to convey the fallen angel's response is very different from those in Book 1:

>   such murmur filled
> The assembly, as when hollow rocks retain
> The sound of blustering winds, which all night long
> Had roused the sea, now with hoarse cadence lull

> Seafaring men o'erwatched, whose bark by chance
> Or pinnace anchors in a craggy bay
> After the tempest.
>
> (2.284–90)

When Satan volunteers his solitary flight to earth, his followers rise, and "their rising all at once was as the sound / Of thunder heard remote" (2.476–77). And when the trumpets' "regal sound" signals the end of the debate, "the hollow abyss / Heard far and wide, and all the host of hell / With deafening shout returned them loud acclaim" (2.515–20).[11] The echoes continue. At the birth of Death, Sin tells us, she "fled, and cried out Death; / Hell trembled at the hideous name, and sighed / From all her caves, and back resounded Death" (2.787–89). Sin is "compassed round" with the "clamours" of her incestuously conceived brood (2.862), and from within her come their howling and hollow sounds:

> about her middle round
> A cry of hell hounds never ceasing barked
> With wide Cerberian mouths full loud, and rung
> A hideous peal: yet, when they list, would creep,
> If aught disturbed their noise, into her womb,
> And kennel there, yet there still barked and howled,
> Within unseen.
>
> (2.653–59)

Or again, there is Sin's own "strange" and "hideous outcry" (2.726, 737), the "lamentation loud" heard on the river Cocytus (2.579), and the "jarring sound" of the doors of hell, which "on their hinges grate / Harsh thunder, that the lowest bottom shook / Of Erebus" (2.880–83).

Finally, there are the "noises loud and ruinous" (2.921) that Satan hears as he approaches chaos, noises we will hear again in Book 12, which opens with the "jangling noise of word unknown," the "hideous gabble," the "din" and "hubbub strange" that turns Babel into "Confusion" (12.55–62):

> At length a universal hubbub wild
> Of stunning sounds and voices all confused
> Borne through the hollow dark assaults his ear

> With loudest vehemence: thither he plies,
> Undaunted to meet there what ever power
> Or spirit of the nethermost abyss
> Might in that noise reside.
>
> (2.951–57)

The spirits that Satan meets in the abyss are the consorts of Chaos, "Tumult and Confusion all embroiled, / And Discord with a thousand various mouths" (2.966–67). Book 2, in short, takes us into a vast echo chamber of mouths within mouths, including, with all the others, the hungery "maw" of Death, with its "ghastly smile" (2.846). The largest of mouths, hell's own "furnace mouth," when opened, casts forth smoke and flame *redounding* (2.888–89), a word that, in this context, suggests that the smoke and flame recoil or return into the mouth from which they spew forth, just as the hellhounds return into the hollow womb of Sin, from whose mouth their howling can still be heard.

But Book 2 is not just about hollow sounds. It is also about the Word. Scripture itself is on trial in Book 2. It is the subject of the infernal debate. Let us return at this point to the opening lines of Book 2, where we meet with a different sort of echo and a different sort of hollowness. The book begins with a caricature, which we will not fully understand until we have read further, of the Son of God:

> High on a throne of a royal state, which far
> Outshone the wealth of Ormus and of Ind,
> Or where the gorgeous East with richest hand
> Showers on her kings barbaric pearl and gold,
> *Satan exalted sat, by merit raised*
> To that bad eminence; and from despair
> Thus high uplifted beyond hope, aspires
> Beyond thus high, insatiate to pursue
> Vain war with heaven, and by success untaught
> His proud imaginations thus displayed.
>
> (2.1–10; my emphasis)

The description is an anticipatory parody of the Father's exaltation of the Son following the latter's offer to ransom mankind: "Because thou hast, though throned in highest bliss / Equal to God.... and hast been found / By merit more than birthright Son of God, / Found worthiest to be so by being good, ... Therefore thy humiliation shall exalt / With thee thy manhood also to this throne" (3.305–14). The contrasts are obvious: Satan's pride and the Son's humility; Satan throned in the gorgeous trappings of wealth, the Son in highest bliss; Satan exalted because he merits a "bad eminence," the Son because he has been "good"; Satan aspiring to rise, the Son willing to "descend ... to assume / Man's nature" (3.303–4). The debased caricature of the Son will resume when Satan alone volunteers to "seek deliverance" for his partners in sin (2.464–65), just as the Son alone will volunteer to seek deliverance for fallen man. It will appear yet again when Satan confronts his offspring, Sin and Death.

The exalting of the Son, which makes him the "head supreme" to whom "all knees ... shall bow" (3.319–21), is in turn an echo of the Father's earliest spoken words, his begetting of the Son, a passage that is, chronologically, the first and hence originating Word of the epic. As Mary Nyquist has shown, it provokes from Satan "a dynamic and dramatic opposition," including his rebellion.[12]

> Hear all ye angels, progeny of light,
> Thrones, dominations, princedoms, virtues, powers,
> Hear my decree, which unrevoked shall stand.
> This day I have begot whom I declare
> My only Son, and on this holy hill
> Him have anointed, whom ye now behold
> At my right hand; your head I him appoint;
> And by my self have sworn to him shall bow
> All knees in heaven, and shall confess him Lord.
>
>   (5.600–607)

The prime scriptural authority for the begetting of the Son is Psalm 2. Milton identifies the fallen "kings of the earth" of the psalm with the fallen angels, just as he turns the "holy hill of Zion" into the "holy hill" in heaven. In the second and third verses of the psalm we read that "the kings of the earth set themselves, and the rulers take counsel together, against the Lord, and against his anointed, saying, Let us break their bands asunder, and cast away their cords from us." The "counsel" would seem to lie behind both the meeting Satan calls following the scene of the begetting, where Satan and Abdiel are the only speakers, and also behind the council or debate that dominates the first half of Book 2. Indeed the debate in hell focuses almost exclusively on the Word, the last four and one-half lines of the irrevocable decree uttered by the Father when he announces his begetting of the Son:

> Him who disobeys
> Me disobeys, breaks union, and that day
> Cast out from God and blessed vision, falls
> Into utter darkness, deep engulfed, his place
> Ordained without redemption, without end.
>
> (5.611–15)

The scriptural authorities for these lines, this doom or sentence against which the fallen angels are struggling, are multiple, including most centrally the following two passages: "God spared not the angels that sinned, but cast them down to hell, and delivered them into chains of darkness to be reserved unto judgment" (2 Pet. 2:4); "Then shall he say also unto them on the left hand, Depart from me, ye cursed, into everlasting fire, prepared for the devil and his angels.... And these shall go away into everlasting punishment...." (Matt. 25:41, 46).

The closing lines of the decree, or variations on their theme, are echoed or referred to again and again in Book 6. The father first assigns the task of driving the rebel angels "out from God and bliss, / Into their place of punishment" to Michael and Gabriel (6.52–53), but he suspends the doom (6.692) in order to transfer it to the Son: "Pursue these sons of darkness, drive them out / From all heaven's bounds into the utter deep" (6.715–17). The Son, in turn, restates it as a promise: "I ... shall soon ... rid heaven of these rebelled, / To their prepared ill mansion driven down / To chains of darkness" (6.736–39).

If Satan and his crew are motivated in Book 1 by what they see around them, in Book 2 they are motivated by the words that they have heard the Father speak, those words being the source of the contention among the participants in the debate, each of whom interprets them according to his nature. Moloch, who initiates the debate in hell by declaring that his own "sentence" is for open war, cites the decree to argue against the fear that God may find some worse way to satisfy his wrath: "What can be worse / Than to dwell here, driven out from bliss, condemned / In this abhorred deep to utter woe"

(2.85–87). The rest of the debate circles around the questions of just how literally meant, and how unchangeable, the decree is, and of how to respond to it. Belial paraphrases the core of Moloch's argument—"Say they who counsel war, we are decreed, / Reserved and destined to eternal woe" (2.160–63)—but takes exception to it, averring, first, that things could be worse:

> Better these [torments] than worse
> By my advice; since fate inevitable
> Subdues us, and omnipotent decree,
> The victor's will.
>
> (2.196–99)

Their present condition, he rightly argues, is the "sentence" of their conqueror, their "doom." Then, however, ignoring or forgetting the fact that their present loss has been "ordained without redemption, without end," he urges patience and expresses the hope that "our supreme foe in time may much remit / His anger" (2.208–11).

Mammon revises Belial's train of thought. Knowing that they could not hope to "disenthrone the king of heaven" unless "everlasting fate" should "yield to fickle chance," and knowing that it never will, and knowing too that even if God were to "publish grace to all" they would not accept it, he dismisses "all thoughts of war." Dwelling on the punishment, the doom itself, he also rejects Belial's hope that the "raging fires" may "slacken" (2.213–14), the darkness grow light (2.220). But he offers his equally misguided hope. If the "piercing fires" themselves do not change, perhaps "our temper" will be "changed / Into their temper; which must needs remove / The sensible of pain" (2.275–78). As for the darkness, he believes, it's all a question of how you look at it:

> This deep world
> Of darkness do we dread? How oft amidst
> Thick clouds and dark doth heaven's all-ruling sire
> Choose to reside, his glory unobscured,
> And with the majesty of darkness round
> Covers his throne....
> As he our darkness, cannot we his light
> Imitate when we please?
>
> (2.262–70)

Beelzebub, knowing better than the others that what God says he means, mocks and rebukes both Mammon and those who applauded his suggestions, charging them with failing to recognize

> that the king of heaven hath doomed
> This place our dungeon, not our safe retreat
> Beyond his potent arm, to live exempt
> From heaven's high jurisdiction, in new league
> Banded against his throne, but to remain
> In strictest bondage, though thus far removed,
> Under the inevitable curb, reserved
> His captive multitude.
>
> (2.316–23)

It is not merely the debate, however, that is haunted by the Father's decree. Satan, who might well regard his "solitary flight" from hell as a welcome escape, no sooner reaches the gates of hell than he is reminded of the decree once again. Death, like the fallen angels, has heard that doom, and when he first sees Satan he hurls it in his face:

> Are thou that traitor angel, art thou he,
> Who first broke peace in heaven and faith, till then
> Unbroken, and in proud rebellious arms
> Drew after him the third part of heaven's sons
> Conjured against the highest, for which both thou
> And they outcast from God, are here condemned
> To waste eternal days in woe and pain?
>
> (2.689–95)

Satan presents himself in this scene, however, not as condemned rebel but as a redeemer and deliverer. He has come to "set free" not only Sin and Death but also "all the heavenly host / Of spirits" who fell with him. He goes on his errand alone, and will, as he says, "one for all / My self expose" (2.824–28). In keeping with that parodic role, as we move further into Satan's meeting with Sin and Death we are brought back to the beginning of God's decree, thus initiating a series of warped echoes of the Word as it appears both in the poem and in the Bible. When Sin, attempting to placate her father and her son, introduces Death to Satan as "thy only son...thine own begotten" (2.728, 782), it is hard not to associate her phrases with the Father's

"I have begotten whom I declare / My only son" (5.603–4), with its source in Psalm 2, "Thou art my son; this day I have begotten thee," as well as with the phrases "only begotten" and "only begotten son," which recur again and again in the New Testament with reference to Christ. The hint of parody, which indirectly links Sin with Mary and Death with Jesus, is important, of course, because Death and his mother Sin are the Son's true adversaries, and it is by defeating them that he will disarm Satan. The resurrection of Christ, "seed" of both Eve and Mary, "shall bruise the head of Satan, crush his strength / Defeating Sin and Death, his two main arms, / And fix far deeper in his head their stings / Than temporal death shall bruise the victor's heel" (12.430–33).

In the description of the births of Sin and Death, too, there is an acting out of the story implicit in James 1:15: "Then when lust hath conceived, it bringeth forth sin: and sin, when it is finished, bringeth forth death." But there are also distorted linguistic remnants of the births of John and Jesus as recorded in the Gospel of Luke. Sin springs from Satan's head surrounded by "all the host of heaven," which does not, of course, like the "heavenly host" at the birth of Jesus, say "Glory to God in the highest," but rather is seized with amazement and recoils in fear (Luke 2:13–14; *PL* 2.758–59). Simeon takes the infant Jesus for a "sign which shall be spoken against," while Sin is taken "for a sign portentous" (Luke 2:34; *PL* 2.76). Death, his mother's "inbred enemy," emerges from his mother's womb "brandishing his fatal dart / Made to destroy," from which she promptly flees (2.785–87). Simeon recognizes Jesus as a sword that "shall pierce through [Mary's] own soul" (Luke 2:35), thus foretelling the afflictions that await her. (See *Paradise Regained* 2.87–89.) Sin, in her womb, "prodigious motion felt and rueful throes" (2.780), but when Elizabeth heard the salutation of Mary "the babe leaped in [her] womb for joy" (Luke 1:44). It may even be that Milton chose the word *pensive* to portray Sin as she sits alone awaiting the onset of labor to remind us of its cognate in the King James Version, where "Mary kept all these things, and *pondered* them in her heart" (Luke 2:19).

Sin declares her own independence of and antagonism toward the Word: "But what owe I to his commands above / Who hates me?" (2.856–57). She is devoted to Satan as the Son is to the Father, and Eve to Adam. She is his "perfect image" (2.764), and she says to him, "Thou art my father, thou my author, thou / My being gavest me;

whom should I obey / But thee, whom follow?" (2.864–66). She dreams of her promised life on earth, "where I shall reign / At thy right hand voluptuous, as beseems / Thy daughter and thy darling, without end" (2.868–70). Her perverse misappropriation of Scripture is best illustrated by the first chapter of Hebrews, with its references to the Son reigning forever at the right hand of God, whose "express image" he is, and to that initiating Word, the exaltation of the Son over the other angels, which prompted Satan's envy and rebellion in the first place. It brings us full circle:

> God...hath in these last days spoken unto us by his Son, whom he hath appointed heir of all things, by whom also he made the worlds; Who being the brightness of his glory, and the express image of his person, and upholding all things by the word of his power, when he had by himself purged our sins, sat down on the right hand of the Majesty on high; Being made so much better than the angels, as he hath by inheritance obtained a more excellent name than they. For unto which of the angels said he at any time, Thou art my Son, this day have I begotten thee?... Unto the Son he saith, Thy throne, O God, is for ever and ever. (1:1–8)

Books 1 and 2, then, have in common with Books 11 and 12 a decided shift from sights of woe to sounds of woe and from nature to Scripture. The unnatural violence, maiming, and brutality of Book 1 reappear with the slaughter, sickness, and inhuman pain that Adam witnesses in Book 11. The "hubbub wild" of chaos in Book 2 becomes the "hubbub strange" of Babel in Book 12. The fallen angels struggle in Book 2 to come to terms with the sentence or doom of their conqueror, just as Adam struggles in Book 12 to understand the doom or curse God had placed on the serpent. What distinguishes the opening from the closing books of the poem is partly the way Book 11 moves toward the rainbow "betokening peace from God, and Covenant new" (866), and Book 12 toward another new beginning. Or, to put the matter differently, there is no Michael in hell, no one to interpret the sights and sounds (including the "doom") for Satan and his followers. Toward the end of Book 2 Satan describes himself as "wandering [a] darksome desert...alone, and without guide, half lost" (973–75). Adam and Eve "take their solitary way" out of Paradise with "wandering steps," but with "providence their guide" (12.647–49).

Having made a preliminary case for regarding the books of nature and Scripture as thematic categories that contribute to the structural plan of *Paradise Lost*, let me reiterate my earlier caveat. The poem is not as rigidly patterned as the nature/Scripture dichotomy might suggest. The categories are neither pure nor impervious. Milton was no Procrustes, and *Paradise Lost* has its own inexhaustible and uncontainable plenitude. But the argument for a kind of order within the plenitude is worth making if it in turn helps make sense of the poem. Whether it does depends chiefly on the chapters that follow.

CHAPTER 4

Meditating on the Creatures, Part 1: The Case of Satan

Truly the light is sweet, and a pleasant thing it is for the eyes to behold the sun.

—(Eccles. 11:7)

As Book 2 ends, Satan's laborious flight has carried him to the point where "nature first begins / Her farthest verge," where light appears, and where the tumult and din that define both hell and chaos diminish (2.104–40). Books 3 through 6, as I have suggested, have nature, or the creation, as their pervasive subject matter. The subject is first set forth in Book 3, a book about the seeing of the world of created beings, a book about the nature and purpose of the creation. That world is "the book of knowledge fair," the book "of nature's works." Beginning with a poignantly personal invocation by a blind man, it includes three characters—the Father, Satan, and Uriel, "the sharpest sighted spirit of all in heaven" (3.691)—who are possessed, in different ways, of perfect vision.

It is a book about seeing and the desire to see, however, and not a book of seeing. Perhaps because it is about "things invisible to mortal sight," it is surprisingly and insistently void of description. Over a third of it (lines 80–343) is taken up with the speeches of the Father and the Son, followed immediately by the angels' hymn of praise to them, and it concludes with another dialogue—that between Satan and Uriel. From time to time we are told what the supernatural beings behold, but we are given remarkably few visual aids. The invocation itself, in immediate response to Milton's prayer for inner sight, launches us suddenly to the "pure empyrean" where the Father "bent down his eye, / His own works and their works at once to view" (3.57–59), and we are given a vision of what is to be seen sub specie aeternitatis:

> on his right
> The radiant image of his glory sat,
> His only Son; on earth he first beheld
> Our two first parents, yet the only two
> Of mankind, in the happy garden placed,
> Reaping immortal fruits of joy and love,
> Uninterrupted joy, unrivalled love
> In blissful solitude; he then surveyed
> Hell and the gulf between, and Satan there
> Coasting the wall of heaven on this side night
> In the dun air sublime, and ready now
> To stoop with wearied wings, and willing feet,
> On the bare outside of this world, that seemed
> Firm land imbosomed without firmament,
> Uncertain which, in ocean or in air.
>
> (3.62–76)

Isabel MacCaffrey has referred to this passage as "reproducing the objects of divine survey" by means of "a static, visually conveyed tableau."[1] But the objects of divine survey are not so much visually conveyed or reproduced as they are named, numbered, and located. There is a calm, grand sweep and scope to the panorama, suggesting reassuringly the totality of the Father's vision. But only Satan, "coasting the wall of heaven on this side night / In the dun air sublime, and ready now / To stoop with wearied wings, and willing feet," receives visual attention, and he is moving, not static. The stress is not on how things look but on the characters' states of mind. If we picture Adam and Eve reaching for real fruits, the picture quickly dematerializes in the presence of the abstractions that follow. And in the concluding lines—"that seemed / Firm land imbosomed without firmament, / Uncertain which, in ocean or in air"—we are led precisely into the realm of the visually indeterminate. Furthermore, as MacCaffrey goes on to say, the passage moves altogether "beyond the power of [human] visualization" toward the Father's beholding of "past, present, future," a timeless vision that gives rise to his strikingly imagined capacity, bodied forth in his subsequent speech, to speak of future events in the past tense, to feel angry at man for what he has not yet done, to feel compassion for those who have not yet suffered, even to express his scorn for those yet unborn who would blame on his foreknowledge what they themselves would will.

The conversation between the Father and the Son is motivated by the sight of Satan winging his way "directly toward the new created world" (3.89), and of the new creation itself. With the exception of his angry and somewhat defensive posture, as in "Ingrate, he had of me / All he could have; I made him just and right" (3.97–8), the Father's first speech is strikingly nonbiblical, nonscriptural.[2] Though not without strong feeling, it is essentially doctrinal. It sets forth the nature of man, the "chief / Of all [God's] works" (7.515–16), declaring him to have been made "just and right, / Sufficient to have stood, though free to fall"; it defines as well the proper relationship between creator and creature, and the Creator's plan with respect to the future of his "creature late so loved." The Son, sensing Satan's intentions, and indeed paraphrasing the relevant passage of Beelzebub's speech (2.365–70), asks the Father, with considerable rhetorical energy, "Wilt thou thy self / Abolish thy creation, and unmake, / For [the adversary], what for thy glory thou hast made?" (3.162–64).

"The great creator" replies with the promise that "man shall not quite be lost," that indeed he will be renewed so that "once more he shall stand / On even ground against his mortal foe"—if there can be found someone able and willing to "pay / The rigid satisfaction, death for death" (3.167–212). The Son accepts the office, and the Father's last speech begins with an expression of his love for all his creatures:

> O thou in heaven and earth the only peace
> Found out for mankind under wrath, O thou
> My sole complacence! well thou knowst how dear
> To me are all my works, nor man the least
> Though last created, that for him I spare
> Thee from my bosom and right hand, to save,
> By losing thee awhile, the whole race lost. . . .
>
> (3.274–80)

The conversation between Father and Son tells "the whole story." It is, in a sense, the poem's last word about the creation, and to it one can return as a standard by which to measure both the conduct and the discourse that ensue. The angelic hymn the angels sing extols the Father in his aspect as Creator, "author of all being, / Fountain of light" (3.374–75), and the Son, "of all creation first" (3.383), as the agent by whom the Father created the "heaven of heavens and all the powers therein" (3.390–91).

Following this conversation, and the Son's sacrificial offering, we are transported, via Satan, to the "opacous globe" (3.418) that divides chaos from the created universe. Here what Milton offers us is virtually unseeable. To Satan himself it seems a "boundless continent / Dark, waste, and wild," with "ever-threatening storms / Of Chaos blustering round" (3.423–26). The elements are mixed and indistinguishable. It is a "windy sea of land" (3.440). And there is literally nothing on it for him to see. It is a creatureless limbo of empty space awaiting the time when it will be filled with more emptiness, or "vanity." Satan is

> Alone, for other creature in this place
> Living or lifeless to be found was none,
> None yet, but store hereafter from the earth
> Up hither like aerial vapours flew
> Of all things transitory and vain, when sin
> With vanity had filled the works of men:
> Both all things vain, and all who in vain things
> Built their fond hopes of glory or lasting fame,
> Or happiness in this or the other life;
> All who have their reward on earth, the fruits
> Of painful superstition and blind zeal,
> Nought seeking but the praise of men, here find
> Fit retribution, empty as their deeds.
>
> (3.442–54)

This is precisely *not* a view of "nature's works," but of "the unaccomplished works of nature's hand, / Abortive, monstrous, or unkindly mixed, / Dissolved" (3.455–57). The sight of nature's works is, for the reader, the telos of Book 3, but lies beyond it.

Satan wanders "long" in this emptiness, "till at last a gleam / Of dawning light" draws his attention to "a structure high"—high, but otherwise indescribable and hence, for the reader, unvisualizable: "inimitable on earth / By model, or by shading pencil drawn" (3.499–509). Reaching the first step of the "structure," he attains a vantage point resembling the Father's, where, like a blind man healed, he "looks down with wonder at the sudden view / Of all this world at once" (3.542–43). Here "the golden sun in splendour likest heaven

/ Allured his eye" (3.572–73). It is light, of course, that Satan seeks, and that draws him on. He, like the poet, has labored "through utter and through middle darkness" to escape the Stygian pool, but unlike the poet, who had "found no dawn," Satan moves from the "dawning gleam" into the full light of day. Alighting on the sun, he finds it "beyond expression bright, / Compared with aught on earth, metal or stone" (3.591–92)—a phrase that once again, as with the "structure high," suggests that indeed what Satan sees lies beyond mortal vision. But if the sun's appearance at such close range is indescribable, as a location from which to see, it affords Satan (though not the reader) all that the eyes could wish:

> Here matter new to gaze the devil met
> Undazzled, far and wide his eye commands,
> For sight no obstacle found here, nor shade,
> But all sunshine, as when his beams at noon
> Culminate from the equator, as they now
> Shot upward still direct, whence no way round
> Shadow from body opaque can fall, and the air,
> No where so clear, sharpened his visual ray
> To objects distant far. . . .
>
> (3.613–21)

Having arrived at the sun, Satan wishes to discover where man dwells. Posing wonderfully as an admirer of the new-created world, he expresses to Uriel his

> Unspeakable desire to see, and know
> All these [God's] wondrous works, but chiefly man,
> His chief delight and favour, him for whom
> All these his works so wondrous he ordained. . . .
>
> (3.662–65)

Fulsomely employing the language of the great psalms of praise— "Sing psalms unto him: talk ye of all his wondrous works" (105:2); "Great is the Lord, and greatly to be praised. . . . I will speak . . . of thy wondrous works" (145:3, 5)[3]—he declares that he desires to explore and learn in order that "the universal maker we may praise. . . . Wise are all his ways" (3.676, 680).

Uriel is thoroughly taken in. "Oft though wisdom wake," Milton explains, "suspicion sleeps / At wisdom's gate" (3.686–87). Uriel recognizes, nevertheless, the propriety of Satan's professed motive:

> Fair angel, thy desire which tends to know
> The works of God, thereby to glorify
> The great *work-master,* leads to no excess
> That reaches blame, but *rather merits praise*
> *The more it seems excess.* . . .
> For wonderful indeed are all his works,
> Pleasant to know, and worthiest to be all
> *Had in remembrance* always with delight.
>
> (3.694–704; my emphasis)

Both Satan's declaration and Uriel's approving response are steeped in the thought and language of biblical Wisdom literature, thus anticipating one of the essential doctrinal features of Raphael's subsequent education of Adam and Eve: the pursuit of knowledge of the created world is good provided it serves to glorify the wisdom of the Creator. Consider, for example, such passages as that in which Solomon urges that those who delight in the beauty of God's works must "acknowledge the workmaster . . . for by the greatness and beauty of the creatures proportionably the maker of them is seen" (Wisd. 13:1, 5); or the advice which concludes the long passage celebrating "the works of the Lord" in Ecclesiasticus: "When ye glorify the Lord, exalt him as much as ye can; for even yet will he far exceed: and when when ye exalt him, put forth all your strength, and be not weary; for ye can never go far enough" (Ecclus. 43:30); or finally Psalm 111: "The works of the lord are great, sought out of all them that have pleasure therein. . . . He hath made his wonderful works to be remembered" (2, 4).

But if the Psalms and Wisdom literature encourage man to search out God's works in order to glorify him, they also, and even more insistently, stress the impossibility of ever achieving full understanding. Uriel goes on to ask: "But what created mind can comprehend / Their number, or the wisdom infinite / That brought them forth, but hid their causes deep" (3.705–7). Versions of this question recur again and again in the Wisdom writings; in God's rebuke to Elihu and Job, for example, or in Job's own question: "But where shall wisdom be found . . . seeing it is hid from the eyes of all living?" (28:12, 21), or in the following passage with which Ecclesiasticus opens: "All wisdom cometh from the Lord, and is with him for ever. Who can number the sand of the sea, and the drops of rain, and the days of eternity? Who can find out the height of heaven, and the breadth of the earth, and the deep, and wisdom?"[4]

Satan and the Sense of Wonder

All these God's wondrous works. The book of knowledge. Nature's works. The works of God. These phrases and their paraphrases, along with expressions of the desire to see, define much of the motivation of Book 3. They also point us toward the dominant motif of the three books that follow, where character is revealed in large measure by one's responses to the visible world, and where the reader is not only given several different perspectives on unfallen nature but is actively trained in what it would be like to see, and to live in, Paradise. Uriel's last speech concludes by directing Satan's gaze and ours toward earthly Paradise, pointing, as it were, toward the subject of Book 4 and toward a location from which "all these God's wondrous works" are visible from a mortal perspective: "Look downward on that globe.... That spot to which I point is Paradise" (3.722, 733).

The impulse toward the sight of nature's works, a movement that we can trace back to the invocation with its image of Milton's eyes rolling in vain to find light's piercing ray, and perhaps even earlier to Satan's first sight of "glimmering dawn" at the end of Book 2, or to Beelzebub's wish for a "brightening orient beam" to "purge off this gloom," is the context in which we should read Satan's address to the sun (4.32–113). For that address begins in a manner very like a Protestant meditation on the book of nature, or a meditation on the creatures, as it was often called. Such meditations received scriptural authority, as we should expect, from Paul's insistence that "the invisible things" of God can be understood "by the things that are made" without the aid of Scripture (Rom. 1:20), but also from the many exhortations toward and examples of such meditation in the Psalms. Indeed the Father's looking down "from the pure empyrean ... his own works and their works at once to view" has its closest scriptural analogue in one of the psalms that meditates on his works: "The Lord looketh from heaven; he beholdeth all the sons of men. From the place of his habitation he looketh upon all the inhabitants of the earth. He fashioneth their hearts alike; he considereth all their works" (Ps. 33:13–15).

Although any of the creatures, rightly seen, could serve as a fit subject for meditation, the sun, moon, and stars were, as one might expect, frequent choices as signs of the glory of God and his works:

> O LORD our Lord, how excellent is thy name in all the earth! who hast set thy glory above the heavens.... When I consider thy heavens, the work of thy fingers, the moon and the stars, which thou hast ordained; What is man, that thou art mindful of him?... (Ps. 8:1–4)

> The heavens declare the glory of God; and the firmament sheweth his handywork. Day unto day uttereth speech, and night unto night sheweth knowledge. There is no speech nor language, where their voice is not heard.... In them hath he set a tabernacle for the sun.... His going forth is from the end of the heaven, and his circuit unto the ends of it: and there is nothing hid from the heat thereof. (Ps. 19:1–6)

Always, of course, the idea is to meditate not just *on* but *through* the creatures, to their maker's goodness, power, mercy, justice, or wisdom, or to that which lies beyond or above mortal sight, or to homely moral wisdom. Among Milton's many near contemporaries who recommended or offered meditations on the sun were Joseph Hall, Lewis Bayly, and Richard Baxter. In one of the earliest Protestant collections of prayers and meditations, Henry Bull included separate groups of meditations on the sun as it rises, as it reaches the meridian, and as it sets.[5] (One thinks of Adam and Eve urging the sun to sound God's praise "both when thou climb'st, / And when high noon hast gained, and when thou fall'st" [5.171–4].) In a work entitled *Meditations, From the Creatures*, Thomas Taylor, a Fellow at Christ's when Milton was there, began a fourteen-page meditation on the sun by declaring: "When I behold the sunne in his wonderful *magnitude*... how can I choose but bee ledde unto the Lord? and say, Great is the Lord, great is his power, and there is no end of his greatnesse. For, how much greater is the Creator of the Sun and Heavens, than the things created?"[6]

Satan's is a failed meditation, to be sure. But we will miss its point if we merely contrast it, as many critics have done, to Milton's invocation at the beginning of Book 3 and do not acknowledge the reverent tone of its opening and the powerfully healing effect, however temporary, that the sight of the sun has on Satan. William Riggs calls the opening lines of Satan's address a "travesty" of Milton's prologue, in which Satan "hurls envious defiance" at the sun.[7] Stephen Wigler calls it a "parody": "Satan's dramatic monologue, ostensibly addressed to the Sun, is an emotionally charged arraignment of the Son and the Father."[8] For Louis Martz the two passages exemplify a running contrast between "the poet's love, the devil's hate":

> Milton has designed Satan's hymn to light...in such a way that we are bound to compare it, point by point, with the feelings and attitudes expressed by the poet in his great prologue to Book 3. Satan's soliloquy begins as a poem of loss, quickly turns to a hymn of hate, and then to an expression of despair. Satan at the outset addresses not the Eternal nor the abstract essence that is God, but simply addresses the physical planet in terms that convey an implicit paganism, sun-worship.[9]

But Satan's lines are neither travesty nor parody, and they are certainly not an arraignment of the Son and the Father. Satan places no blame whatsoever on God, and he arraigns only himself. Milton introduces the passage by reminding us of Satan's troubled thoughts, the workings of his conscience, the awakening of despair and bitter memory. As God's omniscience enabled him to behold past, present, and future, so Satan's conscience here "wakes the bitter memory / Of what he was, what is, and what must be / Worse" (4.24–26). He is "much revolving," just as in *Paradise Regained* the Son is presented as "much revolving" before he enters on his "holy meditations" (1.185, 195):

> Sometimes towards Eden which now in his view
> Lay pleasant, his grieved look he fixes sad,
> Sometimes towards heaven and the full-blazing sun,
> Which now sat high in his meridian tower:
> Then much revolving, thus in sighs began.
>   O thou that with surpassing glory crowned,
> Look'st from thy sole dominion like the God
> Of this new world; at whose sight all the stars

> Hide their diminished heads; to thee I call,
> But with no friendly voice, and add thy name
> O sun, to tell thee how I hate thy beams
> That bring to my remembrance from what state
> I fell, how glorious once above thy sphere;
> Till pride and worse ambition threw me down
> Warring in heaven against heaven's matchless king.
>
> (4.27–41)

If we feel hatred in these words, it is only Satan's hatred of himself. The lines in which he presents himself as hating the sun's beams are curiously detached, void of any felt hatred, envy, or defiance. Consistent with Milton's introduction to the passage, the emotions that are actually expressed, as distinct from merely being named, are deep regret and awe. What Martz takes to be an implicit paganism or sun worship is no more so than Milton's own celebration of the sun, "in splendour likest heaven," in Book 3, lines 572–86, especially when we consider how quickly Satan turns from the sun to "heaven's matchless king." Here, as often elsewhere when he beholds the creation, Satan's thought and language jibes closely with that of his betters. His description, for example, of the stars hiding "their diminished heads" at the sight of the sun takes us back to Milton's description of "the vulgar constellations" keeping "distance due" from the sun's "lordly eye" (3.577–78), and beyond that to the bedazzled seraphim that "veil their eyes" with their wings in the presence of the "eternal King... fountain of light" (3.374–82). Though we understand Satan's sinister motive in telling Uriel of his "unspeakable desire to see, and know" God's "wondrous works" (3.662–63), there is no reason to assume that those works do not win his genuine and profound admiration, or that his desire to see them was not strong.

The memory of his own self-defeat—thrown down by his pride and ambition—leads Satan to wonder why he waged a war at all, and he recognizes the inadequacy, indeed the foolishness, of the only answer he can give:

> Ah wherefore! He deserved no such return
> From me, whom he created what I was
> In that bright eminence, and with his good
> Upbraided none; nor was his service hard.
> What could be less than to afford him praise,

> The easiest recompense, and pay him thanks,
> How due! Yet all his good proved ill in me,
> And wrought but malice; lifted up so high
> I sdeigned subjection, and thought one step higher
> Would set me highest, and in a moment quit
> The debt immense of endless gratitude,
> So burdensome still paying, still to owe;
> Forgetful what from him I still received,
> And understood not that a grateful mind
> By owing owes not, but still pays, at once
> Indebted and discharged; what burden then?
>
> (4.42–57)

Satan remembers here, as he had in his very first speech in hell, how highly favored he had been of God. What he now understands is how easy God's yoke was, how light his burden. His understanding at this point in the meditation seems flawless. As Thomas Merrill points out, Satan's "poignant query, 'Ah wherefore?' turns up no answer that logic can afford to explain the cause of his rebellion. The careful delineation of God's impeccable qualities, far from justifying Satan's sin, only increases its irrationality."[10] He expresses remorse for his rebellion, wishing he had been ordained "some inferior angel" (59), but he realizes quickly that it would have made no difference. He would have freely chosen the rebels' side. Tempted for a moment to curse God's "free love dealt equally to all," he turns the curse upon himself:

> Nay cursed be thou; since against his thy will
> Chose freely what it now so justly rues.
> Me miserable! Which way shall I fly
> Infinite wrath, and infinite despair?
> Which way I fly is hell; my self am hell.
>
> (4.71–75)

"My self am hell." In spite of this piercingly accurate perception we have tended to underestimate the degree of Satan's self-knowledge. The narrator has told us, in a strikingly paradoxical phrase, of the fallen angel's "bitter memory / Of what he was, what is, and what must be / Worse" (4.24–26). In what seems a wishful avoidance of the meaning of the phrase, William Kerrigan asserts that "the surprising

'Worse' of line 26 corrects the momentary suggestion that Satan, like the narrator, remembers his future. No prophet, Satan cannot know what is to be."[11] But Satan does know, both here and elsewhere in the poem, what is to be.[12] He knows that "of worse deeds worse suffering must ensue" (4.26). He knows that his own pride will prevent him from repenting, and that if he were to repent his ambition would cause him to fall again. He knows that the higher he rises in hell the lower he will fall, and the more misery he will experience.

Only at the very end of the meditation, after convincing himself that even repentance would be but the prelude to "a worse relapse / And heavier fall" (100–101), does he reach full despair, and what we hear, even in these concluding lines, is not hatred but a resigned retreat into an earlier state of mind:

> So farewell hope, and with hope farewell fear,
> Farewell remorse: all good to me is lost;
> Evil be thou my good; by thee at least
> Divided empire with heaven's king I hold
> By thee, and more than half perhaps will raign;
> As man ere long, and this new world shall know.
>
> (4.108–13)

It is a clear case of backsliding, and only if we recognize the many stages through which Satan's soliloquy moves on the path from wonder to despair to a rather melancholy resolve to embrace evil as his good can we accurately compare his address to the sun with Milton's address to holy Light.[13] One point of the comparison, surely, is that even Satan can be deeply moved by the beauty of the sun, and the memories it stirs. If that were not the case, the contrast between Milton's conversion of loss into prayer and Satan's conversion of confession into despair would strike us as pat and schematic rather than as exemplary of two similarly human struggles, the first issuing in victory, the second in defeat.

The creatures in *Paradise Lost*, whether they be the heavenly bodies, the trees and flowers of Paradise, or the human face divine, move those who behold them toward wonder, toward love of God, and toward self-knowledge. Satan is susceptible to these motions, but never allows them to prevail.[14] Conflicts like those in his meditation on the sun between, on the one hand, awe, admiration, an impulse to love or to repent, and, on the other, envy, pride, despair, and the determination to destroy, are dramatized again and again.

Wonder is by far the feeling most frequently associated with the sight of God's works, both in the Old Testament and in *Paradise Lost*. Wonder is nonrational. It leaves us susceptible to faith in things unseen, as in the first few minutes of Adam's life, or vulnerable to deception, as in the case of Eve's wonder-filled response to the "brute" serpent's possession of a human voice. We first see Satan wonder-struck in Book 3, when he "looks down with wonder at the sudden view / Of all this world at once":

> As when a scout
> Through dark and desert ways with peril gone
> All night; at last by break of cheerful dawn
> Obtains the brow of some high-climbing hill,
> Which to his eye discovers unaware
> The goodly prospect of some foreign land
> . . . .
> Such wonder seized, though after heaven seen,
> The spirit malign, but much more envy seized,
> At sight of all this world beheld so fair.
>
> (3.542–54)

The last three lines point toward what is perhaps the deepest paradox in Satan's nature, suggestive of what Merrill has called "the mysteriousness of sin."[15] Wonder is so outward-looking, so lacking in self-interest, even in self-awareness. It "abstracts" us from ourselves, as Milton will later point out. Envy, on the other hand, is absorbed in the self and its deficiency. Milton will not quite make explicit the psychology of their simultaneous presence, that "hateful seige of contraries" (9.121–22) within Satan's mind, or of the fact that, at every juncture, it is his evil intent, sustained by envy, that tips the balance. Consider his first sight of the human creatures:

> O hell! What do mine eyes with grief behold,
> Into our room of bliss thus high-advanced
> Creatures of other mould, earth-born perhaps,
> Not spirits, yet to heavenly spirits bright
> Little inferior; whom my thoughts pursue
> With *wonder,* and could love, so lively shine

> In them divine resemblance, and such grace
> The hand that formed them on their shape hath *poured*.
> Ah gentle pair, ye little think how nigh
> Your change approaches, when all these delights
> Will vanish and deliver ye to woe,
> More woe, the more your taste is now of joy;
> Happy, but for so happy ill secured
> Long to continue, and this high seat your heaven
> Ill fenced for heaven to keep out such a foe
> As now is entered; yet no purposed foe
> To you whom I could pity thus forlorn
> Though I unpitied.
>
> (4.358–75; my emphasis)

There is a cut, a gap, after the word *wonder,* as Satan shifts from the declarative into the conditional mood, and another after the word *poured,* as if, in the phrase Patricia Parker uses in her discussion of Eve's fall, the actual movement into sin is "just beyond gradation, beyond language."[16] Since a story that filled in the space would make the movement appear to have been caused, the gap, Parker suggests, "is crucial to the Miltonic premise of freedom." Indeed the impression of Satan's being possessed of freedom of choice is strengthened in this passage (he *could* love, *could* pity them), as he experiences an only slightly controlled sympathy before hardening, once more, into the grimly ironic adversary: "league with you I seek, / And mutual amity so strait, so close . . ." (375–76).[17]

We next see Satan when he returns to Paradise after his weeklong flight around the globe, "as from his inward grief / His bursting passion into plaints thus poured":

> O earth, how like to heaven, if not preferred
> More justly, seat worthier of gods, as built
> With second thoughts, reforming what was old!
> For what god after better worse would build?
> Terrestrial heaven, danced round by other heavens
> That shine, yet bear their bright officious lamps,
> Light above light, for thee alone, as seems,
> In thee concentring all their precious beams
> Of sacred influence: as God in heaven

> Is centre, yet extends to all, so thou
> Centring receivest from all those orbs; in thee,
> Not in themselves, all their known virtue appears
> Productive in herb, plant, and nobler birth
> Of creatures animate with gradual life
> Of growth, sense, reason, all summed up in man.
> With what delight could I have walked thee round,
> If I could joy in aught....
>
> (9.97–115)

Prior to the last two lines, Satan's language expresses, I would suggest, something actually not unlike joy. Forgetting himself, and lost in what he sees, he summarizes so fluidly, with the freshness of wonder rather than the patient care of instruction, so much of what Raphael explains to Adam and Eve! Once again there are readers who find pride, egocentrism, and intellectual confusion in the passage,[18] yet its primary effect, surely, is to convey a sense of just how heavenly this earth seems even to one who has witnessed heaven and has defined himself in opposition to all that is good. Nor, in these lines, is Satan appreciative of appearances only, but of the earth's sacred place in God's design and of its ordered, ascending, productive plenitude. He knows the value and virtue of what he sees. His unquestioning geocentrism, which Fowler calls "perverse," is not astronomical but teleological, similar to that implicit in the almighty's creation of the sun, moon, and stars "to give light on the earth," setting them "in the firmament of heaven / To illuminate the earth" (7.345, 349–50). For Satan, as for God and Raphael, the earth, with its prime inhabitant man, is the centerpiece of the new creation. Furthermore, as Elizabeth Fuller has pointed out, he expresses with great clarity the "reciprocity of heaven and earth."[19] The earth receives the "sacred influence" of light and imparts its "virtue" to herb, plant, and "creatures animate," just as, on the fourth day of the creation, the sun is made "to receive and drink the liquid light," and from the sun, in turn, "as to their fountain other stars / Repairing, in their golden urns draw light" (7.362–65).

Milton precedes Satan's final soliloquy by explaining the effect on him of Eve's "heavenly form / Angelic, but more soft, and feminine," a phrase that almost suggests *even* more soft and feminine, *even* more lovely. Her "graceful innocence" overawes his malice, "abstracts" him from his evil, "disarms" him of enmity, hate, envy, and revenge (9.457–66). He remembers himself, to be sure, as he always does, and becomes again the arch rebel, deceiver, and destroyer. He serves, nevertheless, as a continuing though unwitting participant in the celebration of "all these God's wondrous works." In soliloquy, and with nothing to gain but anguish from indulging in the wonders of the creation, Satan has his own credibility.

Satan Agonistes

Where does this capacity in Satan come from, this better self against which he repeatedly has to struggle? Is he, in effect, a different Satan from the Satan we meet in hell? The question is pressing enough to merit a brief digression. Thirty years ago A. J. A. Waldock remarked that "everybody feels that the Satan of the first two books stands alone; after them comes a break, and he is never as impressive again.... It is not merely that the Satan of the first two books reenters altered: the Satan of the first two books to all intents and purposes *disappears:* I do not think that in any true sense we ever see him again."[20] And more recently Harold Bloom, speaking of Satan's address to the sun, has claimed that "here Satan makes his last choice, and ceases to be what he was in the early books of the poem.... Nothing that can be regenerated remains in Satan."[21]

We will not, I think be able to grasp the consistency of Milton's characterization of Satan unless we can move beyond the dichotomous thinking that has, from the beginning, informed "the Satan controversy," the kind of thinking represented by the question Bloom himself characterizes as the most "vexing of critical problems concerning *Paradise Lost.* ... Is Satan in some sense heroic, or is he merely a fool?"[22]

Roland Mushat Frye's article on Satan in *A Milton Encyclopedia* offers an admirably accurate summary of the state of critical affairs:

> The Satan whom we encounter in *PL* 1 and 2 has the accoutrements of the great leader, the attractiveness of an epic adventurer.... Books 1 and 2 reveal a heroic self-assertion, self-reliance, and self-deification that we find not only exciting (both aesthetically and intellectually) but with which we in varying degrees identify. Milton's introduction of Satan is thus designed to make him

attractive—for temptation rarely if ever comes to man in unattractive form—and yet at the same time Milton, even in the opening Books, is ironically undercutting Satan's magnificence by linking him repeatedly to tyranny, deceit, and destruction.... The only way Milton could present this Christian conception adequately was through a characterization that readers would in many ways find both magnificent and appealing. At the same time, the stature of Satan is undercut by irony and by narrative comment.... The degeneration of Satan's character in the epic is brilliantly conceived and executed.... He declares his hatred of the sun's light (4.37), and demonstrates a hatred of all life, a general antagonism to all that lives.[23]

One can hear behind Frye's account some of the most distinguished Miltonists of our century: Waldock, Davis Harding, and Balachandra Rajan on Satan's heroic qualities; Douglas Bush on the importance of making evil attractive; Stanley Fish on Satan's stature being undercut by narrative comment; C. S. Lewis on his degeneration; John Steadman on his tyranny and deceitfulness.[24]

What gets left out of all this, of course, is the impressive Satan we have been talking about, the Satan who has it within himself to sigh "Ah wherefore!", to "melt" at the thought of Adam and Eve's "harmless innocence" (4.389), and to recognize, just as the poet does, that the influence of light is "sacred." What gets left out is the Satan whose dramatization, as Catherine Belsey reminds us, owes so much to Shakespeare and the other Elizabethans who knew how to represent the thinking and feeling human mind.[25]

To find that Satan in hell we must look more closely at what he says there, and how he says it, than readers caught up in the terms of the Satan controversy have been free to do. The only differences between Satan in hell and Satan on earth are those that parallel the differences between the two locations, and between dialogue and monologue. The movement from wonder to envy to self-redefinition has its analogue, in hell, as he struggles to control what Dr. Johnson might have called "the perplexity of contending passions," and Milton "the refluxes of mans thoughts from within."[26]

Consider, for example, Satan's first speech, impressive, according to Stanley Fish, "as a *performance* that commands attention as would any forensic *tour de force*."[27] Certainly Milton prepares us not for a public performance but for a character torn by contending passions, a character not just in physical but in mental agony:

> for now the thought
> Both of lost happiness and lasting pain
> Torments him; round he throws his baleful eyes
> That witnessed huge affliction and dismay
> Mixed with obdurate pride and steadfast hate....
>
> (1.54–58)

The very order of the substantives—lost happiness, pain, affliction, dismay, pride, and steadfast hate—parallels the movement of the speech that is about to follow. We are prepared for an astonished, pained outburst, and when Satan speaks we hear it:

> If thou beest he; but O how fallen! how changed
> From him, who in the happy realms of light
> Clothed with transcendent brightness didst outshine
> Myriads though bright: If he whom mutual league,
> United thoughts and counsels, equal hope
> And hazard in the glorious enterprise,
> Joined with me once, now misery hath joined
> In equal ruin: into what pit thou seest
> From what highth fallen, so much the stronger proved
> He with his thunder: and till then who knew
> The force of those dire arms?
>
> (1.84–94)

Arnold Stein notes that "the opening lines keep trying for Satan's characteristic orchestration and assertiveness of rhythm, but lose their way and falter in a dazed and confused syntax."[28] Satan indeed can scarcely recognize his mate and is aghast at the change that has taken place in him. This is dismay indeed—a sense of powerlessness and great loss. Satan's first recollection, intensified by the sight of his new surroundings, is of the happiness that was theirs in heaven, of how they were once "clothed with transcendent brightness," testifying to his sense of the honored place they held, outshining "myriads though bright," in the heavenly hierarchy. He can still refer to "the glorious enterprise," though almost as a proper name that, given the results, has nearly lost its meaning. His exclamatory locutions ("into what pit thou seest / From what highth fallen") emphasize his shock and horror at what Beelzebub will call their "foul defeat."

Bush said of this speech that "in every line [it] should arouse horror and repulsion. It is a dramatic revelation of nothing but egoistic pride and passion, of complete spiritual blindness."[29] But surely there is little in these lines to repel us, for we are watching a man reeling under the devastating impact of what he sees, and overcome by spiritual insight he never had before. It is the first instance in the poem of "knowledge of good bought dear by knowing ill" (4.222).

At this point Satan begins, in Stein's phrase, to "pull himself together." The first course of action that comes to his mind, and one that continues to exert pressure on him, is that of repentance, and it is immediately rejected. He powerfully asserts the fixedness of his mind. But to do so is difficult. What he displays here is not rhetorical skill, but the triumph of will over knowledge, the muscular suppression of the dismay his opening lines have revealed. His pride swells ("Vaunting aloud," in Milton's phrase) as he remembers how his "fixed mind / And high disdain" won over numberless others who "durst dislike [God's] reign" and recollects, whether accurately or not, their near success. He alludes very briefly to the source of his disdain, a *sense* of "injured merit," as if he remembers but no longer quite feels what he then felt. And then, with still greater assurance, he begins to imagine a goal; not an action, but a peculiarly negative state of mind:

> What though the field be lost?
> All is not lost; the unconquerable will,
> And study of revenge, immortal hate,
> And courage never to submit or yield:
> And what is else not to be overcome?
> That glory never shall his wrath or might
> Extort from me.
>
> (1.105–11)

In the lines that immediately follow, not being overcome is redefined yet again as not bowing and suing for grace "with suppliant knee," for that would be "low indeed, ... an ignominy and shame beneath / This downfall." And as the speech concludes, Satan moves forward to persuade himself for the first time, drawing on his experience, that it may be possible to act:

> since by fate the strength of gods
> And this empyreal substance cannot fail,
> Since through experience of this great event
> In arms not worse, in foresight much advanced,
> We may with more successful hope resolve
> To wage by force or guile eternal war
> Irreconcilable, to our grand foe,
> Who now triumphs, and in the excess of joy
> Sole reigning holds the tyranny of heaven.
>
> (1.116–24)

Taken as a whole, this first speech is striking for the rapidity with which Satan manages to suppress the "deep despair" implicit in the opening lines, moving from "so much the stronger proved / He with his thunder" to "dubious battle" and "shook his throne" in only eleven lines. It is a compressed speech, a struggle that succeeds, temporarily, by boldly rewriting history, transforming "the happy realms of light" to "the tyranny of heaven." In its compression what it omits, of course, is any persuasive account of what motivated Satan's rebellion, or of what he hopes to achieve other than the avoidance of the "ignominy and shame" that, in his eyes, would accompany repentance, and revenge for the ignominy and shame that his defeat has already brought upon him. Certainly there is little sense that God has wronged him, only that he has defeated him. The speech is impressive, to be sure, and at times eloquent. But Satan is not performing for the public here. If the speech succeeds as rhetoric, its only convert must be Satan himself, for Beelzebub is neither cheered nor persuaded by his leader. He knows that all their glory is extinct, and, like Satan, he knows that what they have lost is happiness itself:

> Too well I see and rue the dire event,
> That with sad overthrow and foul defeat
> Hath lost us heaven, and all this mighty host
> In horrible destruction laid thus low,
> As far as gods and heavenly essences
> Can perish: for the mind and spirit remains
> Invincible, and vigour soon returns,
> Though all our glory extinct, and happy state
> Here swallowed up in endless misery.
>
> (1.134–42)

Like Moloch and Belial in the debate of Book 2, Beelzebub is uncertain of their conqueror's intentions, and hence fearful of what worse may follow. His concluding lines are pure despair:

> What can it then avail though yet we feel
> Strength undiminished, or eternal being
> To undergo eternal punishment?
>
> (1.153–55)

Satan responds with an attempt to find a more persuasive definition of their mission. He does so in highly abstract terms. He neither indicts God nor tries to put a fair coloring on his own motives; he testifies to the goodness of God's intentions and the evil of his own, as if he were accepting for himself the only logical category (contrariness) left for him to inhabit:

> But of this be sure,
> To do aught good never will be our task,
> But ever to do ill our sole delight,
> As being the contrary to his high will
> Whom we resist. If then his providence
> Out of our evil seek to bring forth good,
> Our labor must be to pervert that end,
> And out of good still to find means of evil;
> Which oft-times may succeed, so as perhaps
> Shall grieve him, if I fail not, and disturb
> His inmost counsels from their destined aim.
>
> (1.158–68)

In his contempt for weakness, and in his setting himself up as the contrary of God and goodness, Satan bears some resemblance to the type of the "ungodly" man, who says, in The Wisdom of Solomon: "Let our strength be the law of justice: for that which is feeble is found to be nothing worth. Therefore let us lie in wait for the righteous; because he is not for our turn, and he is clean contrary to our doings." What is remarkable about Satan's lines is that in spite of their declaring something so significant as the opposition between good and evil which shall control human history until the end of time, they come across as being so human, so conversational, as if he were thinking aloud, figuring out a resolution to an apparent dilemma. The opposition is put forward as if Satan honestly believed it would be reassuring ("But of this be sure") and lead to "delight," a term oddly unadulterated by suggestions of either malicious or selfish intent. But the assuredness gives way, in the last three lines, to a sense of uncertain purpose and of slightly faltering confidence beneath the determination. *Perhaps* he shall grieve God, *if* he fail not. And "disturb" implies only the temporary interruption, not the destruction, of God's "destined aim." Here as elsewhere he is struggling unsuccessfully to find a compelling voice and mission for himself.

That Satan feels the likely futility of his intentions is indicated once again by "But":

> But see the angry victor hath recalled
> His ministers of vengeance and pursuit
> Back to the gates of heaven.
>
> (1.169–71)

This is as much as to say, "These words may be disheartening, *but* take hope from the following." "The thunder . . . perhaps hath spent his shafts." Then, gloomily surveying his surroundings ("dreary," "forlorn," "wild," "desolate," "dreadful"), he concludes his speech in lines that continue to bespeak little but continuing doubt and discouragement:

> Thither let us tend
> From off the tossings of these fiery waves,
> There rest, if any rest can harbour there,
> And reassembling our afflicted powers,
> Consult how we may henceforth most offend
> Our enemy, our own loss how repair,
> How overcome this dire calamity,
> What reinforcement we may gain from hope,
> If not what resolution from despair.
>
> (1.183–91)

My point is not that Satan and Beelzebub are weak or lacking in courage. It is that even in hell they are inwardly tormented—and their speech shows it—by a much sharper awareness of the good, the happiness, they have lost, and of the hopelessness of their present state, than they are usually given credit for possessing. For all his resolve there is something humanly pathetic about Satan in these passages, something decidedly un-Promethean in his uncertainty about what to do (if indeed there is anything to be done), and certainly in the defeated but touchingly elegiac tone of the words he utters when at last he stands at the edge of the burning pool looking toward land:

> Is this the region, this the soil, the clime,
> Said then the lost archangel, this the seat
> That we must change for heaven, this mournful gloom
> For that celestial light? Be it so, since he
> Who now is sovereign can dispose and bid
> What shall be right: furthest from him is best
> Whom reason hath equalled, force hath made supreme
> Above his equals. Farewell happy fields
> Where joy for ever dwells: hail horrors, hail
> Infernal world, and thou profoundest hell
> Receive thy new possessor: one who brings
> A mind not to be changed by place or time.
> The mind is its own place, and in itself
> Can make a heaven of hell, a hell of heaven.
>
> (1.242–55)

There is deep sadness in the repeated, stressed demonstratives of the first four lines, and defeat in the lines that follow, as if Satan cannot take his eye or mind off the surrounding "mournful gloom." If the salutation "hail horrors, hail / Infernal world" were met out of context, it might be thought to resound with rebellious, proud determination. But coming where it does, the willed courage it conveys is considerably muted by a tone of resignation.

Satan's initial thoughts in this passage are dominated by his sense of the overriding significance of place: "*furthest* from him is best," "*fields / Where* joy forever dwells." He struggles against this perception and thinks, fleetingly, that location does not matter. But he can find no substitutes for the place words *heaven* and *hell* to designate his desires. Later of course he will discover that his mind *is* its own place insofar as he carries hell within it, even into Paradise. But here he cannot but succumb to place. There is something sadly comical about his feeble attempt to wring advantage from this place—"Here at least / We shall be free; the almighty hath not built / Here for his envy, will not drive us hence" (1.258–60)—as if he knows his joke is on himself. The speech closes on that note of brooding regret and yearning that casts a shadow over almost every speech in Books 1 and 2, as he determines to call upon his partners "to share with us their part / In this unhappy mansion." The upward thrust of "once more / With rallied arms to try what may be yet / Regained in heaven" (insisting again on the importance of place) cannot be sustained, but falls back into "or what more lost in hell."

It is Beelzebub who, for the moment, strikes the more positive note: "If once they hear that voice... they will soon resume / New courage and revive." But he too gives way:

> though now they lie
> Grovelling and prostrate on yon lake of fire,
> As we erewhile, astounded and amazed,
> No wonder, fallen such a pernicious highth.
>
> (1.279–82)

Beelzebub's remarks are followed immediately by the wonderful description of Satan moving toward the shore, a description which visually, almost kinesthetically, reinforces our sense of his laborious inward struggle. It is a picture of massive awkwardness, as awkward to read as to visualize:

> His ponderous shield
> Ethereal temper, massy, large, and round,
> Behind him cast; the broad circumference
> Hung on his shoulders like the moon, whose orb
> Through optic glass the Tuscan artist views
> At evening from the top of Fesole,
> Or in Valdarno, to descry new lands,
> Rivers or mountains in her spotty globe.
> His spear, to equal which the tallest pine
> Hewn on Norwegian hills, to be the mast
> Of some great ammiral, were but a wand,
> He walked with to support uneasy steps
> Over the burning marl.
>
> (1.284–96)

The unwieldy shield "behind him cast" is of no use, a weighty nuisance. Whatever suggestions of heroic stature the similes may send off are diminished if not altogether canceled as the lines progress. The shield, whose heft we can almost feel dragging Satan down at first, is both distanced and domesticated, becoming the object of the curious Galileo, as he might view it from afar.[30] The first three lines describing the great spear, to "equal which the tallest pine ... were but a wand," soar toward the heroic, but the main clause that follows brings us down at once. The spear is a walking stick, supporting "uneasy steps / Over the burning marl." The implements of war—the one now a useless impediment, the other turned to ungainly use—serve but to point up the odds against their wielder's ever taking on heroic proportions again. The simile comparing shield and moon recalls Achilles arming himself for battle, and the contrast between the two descriptions could not be greater—Satan stumbling and weighted down, Achilles graceful and almost airborn:

> And about his shoulders he cast the silver-studded sword of bronze, and thereafter grasped the shield great and sturdy, wherefrom went forth afar a gleam as of the moon.... From the shield of Achilles went up a gleam to heaven, from that shield fair and richly-dight.... And goodly Achilles made proof of himself in his armour, whether it fitted him, and his glorious limbs moved free; and it became as it were wings to him, and lifted up the shepherd of the people.[31]

If there is one speech in the first book in which Satan can be said to be in full control, Fish's orator par excellence, it is the speech in which he rouses his followers from their stupor (1.315–30). It is, significantly, a speech dependent for its power entirely on sarcasm and mockery. (E.g., "Or have ye chosen this place / After the toil of battle to repose / Your wearied virtue, for the ease you find / To slumber here?") That is, Satan need not rely in it on any positive statement of purpose, the expression of which always eludes him and proves self-defeating. Instead he fills them with a sense of shame, the avoidance of which has provided him with his own only sustained motive. He can imply the need for action without designating any ("Awake, arise, or be for ever fallen") and turn their ignominy to good rhetorical use.

The speech succeeds. "They heard, and were abashed, and up they sprung / Upon the wing." And the long narrative passage that follows describes the gathering of the troops in grand epic style. If ever we might expect the splendid appearance of "a commanding general reviewing defeated troops," "the magnificent rebel," or a display of "remarkable powers of rising to an occasion,"[32] it might be now. But the Satan we see and hear is far otherwise. Milton precedes Satan's oration with a description (589–612) that stresses, with its series of disjunctions, the conflicting emotions that can be seen in his countenance: pain, care, courage, pride, cruelty, but most of all, with no hint that they are disingenuous, feelings of "remorse and passion" for what his "fellows" are suffering "for his fault." So overpowered is he that

> Thrice he essayed, and thrice in spite of scorn,
> Tears such as angels weep, burst forth: at last
> Words interwove with sighs found out their way.
>
> (1.619–21)

The sighs and tears of remorse are not, as some have called them, "spurious."[33] Nor is Satan able to "convert [them] to oratory," as Stein once alleged.[34] They seem, rather, to take control over the fine opening lines of the speech, where Satan struggles to get a purchase on his feelings and move beyond them, but instead slides back as each phrase qualifies and weakens its predecessor and yields to a truer description of what in fact transpired:

> O myriads of immortal spirits, O powers
> Matchless, but with the almighty, and that strife
> Was not inglorious, though the event was dire,
> As this place testifies, and this dire change
> Hateful to utter.
>
> (1.622–26)

The grand vocatives are qualified ("Matchless, but with the almighty"). The "glorious enterprise" of his first speech has become a "not inglorious" strife, and even the diminished strength of that assertion is further qualified by "though the event was dire, / As this place testifies." The sight of this place exerts its characteristic pressure on Satan, and it is hard not to feel that at this point he has been distracted from whatever he may have planned to say. Whatever rousing exhortation the opening address may have led one to expect never materializes, but gives way to genuine, embarrassed questions, forced out of him by what he sees and knows. In his previous speech he had addressed his followers as "ye" and "you." But here it is almost as if he is brooding out loud on *these* legions, neglectful of his audience:

> but what power of mind
> Foreseeing or presaging, from the depth
> Of knowledge past or present, could have feared,
> How such united force of gods, how such
> As stood like these, could ever know repulse?
> For who can yet believe, though after loss,
> That all these puissant legions, whose exile
> Hath emptied heaven, shall fail to re-ascend
> Self-raised, and repossess their native seat?
> For me be witness all the host of heaven,
> If counsels different, or danger shunned
> By me, have lost our hopes.
>
> (1.626–37)

In the last three lines Satan's feelings of remorse awaken a fear of impending blame, and he moves to exculpate himself. In doing so he ironically calls upon the host of heaven to bear him witness and acknowledges their present despair. In the lines that follow, he regains some mastery over his speech, pointing the finger of accusation at God. It should be noted that this feeble charge marks the only attempt by any of the fallen angels to make God out to be unjust, the only attempt to portray themselves as having been wronged. But even if his argument is a piece of blatant rationalization, at least it enables Satan to turn his attention away from their predicament and toward the future:

> But he who reigns
> Monarch in heaven, till then as one secure
> Sat on his throne, upheld by old repute,
> Consent or custom, and his regal state
> Put forth at full, but still his strength concealed,
> Which tempted our attempt, and wrought our fall.
> Henceforth his might we know, and know our own.
>
> (1.637–43)

In the last line of the passage, and for the first time in the speech, we find a clarity and decisiveness that might inspire some confidence, and we can say that at least for the rest of the speech, concluding with the determination of "war then, war / Open or understood must be resolved," he refuses to look back. But even as Satan expounds his plan, his conception emerges in terms that must deflate it even as they are uttered, terms hardly suggestive of a second glorious enterprise:

> Thither, if but to pry, shall be perhaps
> Our first eruption, thither or elsewhere.
>
> (1.655–56)

If Satan, then, has been struggling to achieve heroism in Book 1, what he has been struggling against includes at least the following: his memory of the "happy realms of light" and the honored place he held there, his recognition of God's surpassing strength, his own shame and despair and remorse, and his inability to conceive of or articulate any concrete goal that does not ring either hollow or petty (as in the case of "pry").

In Book 2, as John Peter has noted,[35] the drama has passed to Moloch, Belial, Mammon, and Beelzebub, who in diverse ways act out feelings Satan has already expressed. Moloch's voice, in keeping with the narrator's description of him, starts out "strong" and "fierce," scornful of weakness, full of confidence. One senses, perhaps, the voice that Satan's intelligence, his recognition that God proved "so much the stronger," prevented him from mustering:

> No, let us rather choose
> Armed with hell flames and fury all at once
> O'er heaven's high towers to force resistless way,
> Turning our tortures into horrid arms
> Against the torturer....
>
> (2.60–64)

His speech ends, however, with claims far less grandiose than those with which he began:

> By proof we feel
> Our power sufficient to disturb his heaven,

> And with perpetual inroads to alarm,
> Though inaccessible, his fatal throne:
> Which if not victory is yet revenge.
>
> (2.101–5)

"Disturb" and "alarm" are a comedown, precisely the sort of linguistic attrition we heard in Book 1, and God's throne, which he had earlier thought to mix "with Tartarean sulphur, and strange fire" (2.69), is now described as "inaccessible." If we cannot have victory, at least we can have revenge.

It is at this point that Beelzebub puts forward again Satan's proposal to "pry" into the newly created world, like heaven, by all reports, a "happy seat." The ultimate goal, reminding us of Satan's proposal to "disturb / [God's] inmost counsels" and Moloch's to "disturb his heaven," is to "interrupt his joy / In our confusion, and our joy upraise / In his disturbance" (2.371–73). All three formulations acknowledge that whatever success they have will be short-lived. Like the "turbulent wits" mentioned by Richard Hooker, they "thought the very disturbance of things established an hire sufficient to set them on work."[36] The means toward that end are as yet undetermined: "Perhaps / Some advantageous act may be achieved," either to destroy the place, or to possess it, or to drive out the "puny habitants," or "seduce them to our party." Apparently it makes little difference, for the fallen angels, "pleased highly," adopt the plan.

Satan is magnificently drawn in Book 1, but that magnificence lies as much in his agony, his despair, his remorse, his keen sense of the happiness he lost, as in any qualities of leadership he may from time to time exhibit. I mean by this, and by my emphasis on the labored qualities of his speech, to suggest how much more complexly human he is than he is customarily said to be. We do not merely admire him for his rhetorical skill or his strong determination (though there are touches of both); nor do we merely mark with abhorrence his errors, his heresies, his mendacity, his destructive designs on the human race. We also, and simultaneously, pity him. Milton presents him initially, that is, as a figure of tragic pathos, aware of his mistake, suffering mightily for it, and yet determined, like Macbeth, to persist in a course of action in the justice of which he has no conviction, and in the ultimate success of which he has scant belief. As with Macbeth, too, we receive in some measure what A. C. Bradley called the "central" tragic impression, the impression of "the possibilities of human nature" gone to "waste."[37] Those possibilities, in Satan's case, are nowhere more evident than in his enduring capacity to be moved by the wondrous beauty of the creation.

In this context Satan's meditation on the sun in Book 4 surprises us, no doubt, with its completeness and openness, but it is a fulfillment, not a contradiction, of what we already know. The memories of that "glorious state" had shown themselves in his very first lines, and we have already observed his capacity for remorse. "Heaven's matchless king" is simply the obverse of "matchless but with the almighty," though of course the moral connotations of the word receive their full weight in the meditation. Even his exoneration of God seems to follow naturally enough from his earlier failure to hold God responsible for what befell him. It is hard to see the soliloquies of Book 4 as marking anything like a degeneration. They seem much rather a simultaneous intensification and a freeing up of what he had labored to hold in. It is as if he had felt "the sacred influence / Of light" (2.1034–35), an influence that, in Beelzebub's words, purges and heals. Its intensity is all the more poignant because of his inability, even here, to keep it alive.

By the time we read, in Book 5, of Satan's original rebellion, prompted by the Father's exalting his Son above the angels, we have not only heard the Son plead in man's behalf and offer to die that we might be saved; we have been given every reason to suspect that the rebellion was an altogether misguided affair. We have heard even Belial refer to God as wise, and though Satan and Moloch both refer to the government of heaven as a tyranny, they do not even pretend to justify the term. No doubt they take it as a given, but when even Moloch can go on to refer to life in heaven as "bliss," the reader must ask what sort of tyranny it was. Satan refers to "the happier state / In heaven, which follows dignity [i.e., worth]" (2.24–25), and acknowledges that he himself, "clothed with transcendent brightness didst outshine / Myriads though bright." If this were not enough, we have heard Satan's regretful sigh, "Ah wherefore! he deserved no such return." It is hard to think of a fitter means for initiating the justification of God's ways than to have it emerge from the mouths of Satan and his followers.

CHAPTER 5

Meditating on the Creatures, Part 2: Milton, Eve, Adam, Raphael

Milton: Losing the Reader in Paradise

Satan is not, of course, the only beholder of Eden, nor the only one to sing its praises. The reader's own desire to see Paradise or to "sense" its nature, however, is fulfilled first not by Satan, but by the narrator, who gives us, before introducing us to Adam and Eve, two breathtaking descriptive passages, relatively free of analysis and commentary, of some forty and sixty lines respectively.

In these passages Milton is not so much reading the book of nature as writing it, giving the reader the literary equivalent of seeing and trying to understand. He controls and guides the sequential workings of our visual imaginations in a way no painter could do. I say *workings* because Milton's descriptions exercise our apprehension hard. They take us further into the sensation of trying to see something than vividness, definiteness, or detail—the qualities that Eliot, for one, found lacking in *Paradise Lost*[1]—could possibly do. These, after all, are qualities that, in poetry, can work against sensuousness, and against visualization, as easily as for them. It is easier to visualize a daisy than to visualize a daisy with eleven petals. And Milton's valley with "flowers of all hue" is at least as persuasively colorful as it would have been had he named all the hues. Like Robert Frost's more intimate "all shapes and colors of flowers, / I needn't call you by name" (from "The Last Mowing"), it works as description by expressing the observer's sense of a profusion that exceeds the capacity, or obviates the necessity, for naming or numbering. Though a poet may accomplish something by numbering the streaks of the tulip, it will not be ease of visualization.

Eliot came closest to defining the effect Milton's scenes have on us when he conceded that perhaps they should be accepted as "shifting phantasmagory."[2] The key to Milton's description of Eden is motion and variety, though the motion refers not just to the motion of the presented objects, but to the shifting point of view of the narrator and hence of the reader's sense of where he or she is located. Northrop Frye may have been right when he wrote that "every act of the free intelligence, including the poetic intelligence, is an attempt to return to Eden, a world in the human form of a garden, where we may wander as we please but cannot lose our way."[3] But Milton did not design his Eden as a safe haven. Certainly Adam and Eve lose their way in it, and Roy Daniells has nicely observed of Adam and Eve's bower—that prime nesting place of the garden—that "we are never told precisely where it is in relation to anything else."[4] For Milton, who, like his God, valued freedom over security, an Eden in which one could not get lost would be anything but perfect. He designed his description of Eden to give us the sense of being lost in nature's works.

That losing us is part of the design of Book 4 is strongly suggested by its opening lines, though there we are temporally rather than spatially lost. The word *now* occurs no less than seven times in the first thirty lines—often in a heavily stressed position—even as the narrator takes us backward and forward through several layers of times past and future. The passage begins with a ringing phrase that places us very much in the narrator's present and presence:

> O for that warning voice, which he who saw
> The Apocalypse, heard cry in heaven aloud,
> Then when the dragon, put to second rout,
> Came furious down to be revenged on men,
> *Woe to the inhabitants on earth!* that now,
> While time was, our first parents had been warned
> The coming of their secret foe, and scaped
> Haply so scaped his mortal snare; for now
> Satan, now first inflamed with rage, came down,
> The tempter ere the accuser of mankind,
> To wreak on innocent frail man his loss
> Of that first battle, and his flight to hell. . . .
>
> (4.1–12)

But if the passage seems to place us dramatically in the poet's presence, it places the poet himself into an imagined past. Milton's *now* is the time of Satan's first arrival on earth. The warning voice the poet calls for is a voice from the past, from the Book of Revelation, that is also a voice fore-heard, so to speak, from the future end of time itself. After the poet narrates the future event—the dragon's "second rout"—in the past tense, we come to the striking, jarring clause, "that now, / While time was, our first parents had been warned." Where are we? Or rather, when are we? Milton collapses the present into the past and brings the moment of Satan's approach into the present, where, indeed, it belongs. The temptation happened, Milton is saying, and there is nothing that can prevent it, and it is happening now, and will happen, and something can be done if we can hear the warning. Like Satan's paradoxical "bitter memory / Of what he was, what is, and what must be / Worse" (4.24–26), the passage insists on the presentness to our minds of past and future.

The present is the time of drama, the past the time of narration. What intervenes between this opening paragraph and the description of Eden is Satan's long meditation. The act of following him through his intricate progress and regress of thought and feeling suspends our sense of the pastness of his crime, just as every soliloquy and conversation in the poem puts us in the presence of decisions being made, quarrels struggling toward resolution, knowledge being imparted.

Milton leads us into Paradise with a shifting and phantasmagorical view of Eden.[5] As we enter Eden, Satan himself, "alone, / As he supposed, all unobserved, unseen," is what we first observe:

> So on he fares, and to the border comes,
> Of Eden, where delicious Paradise,
> Now nearer, crowns with her enclosure green,
> As with a rural mound the champaign head
> Of a steep wilderness, whose hairy sides
> With thicket overgrown, grotesque and wild,
> Access denied; and over head up grew
> Insuperable highth of loftiest shade,
> Cedar, and pine, and fir, and branching palm,
> A sylvan scene, and as the ranks ascend
> Shade above shade, a woody theatre

> Of stateliest view. Yet higher than their tops
> The verdurous wall of Paradise up sprung:
> Which to our general sire gave prospect large
> Into his nether empire neighbouring round.
> And higher than that wall a circling row
> Of goodliest trees loaden with fairest fruit. . . .
>
> (4.131–47)

As C. S. Lewis pointed out in a marvellous commentary on this passage, Milton "begins playing on the note of progression—upward progression, a vertical serialism."[6] We begin, as it were, at the very top, with Paradise, the crown of Eden, and are then led in an instant down to the steep sides of the mountain. We are then made to look, or think, upward toward the trees growing "over head," trees which themselves are planted in ascending ranks, "shade above shade." But these trees turn out not to be, as they are called, of insuperable height, for "yet higher than their tops / The verdurous wall of Paradise up sprung," from which wall Adam can look down. Nor, as Lewis points out, is that wall the real top. For still "higher than that wall" are the trees of Paradise itself. Our imaginations are strained, in other words, and the progressive description tempts us now and then to feel that we have come to the end of a sequence but then denies us that stability. Lewis says that the passage is designed to make us feel as if our necks ached as we read. It is designed, too, to defer any sense of precise location. The passage works as much on our spatial as on our visual imaginations, our effort not just to see things, but to see where things are in relation to each other. Not only is the prospect itself in motion ("up grew . . . ascend . . . up sprung"); it forces us to move upward as we read.

When we reach the "circling row / Of goodliest trees," we receive a moment's rest. Supposedly safe within the circle, we are also within a world artfully designed for human pleasure:

> Blossoms and fruits at once of golden hue
> Appeared, with gay enamelled colours mixed:
> On which the sun more glad impressed his beams
> Than in fair evening cloud, or humid bow,
> When God hath showered the earth; so lovely seemed
> That landscape: and of pure now purer air
> Meets his [Satan's] approach, and to the heart inspires

> Vernal delight and joy, able to drive
> All sadness but despair: now gentle gales
> Fanning their odoriferous wings dispense
> Native perfumes, and whisper whence they stole
> Those balmy spoils.
>
> (4.148–59)

This is a world intensely gentle: goodly, fair, gay, glad, lovely, pure, gentle, balmy. Milton's reference to *the* heart rather than to his [Satan's] heart hedges on the question of whether Satan felt delight and joy, but insists on the present power of pure air to inspire delight and joy in any human heart. It is another way of asserting that the loss of Paradise, while it indeed took place, still can take place. It is a kind of triumph over the elegiac tone of the prologue to Book 3 ("But not to me returns / Day, or the sweet approach of even or morn"). We hear present delight, even excitement, in Milton's voice when he speaks of "Eden, where delicious Paradise, / Now nearer, crowns..." (4.132–33), or when he draws images from *our* present ["fair evening cloud, or humid bow, / When God hath showered the earth" (4.151–52)] to show just how lovely the Edenic landscape seemed. Eliot excused what he took to be Milton's neglect of the visual on the grounds that "a more detailed account...could only have assimilated Eden to the landscapes of earth with which we are familiar."[7] Such assimilation, however, is just what Milton was striving for, and what he achieved.

The description is so absorbing that we may do a momentary double take at the reference to Satan's approach, and indeed our sense of enclosure is threatened, in the last two lines, by the suggestion of other and unknown places. That is, just as Milton's camera has been focusing in on Paradise, it reminds us of the Satanic threat, of stolen spoils, and of the world beyond Eden. And the similes that follow rapidly carry us into those lands and into the world of modern geography and commerce and of violent biblical history:

> As when to them who sail
> Beyond the Cape of Hope, and now are past
> Mozambic, off at sea north-east winds blow
> Sabean odours from the spicy shore
> Of Arabie the blest, with such delay

> Well pleased they slack their course, and many a league
> Cheered with the grateful smell old Ocean smiles.
> So entertained those odorous sweets the fiend
> Who came their bane, though with them better pleased
> Than Asmodeus with the fishy fume,
> That drove him, though enamoured, from the spouse
> Of Tobit's son, and with a vengeance sent
> From Media post to Aegypt, there fast bound.
>
> (4.159–71)

The similes disrupt our sense of time as well as of place. The present tense, and especially the *now* of line 160, echoing *now* in line 156, prevents an easy transition from the more distant to the less distant past. But temporal hovering between fictional present and historical past has in fact been with us all along, for in the descriptive passage itself we have no less than four shifts in tense and hence in the reader's temporal point of view, from "Now nearer, crowns," to "access denied," to "ranks ascend," to "up sprung," to "meets his approach."

The second and very different descriptive passage, following Satan's easy leap into the very middle of the garden, begins as if we were going to share his own point of view:

> Beneath him with new wonder now he views
> To all delight of human sense exposed
> In narrow room nature's whole wealth, yea more,
> A heaven on earth....
>
> (4.205–8)

But Milton at once pulls us back and away from Satan, and the voice we hear is that of the detached and learned historian locating Eden firmly in known postlapsarian boundaries:

> for blissful Paradise
> Of God the garden was, by him in the east
> Of Eden planted; Eden stretched her line
> From Auran eastward to the royal towers
> Of great Seleucia, built by Grecian kings,
> Or where the sons of Eden long before
> Dwelt in Telassar: in this pleasant soil

> His far more pleasant garden God ordained;
> Out of the fertile ground he caused to grow
> All trees of noblest kind for sight, smell, taste;
> And all amid them stood the tree of life,
> High eminent, blooming ambrosial fruit
> Of vegetable gold; and next to life
> Our death the tree of knowledge grew fast by,
> Knowledge of good bought dear by knowing ill.
> Southward through Eden went a river large,
> Nor changed his course. . . .
>
> (4.208–24)

These lines suggest a definiteness about the locations of the things within this garden God "ordained," i.e., not only decreed but arranged in order. Amid the trees is the tree of life, next to it the tree of knowledge. The river ran southward. The lines that locate Eden geographically are framed by lines that follow Genesis 2:8–10 with reassuring accuracy. ("And the Lord God planted a garden eastward in Eden. . . . And out of the ground made the Lord God to grow every tree that is pleasant to the sight, and good for food; the tree of life also in the midst of the garden, and the tree of knowledge of good and evil. And a river went out of Eden. . . .") The reader, whether or not he or she has ever heard of Seleucia or Telassar, surely feels securely in the hands of a narrator who is absolutely certain about the arrangement and location of the setting of his story.

But at this point the description breaks loose, both from Scripture and from that sense of clear boundaries, as the very syntax of the long, difficult sentence seems to follow the divers and dispersed courses of the river:

> Southward through Eden went a river large,
> Nor changed his course, but through the shaggy hill
> Passed underneath ingulfed, for God had thrown
> That mountain as his garden mould high raised
> Upon the rapid current, which through veins
> Of porous earth with kindly thirst up drawn,
> Rose a fresh fountain, and with many a rill
> Watered the garden; thence united fell
> Down the steep glade, and met the nether flood,
> Which from his darksome passage now appears,

> And now divided into four main streams,
> Runs diverse, wandering many a famous realm
> And country whereof here needs no account,
> But rather to tell how, if art could tell,
> How from that sapphire fount the crisped brooks,
> Rolling on orient pearl and sands of gold,
> With mazy error under pendant shades
> Ran nectar, visiting each plant, and fed
> Flowers worthy of Paradise which not nice art
> In beds and curious knots, but nature boon
> Poured forth profuse on hill and dale and plain,
> Both where the morning sun first warmly smote
> The open field, and where the unpierced shade
> Embrowned the noontide bowers.
>
> (4.223–46)

The first line and a half create the impression that we know exactly where we are heading: southward, and in a straight line. But we quickly lose sight of the river in the image of God's throwing (not placing or building) that mountain upon the rapid current. We are led to think that the river does change its course, "up-drawn" through the porous earth. It "rose a fresh fountain" and then disperses itself into "many a rill," which then, strangely, reunite, fall, and meet "the nether flood, / Which from his darksome passage now appears, / And now divided into four main streams, / Runs diverse." We have to labor to understand how the river both did and did not change its course. The two uses of the temporal adverb *now* imply that we are on hand to see what is happening, that we are following with our eyes the river's flow from place to place, but that sense is illusory, just as illusory as the sense that we are aided in locating places visually by being directed toward those areas where the sun first smote and where the shade embrowned the noontide bowers. The guide sees; we do not. Then, just as the waterfall rejoins the river and we think we know where we are, or it is, the river divides, runs diverse, "wandering" many a country whereof "here needs no account." What Helen Gardner says of Milton's descriptions of the vast cosmic spaces of the universe is equally true of his descriptions of Eden: "He continually satisfies and then defeats our powers of visualization."[8]

That the river "rose a fresh fountain" is something of a miracle. Arnold Stein was probably right in suggesting that the upward course of the stream signifies "the kindly-natural thirst of growing things for water, and the kindly-beneficent-natural thirst of the waters below the earth for growing things." And Roland Mushat Frye has pointed out that the passage "corresponds to the taste for fountains designed to appear natural which [Milton] would have encountered in Italy."⁹ But no natural thirst will account for rivers that rise a fountain, and yet we are precisely not to see it as the product of "nice art." Things in the garden have a way of taking on second natures. Water runs nectar, the fountain is sapphire, the pebbles are pearls, the sands gold, and the poetry refuses to commit itself as to whether it is reporting actual minerals or visual appearances.

Even if we try, as various critics think we are supposed to do, to exclude the "tainted," "bad," "guilty," or "evil" meanings of the oft-discussed phrase "mazy error,"¹⁰ there are no meanings we could attach to it that would not leave us with the correct view that Eden is bewildering, a place in which one can get lost. Robert Crosman, who has discussed the landscapes of Eden with great skill, nevertheless errs, I think, when he poses the question "Why does innocence appear so *fallen*?" and lets the assumption buried in the question determine the terms of the answer: "There is *no* way for Milton, or for any other poet since Adam's fall, to present an Eden untinged with defect."¹¹ There is simply no reason, however, to think that Milton would have regarded places where one might get lost, or people who might get lost (whether physically or spiritually) as defective.

As the description proceeds we are given a very brief respite— "Thus was this place, / A happy rural seat of various view"—but though the landscape that we next encounter is more gently pastoral, the indefiniteness of the spatial relations increases. There are "groves" of "rich trees," and

> Betwixt them lawns, *or* level downs, and flocks
> Grazing the tender herb, were interposed,
> *Or* palmy hillock, *or* the flowery lap
> Of *some* irriguous valley spread her store,
> Flowers of all hue, and without thorn the rose:
> *Another side*, umbrageous grots and caves
> Of cool recess, o'er which the mantling vine
> Lays forth her purple grape, and gently creeps
> Luxuriant.
>
> (4.252–60; my emphasis)

We are given almost too much to visualize in these lines, and in almost too-rapid succession; the processes of reading and locating are severely disrupted by such profusion. The abundant *or*'s all but get us lost. John Knott suggests that the use of *or* as a connective "makes the parts of the landscape seem interchangeable, as if to suggest that all views are equally pleasant."[12] It also suggests, I think, that the narrator is almost overcome by the variety. "Lawns, or level downs" may imply that both lawns and downs are there to be seen, but it equally suggests, lawns and downs being difficult to distinguish at a distance, that the narrator cannot be sure which he is seeing, something in the spirit of Wordsworth's "hedge-rows, hardly hedge-rows, little lines / Of sportive wood run wild" (from "Lines Composed a Few Miles above Tintern Abbey"). *Some* irriguous valley is not a valley we could locate, nor is *another* side a side we could be sure we had found. The concluding lines, in which the mirroring lake doubles the image of the bank even as it unites the streams, are perhaps the most disorienting of all.

> mean while murmuring waters fall
> Down the slope hills, dispersed, or in a lake,
> That to the fringed bank with myrtle crowned,
> Her crystal mirror holds, unite their streams.
>
> (4.260–63)

As Paul Alpers points out:

> These lines display Miltonic syntax and word order with a vengeance. The main verb phrase, "unite their streams," is produced so as not only to surprise, but also to increase the sense of difficulty in the passage. The effect occurs not simply because the main verb comes pressing upon the verb of the relative clause, but also because we were scarcely aware that a main verb was necessary or appropriate. Up to this point we took "In a lake" and the rest as simply dependent on "fall," so that the grammatical turn directly mimes the attribution of positive activity to the streams—*uniting*, rather than merely falling in one direction instead of another. ... The syntactic difficulty in the last line corresponds to a reversal in the experiences of participation and control.[13]

Both this and the earlier passage, then, gradually lose the reader, "overwhelm" us, as Knott observes, with their sensuousness. And both passages include, almost as if Prospero were in charge, a movement toward dissolution, a dissolving of the world of sights and places and objects into air. Our earlier struggle up the "steep wilderness" ends in "purer air," surrounded only by the perfume brought from we know not where by "gentle gales." Our increasingly dislocating journey through the lawns, hills, and valleys of Eden ends with sounds that become airs, airs that breathe smells and attune trembling leaves, and a masque-like "sight" such as no one can see:

> The birds their choir apply; airs, vernal airs,
> Breathing the smell of field and grove, attune
> The trembling leaves, while universal Pan
> Knit with the Graces and the Hours in dance
> Led on the eternal spring.
>
> (4.264–68)

Of the many critics who have described the particular pleasures Milton's descriptions of Eden afford the reader, it was Addison who came closest when he praised those natural landscapes where "the Eye has Room . . . to lose itself amidst the Variety of Objects that offer themselves to its Observation," landscapes "where the Scene is perpetually shifting, and entertaining the Sight every Moment with something that is new." We "find our Thoughts a little agitated," according to Addison, "at the sight of such Objects as are ever in Motion and sliding away from beneath the Eye of the Beholder." Because poetry itself is always in motion, it is poetry, not painting, that can best imitate and produce such effects, and, Addison later remarks, "If I were to name a Poet that is a perfect Master in all these Arts of working on the Imagination, I think Milton may pass for one."[14]

Milton's first descriptions of Adam and Eve repeat or imitate the pattern that we have seen him follow in his landscapes, the movement from orderliness toward unarranged profusion, just as the river began in an unchanging course and ended up running "diverse, wandering many a famous realm." The couple is initially presented as one, as undifferentiated:

> Two of far nobler shape erect and tall,
> Godlike erect, with native honour clad
> In naked majesty seemed lords of all,
> And worthy seemed, for in their looks divine
> The image of their glorious maker shone,
> Truth, wisdom, sanctitude severe and pure,
> Severe but in true filial freedom placed;
> Whence true authority in men.
>
> (4.288–95)

Their distinguishing attributes are initially presented abstractly, with balanced phrases that suggest a kind of equivalence within difference: "though both / Not equal, as their sex not equal seemed; / For contemplation he and valour formed, / For softness she and sweet attractive grace, / He for God only, she for God in him" (4.295–99). Adam himself is described briefly, and seems to run in an unchanging, unambiguous course, with only a slight hint, given by the word *but* in the last line, of a tension between natural growth and restraint:

> His fair large front and eye sublime declared
> Absolute rule; and hyacinthine locks
> Round from his parted forelock manly hung
> Clustering, but not beneath his shoulders broad.
>
> (4.300–303)

But not so Eve:

> She as a veil down to the slender waist
> Her unadorned golden tresses wore
> Dishevelled, but in wanton ringlets waved
> As the vine curls her tendrils, which implied
> Subjection, but required with gentle sway,
> And by her yielded, by him best received,
> Yielded with coy submission, modest pride,
> And sweet reluctant amorous delay.
>
> (4.304–11)

Whereas the *but* in the lines on Adam's hair merely places a limit on its length, the two *but*'s it takes to get Eve's hair unraveled qualify in a far more complicated way; first, in a simile, followed by a clause that explicates or unfolds the meaning or "implication" of her hair; second, in a series of phrases that further qualify that meaning: not just subjection, but subjection required with gentle sway, and so on. There is no doubt some truth in the notion that words like *dishevelled* and *wanton* are susceptible of interpretations (e.g., wanton as *lascivious* vs. wanton as *unrestrained*) that would attribute to Eve qualities that seem out of place in the unfallen world.[15] But the struggle to hold on for dear life to the unfallen or innocent meanings should not distract us from the point that the entire passage more explicitly reiterates: Eve is a complex creature, delicately poised, interesting enough to be a challenge, and challenging enough to be interesting. Her complexity requires a poised, calibrated response (gentle sway) from her husband. She holds heterogeneous qualities in equilibrium: submissive but not merely or excessively submissive; proud, but properly, not immodestly so. None of the words in line 311 ("And sweet reluctant amorous delay") *has* a fallen meaning, but the conjunction of those qualities—morally neutral every one of them—creates an attractive network of interrelated impulses that quietly tug against each other. Adam himself will pay handsome tribute to "her virtue and the conscience of her worth, / That would be wooed, and not unsought be won, / Not obvious, not obtrusive, but retired, / The more desirable" (8.502–4). Eve's coyness and delay, William Kerrigan and Gordon Braden have argued, protect sexuality in Eden from the dangers of satiety, so often lamented in Renaissance erotic poetry, "by incorporating an obstacle into a sexual life of satisfied consummation."[16]

The delicately balanced qualities that make Eve so winning are reflected not only in her demeanor, but also in her ways of speaking. The lyrical and spontaneously artful qualities of her poetry are sharply distinguished from those of her prosaic husband's. As storyteller and descriptive poet she patterns her speech according to the order of events related.[17] Many of her most memorable phrases are achieved through graceful chiasmus and repetition: "Sweet is the breath of morn, her rising sweet"; "Pleased I soon returned, / Pleased it returned as soon." The composure, both mental and verbal, with which she tells the story of her creation is perfect, and like the lines in which she later expresses her love for Adam, the story gives the impression of having been composed, but entirely without effort. The rhythms of her speech tend to mimic the excitement she must have felt during the experiences she is narrating as if they still exerted pressure on her and she were reliving them, a fact that may explain why some readers have been inclined to see her as, if not already fallen, at least as likely to fall:

> As I bent down to look, just opposite,
> A shape within the watery gleam appeared
> Bending to look on me, I started back,
> It started back, but pleased I soon returned,
> Pleased it returned as soon with answering looks
> Of sympathy and love; there I had fixed
> Mine eyes till now, and pined with vain desire
> Had not a voice thus warned me, *What thou seest,*
> *What there thou seest fair creature is thyself,*
> *With thee it came and goes: but follow me,*
> *And I will bring thee where no shadow stays*
> *Thy coming, and thy soft embraces, he*
> *Whose image thou art, him thou shall enjoy*
> *Inseparably thine, to him shalt bear*
> *Multitudes like thyself, and thence be called*
> *Mother of human race:* What could I do,
> But follow straight, invisibly thus led?
> Till I espied thee, fair indeed and tall,
> Under a platan, yet methought less fair,
> Less winning soft, less amiably mild,
> Than that smooth watery image; back I turned,
> Thou following cried'st aloud, *Return fair Eve,*
> *Whom fly'st thou? Whom thou fly'st, of him thou art,*
> *His flesh, his bone; to give thee being I lent*
> *Out of my side to thee, nearest my heart*
> *Substantial life, to have thee by my side*
> *Henceforth an individual solace dear;*
> *Part of my soul I seek thee, and thee claim*
> *My other half:* with that thy gentle hand
> Seized mine, I yielded, and from that time see
> How beauty is excelled by manly grace
> And wisdom, which alone is truly fair.
>
> (4.460–91; my emphasis)

Just as Milton's earlier description of Eve's yielding herself to Adam "with coy submission, modest pride, / And sweet reluctant amorous delay" seems to change direction almost word by word, caught up in the rhythm of giving and holding back, moving forward and pulling away, so she describes her own movements toward and away from her mirror image in the water. So too does she enact that rhythm in her response to the warning voice. We should note how her question—"What could I do?"—expresses her sense of having been led against her will; how the word *indeed* two lines later, hovering somewhere between the meanings "to be sure" and "admittedly," hints at the ambivalence she felt; how the increasing length of the three phrases—"less fair, / Less winning soft, less amiably mild"— suggests a sort of retrospective indulgence and gradual immersion in the beauty of her own image. At the end of her speech it is clear that she has learned what, from God's point of view, she presumably ought to have learned: "With that thy gentle hand / Seized mine, I yielded, and from that time see / How beauty is excelled by manly grace / And wisdom, which alone is truly fair." But the process of learning is left somewhat mysteriously embedded in the visual word *see*. Does she see because she has figured it out, or because she literally sees Adam's manly grace as fair, or because she has felt the strength of Adam's gentle hand *seizing* hers?

Milton rewrites Ovid's sad story of Echo and Narcissus delightfully here, giving it, if not the happiest possible ending from a twentieth century perspective, at least a much happier ending than that of the original. If the girlish Eve is the boyish Narcissus while bending over the "watery gleam," Milton undoes the gender mix-up. Echo's frustrated wish to throw her arms around Narcissus' neck is, in Eve's case, granted, as her heavenly maker leads her where no shadow will stay her "soft embraces," and Adam, in turn, echoes Narcissus' cry to Echo (*Quid me fugis*) with his own "whom fly'st thou?" Within the passage, in other words, Adam is metamorphosed into Narcissus, and Eve becomes Echo—not the Echo doomed to speak only the last few words she has heard, but one who remembers, interprets, and can repeat precisely what God and Adam had said to her that day, echoing even their un-Eve-like enjambments and syntactical inversions. The double act of remembering and re-presenting is a more dramatic, more audible, enactment of Eve's closeness to God, and her oneness with Adam, than is the unison with which Adam and Eve say and sing their evening and morning hymns of adoration and praise.

The fact that in Milton's revision of Ovid's story Eve becomes Echo can itself be viewed from various perspectives. It is true, as Christine Froula has suggested, that the italicized passages represent "patriarchal discourse." They had the effect when Eve first heard them (though Adam's tone is pleading rather than pedagogical) of educating her "to her secondariness." But that discourse ("part of my soul . . . my other half") both implies and was initiated by Adam's own "single imperfection," his "deficience" (8.415–26). If Eve, in Froula's words, is "not a self, a subject" until she is united to Adam,[18] it is also true that Adam is not a self without Eve. "To lose thee," he will later tell her, "were to lose my self" (9.959). To avoid that loss he falls, not into a "clear, / Smooth lake" (4.458–59), but into "a troubled sea of passion" where, in soliloquy ("from deep to deeper plunged") and in his venomous attack on Eve, he will act out his own narcissistic despair and self-righteous hatred, an "abyss" of emotions (10.718–908) from which he will be rescued only by Eve's remembering and echoing of the words the patriarch spoke in cursing the serpent.

The Amiable Fruits of Eden

Within the ever-shifting variety and abundance of Eden certain images recur and by their repetition characterize, even if vaguely, the appearance of the landscape. These images reinforce our sense of Eden as a dynamic place in which losing one's way, or yielding to temptation, is always possible, and as the poem progresses toward the Fall, the images become increasingly laden with connotations of sensuous excess. The dominant image (if one can be sure of what is dominant in such a landscape) is that of a partly sheltered, shaded enclosure within which, or into which, heavy boughs or fruits or flowers offer themselves. The brook runs nectar "under pendant shades." The fruit hangs "amiable" on the trees. The "mantling" (i.e., enveloping) vine "lays forth her purple grape, and gently creeps / Luxuriant," as if in invitation, over the "grots and caves." The "flowery lap" of a valley "spred her store." The images anticipate the "tuft of shade" where, at noon, Adam and Eve enjoy the "nectarine fruits which the compliant boughs / Yielded them" (4.332–33), as well as the "close recess" of the "shady bower," which Eve, in imitation of her maker, has decked with "flowers, garlands, and sweet-smelling herbs" (4.705–9). The amiable fruits and the compliant, yielding boughs link the garden with Adam, whose grapelike locks "hung / Clustering," and with the yielding Eve, whose "wanton ringlets waved / As the vine curls her tendrils."

Anne Ferry points out that in Eden a shaded place "is a region holy, refreshing, benevolent, protected." "The word 'shade' in its variety of forms," she writes, "is used with pointed frequency and emphasis in the narrator's descriptions of Eden until it grows in meanings with the effect of a sacred metaphor." At the same time, however, "a terrible threat hangs over man, hidden in those very 'shades' of Eden which seem simply to shield and refresh him."[19] The brooks run "with mazy error" under those pendant shades, and the images of the shaded recess are also images of temptation, and of considerable, almost erotic luxuriance. After Eve's dream of being tempted by one whose "dewy locks distilled / Ambrosia" (5.56–57), and within their bower, Adam himself becomes the shade-giving, cordial fruit "hung amiable" over a discomposed and glowing Eve:

> His wonder was to find unwakened Eve
> With tresses discomposed, and glowing cheek,
> As through unquiet rest: he on his side
> Leaning half-raised, with looks of cordial love
> Hung over her enamoured, and beheld
> Beauty, which whether waking or asleep,
> Shot forth peculiar graces.
>
> (5.9–15)

Adam, as Ferry points out, is Eve's protector, but there is an anticipatory tension in this vignette. What Adam beheld as he looked upon her was neither, as we might have expected, her discomposure, nor her appearance, but beauty personified, beauty enhanced and eroticized by that glowing cheek—the effect of causes Adam cannot discern. Milton will recall the passage twice in Book 9: first when the fallen Eve returns to Adam and "in her cheek distemper flushing glowed" (887); and again when, after a night "encumbered" by dreams, they rise "as from unrest" (1052). Eve herself is in a "sweet recess" when Satan spies her alone, "veiled in a cloud of fragrance, ... so thick the roses bushing round / About her glowed" (9.456, 425–27).

When Satan describes the forbidden fruit to Eve in her dream, he takes the amiability and compliance of the fruits in Eden one step further and suggests that the fruit is so heavy and swollen, the branches so burdened with weight, that it will be a kindness to eat thereof: "And O fair plant, said he, with fruit surcharged, / Deigns none to ease thy load and taste thy sweet?" (5.58–59). If there is an ever-so-slight suggestion in these words of a sort of kinesthetic sexuality, of tumescence seeking release, it is intensified when we come to the temptation itself:

> I nearer drew to gaze;
> When from the boughs a savoury odour blown,
> Grateful to appetite, more pleased my sense
> Than smell of sweetest fennel or the teats
> Of ewe or goat dropping with milk at even,
> Unsucked of lamb or kid, that tend their play.
>
> (9.578–83)

Eve accepts Satan's logic and vows to the tree, after eating the fruit, that she will "each morning... the fertile burden ease / Of thy full branches offered free to all" (9.800–802). She will serve the tree, as the lamb serves the ewe, the child its mother. The shelter so generously provided by Eden's landscape will not protect man from what Adam will later call the danger that lies "within himself." When, after the Fall, we arrive at the "shady bank, / Thick overhead with verdant roof embowered" to which Adam leads Eve in order to satisfy the lust in which "they burn" (9.1037–38, 1015), the shadier connotations of the Edenic shades, which had been present from the beginning, should not surprise us. "The real protection of the Garden," as G. K. Hunter has written, lies "in the perpetual vigilance of the human minds. This is the price of freedom, then as now."[20] The freedom to lose one's way in Eden, as Adam and Eve will lose theirs, is for Milton a positive, defining, integral feature of its perfection. It is pictured for us in its landscape and its inhabitants, and we, as readers, experience the possibility by coming close to losing *our* way. As a lesson in reading the book of the creatures it suggests that the Creator provided us with extraordinary abundance and variety, with food and shelter, and left us free to find or lose ourselves, to use or misuse his gifts.

Eden at Night

Paradise Lost, as many readers have observed, is a poem that repeatedly echoes itself, recalling an earlier passage and leading the reader to reconsider and reassess the ground already covered and the road that lies ahead. The more one reads the poem, and the more deeply it takes a hold on the memory, the more convinced one becomes of its intricate density. Like the river in the garden, an image, gesture, or phrase can go underground for a while and then rise up a fountain or divide into divergent streams. We turn next to what is in fact a series of closely related descriptive passages through which Milton creates what we might think of as a stereoscopic effect, a sense of looking at the same objects from slightly different angles. The viewers include the poet, Eve, Adam, Satan, and Raphael. And to begin we should return to that scene in the prologue to Book 3 in which Milton presents himself as immersed in the process of composing his poem. The poet is out of doors, surrounded by nature's works, wandering, by day, among "clear spring, or shady grove, or sunny hill" and visiting, nightly, Sion and its "flowery brooks." The scene of composition is a night scene, literally because the poet composes at night, and metaphorically because the poet is blind and finds "no dawn." As the doubly functioning word *as* suggests, the poet's singing is like the nightingale's, and he sings while the nightingale sings:

> Then feed on thoughts, that voluntary move
> Harmonious numbers; as the wakeful bird
> Sings darkling, and in shadiest covert hid
> Tunes her nocturnal note.
>
> (3.37–40)

One of the songs he sings, even as he tells of its making, is a lament for the world he cannot see:

> Thus with the year
> Seasons return, but not to me returns
> Day, or the sweet approach of even or morn,
> Or sight of vernal bloom, or summer's rose,
> Or flocks, or herds, or human face divine.
>
> (3.40–44)

The passage begins by establishing a strong, balanced rhythm—"Thus with the year / Seasons return"—the repetition providing its own slow return. The syntax of the clause, as of the entire passage, is far simpler than that of the preceding lines, with the verb *returns* followed by an unbroken string of subjects joined by *or*'s. The list takes us gently up the scale of earthly life from plant to animal to human. The rhythm, after the heavy stress on *Day*, remains uninterruptedly iambic. The phrases diminish steadily in length, retarding the movement and suggesting that the series is reaching its terminus, so that the longer final phrase with its split adjectives—"or human face divine"—takes on unusual force. The poet knows of the passage of time—"seasons return"—but he can only remember the visual evidence for it, the "sweet approach of even or morn," the change from the bloom of spring to the rose of summer.

In Book 4, as Adam and Eve are about to retire to their bower, the scene of the prologue is repeated. Again it is night, and the "wakeful nightingale" sings her "amorous descant," a descant to Eve's own tribute to nature and to Adam:

> With thee conversing I forget all time,
> All seasons and their change, all please alike.
> Sweet is the breath of morn, her rising sweet,
> With charm of earliest birds; pleasant the sun
> When first on this delightful land he spreads
> His orient beams, on herb, tree, fruit, and flower,
> Glistering with dew; fragrant the fertile earth
> After soft showers; and sweet the coming on
> Of grateful evening mild, then silent night
> With this her solemn bird and this fair moon,
> And these the gems of heaven, her starry train:
> But neither breath of morn when she ascends
> With charm of earliest birds, nor rising sun
> On this delightful land, nor herb, fruit, flower,
> Glistering with dew, nor fragrance after showers,
> Nor grateful evening mild, nor silent night
> With this her solemn bird, nor walk by moon,
> Or glittering starlight without thee is sweet.
>
> (4.639–56)

Milton's "sweet approach of even or morn" is expanded into Eve's "Sweet is the breath of morn, her rising sweet . . . and sweet the coming on / Of grateful evening mild." Her syntax throughout is, like that of Milton's brief lament, simple, her rhythms lyrical, though more relaxed and luxuriant, and in the last seven lines her repeated *nor*'s create an almost elegiac echo of his, as they suggest how ephemeral these pleasures are, and how entirely dependent on Adam's company. The song joins the unfallen Eve, as its singer, in sympathetic union with the blind and fallen poet,[21] and this union is strengthened by the congruence between Eve's phrasings and the phrasings of the narrator's description of the setting. Though there is perhaps no change of season in Eden, and though Fowler and Hughes gloss Eve's use of *season* as referring to periods of the day,[22] her poetry creates the effect of seasons returning by means of its unhurried repetitions: "herb, tree, fruit, and flower... herb, fruit, flower"; "fragrant the fertile earth / After soft showers... fragrance after showers."

This is the epic's most poignant evocation of the beauty of Eden, as opposed to its splendor or variety, and it is crucial to see how different it is from the others we have examined. It is a tribute to the aesthetic qualities of Eden, its gentle appeal to the senses. It is altogether an earthy description, with nothing exotic or miraculous about it, no magical river rising a fountain, no ambrosia or burnished fruit or orient pearl. Instead of "odorous gums and balm" or perfumes whispering "whence they stole those balmy spoils," we find "fragrant the fertile earth." Eve's appreciative modifiers are uniformly modest: *sweet, pleasant, delightful, grateful, fair.* While she takes us twice through the cycle of a whole day, suggesting the stable regularity of her seasons, what she singles out and relishes are the fleeting moments and sensations, the *breath* of morn, the charm of *earliest* birds, the sun's *first* beams, the *coming on* of evening, the *glistering* dew and *glittering* starlight—all that is transitional, ephemeral, shimmering. Ferry has suggested that when Adam and Eve fall they are driven down "into the world of chance and change, the world in which the reader and the blind speaker now live."[23] Eve's song, both in itself and in its resonance with Milton's own, stresses the proximity of the world she will leave to the one she will enter.

Adam's way of responding to the book of nature is different from Eve's, less aesthetic, we might say, and more scientific. He is interested less in the objects of experience themselves than in the relations among them. Eve's song had ended with a question about the "glittering starlight": "But wherefore all night long shine these, for whom /

This glorious sight, when sleep hath shut all eyes?" To see how Adam's viewpoint, like Eve's, derives from the invocation of Book 3, we must return to Milton's references to the sun, that "vital lamp," and its "piercing ray"; to his prayer to the "celestial Light" to "shine inward, and the mind through all her powers / Irradiate, there plant eyes"; and to his later account of how the sun "gently warms / The universe, and to each inward part / With gentle penetration, though unseen, / Shoots invisible virtue even to the deep" (3.583–86). What Adam shares with Milton and with Satan is an interest in that which lies beneath and beyond surfaces. He sees causes and effects, infers the unseen from the seen, recognizes the cooperative relationship between stars and sun as they interact with life on earth. In answer to Eve's question he speaks of the

> life
> In nature and all things, which these soft fires
> Not only enlighten, but with kindly heat
> Of various influence foment and warm,
> Temper or nourish, or in part shed down
> Their stellar virtue on all kinds that grow
> On earth, made hereby apter to receive
> Perfection from the sun's more potent ray.
> These then, though unbeheld in deep of night,
> Shine not in vain, nor think, though men were none,
> That heaven would want spectators, God want praise.
>
> (4.666–76)

This passage is highly characteristic of Adam's way of reading nature. We see it again in his understanding of the psychology that lies behind Eve's dream (5.95–119); in the questions he puts to Raphael, from whom he wants to learn "how this world / Of heaven and earth conspicuous first began, / When, and whereof created, for what cause" (7.62–64); and, developed almost to excess, in his questions regarding the movement of the heavenly bodies and the vehemence of the effect on him of Eve's loveliness. The motives that lie behind Adam's ways of interpreting the creation are neatly summarized in a passage from the great naturalist Sir Thomas Browne:

> Every Essence, created or uncreated, hath its finall cause, and some positive end both of its Essence and operation; This is the cause I

grope after in the works of nature, on this hangs the providence of God; to raise so beauteous a structure, as the world and the creatures thereof, was but his Art; but their sundry and divided operations with their predestinated ends, are from the treasury of his wisedome. In the causes, nature, and affections of the Eclipse of [the] Sunne and Moone, there is most excellent speculation; but to profound farther, and to contemplate a reason why his providence hath so disposed and ordered their motions in that vast circle, as to conjoyne and obscure each other, is a sweeter piece of reason, and a diviner point of philosophy....[24]

Just as Eve's song and Adam's reply to her concluding question enlarge upon and transform Milton's prologue, so the scene of the prologue evolves into the following more expansive scene, described by the narrator, in which Adam and Eve converse:

> Now came still evening on, and twilight grey
> Had in her sober livery all things clad;
> Silence accompanied, for beast and bird,
> They to their grassy couch, these to their nests
> Were slunk, all but the wakeful nightingale;
> She all night long her amorous descant sung;
> Silence was pleased: now glowed the firmament
> With living sapphires: Hesperus that led
> The starry host, rode brightest, till the moon
> Rising in clouded majesty, at length
> Apparent queen unveiled her peerless light,
> And o'er the dark her silver mantle threw.
>   (4.598–609)

This setting, too, reappears, in Eve's dream (it is, after all, the same night, the same place), but it is subtly transformed by the Satanic voice she hears, the voice she mistakes for Adam's:

> Now is the pleasant time,
> The cool, the silent, save where silence yields
> To the night-warbling bird, that now awake
> Tunes sweetest his love-laboured song; now reigns
> Full-orbed the moon, and with more pleasing light
> Shadowy sets off the face of things; in vain,

If none regard, heaven wakes with all his eyes,
Whom to behold but thee, nature's desire,
In whose sight all things joy, with ravishment
Attracted by thy beauty still to gaze.

(5.38–47)

In the first of these two passages the bird's song is "amorous"; in the second it is "love-laboured." The first, in harmony with Eve's love song, presents a changing scene, catching the gradual coming on of night, the movement from twilight, through the appearance of the evening star, through the moon's regal progress rising through the clouds to her full unveiling.[25] The heavens protectively clothe the earth, first in the sober gray livery of twilight, later in the "silver mantle" of the moon's "peerless light," as if in imitation of "holy Light" when it "as with a mantle didst invest / The rising world of waters dark and deep" (3.10–11). The second passage, on the other hand, is static, catching a frozen moment. The function of the light is not to clothe, but to enhance appearances, to "set off the face of things." If the first directs our eyes upward toward the queenly moon, the second directs them finally downward toward Eve. The stars in the first passage are there to be seen, "living sapphires" in the distance; in the second they are there to see, to gaze down on Eve's beauty.

There was sensuous potential in Eve's lyrical song, but her restrained adjectives kept her an appreciative observer, sensing from a distance, rather than a partaker. Throughout her dream, however, what had been potential becomes actual. Eve's favorite adjectives are intensified: "sweetest," "more pleasing," "much fairer." The glistering dew of her song reappears in her subsequent description of her suitor: "His dewy locks distilled / Ambrosia." Satan uses *sweet* repeatedly with reference to taste, whereas Eve and Milton had used it, beautifully, to describe the approach or breath or coming on of morning and evening. The fruit that had merely been named, along with tree and flower, as one of the visual delights of Eden, becomes singled out as "fruit surcharged," "fruit divine, / Sweet of thy self, but much more sweet thus cropt." The fragrance of the moist earth becomes the fruit's "pleasant savoury smell" that "quickens appetite." And the upward movement in Book 4—the rising and ascending of both morn and moon—is, within the dream, transferred to Eve herself: "Ascend to heaven," the voice suggests, and "Forthwith [as if to rise like the majestic moon] up to the clouds / With him I flew."

The War in Heaven: Nature's Works Expunged and Razed

What we have witnessed in these several descriptions of Eden is a dynamic series of transformations: in the poet's descriptions an accelerating movement from orderliness toward profusion and dislocation, such that, to borrow another phrase from Frost, we "feel our standpoint shaken" (from "One Step Backward Taken"); in the increasingly swollen amiability of the fruits of Eden and the evolving versions of the prologue, movements from passive, aesthetic appreciation to active, appetitive indulgence, from the amorous to the love-labored, from change and growth to stasis and ripeness.

The final Edenic scene in these four books on nature's works is not in Eden, but in heaven, and it is given us by Raphael. More than simply an expansion of or variation on the scenes we have examined, it absorbs image after image not only from the invocation to Book 3 but from all we remember of Eden. It occurs in Raphael's account of how the angels celebrate the solemn day on which the Father "begets" and "anoints" his "only Son":

> That day, as other solemn days, they spent
> In song and dance about the sacred hill,
> Mystical dance, which yonder starry sphere
> Of planets and of fixed in all her wheels
> Resembles nearest, mazes intricate,
> Eccentric, intervolved, yet regular
> Then most, when most irregular they seem,
> And in their motions harmony divine
> So smooths her charming tones, that God's own ear
> Listens delighted.
>
> (5.618–27)

The bird, whether tuning her nocturnal note, singing her amorous descant, or tuning sweetest his love-laboured song, has been replaced by harmony divine, smoothing her charming tones. If silence was pleased by the nightingale, now "God's own ear / Listens delighted." The Sion Milton visits nightly has been replaced by another "sacred hill." If Milton's thoughts moved "harmonious numbers," and Adam had heard celestial spirits "in full harmonic number joined," so here the motions of the "mystical dance" create a "harmony divine." The dance itself takes us back to the "mystic dance" of the five planets that Adam and Eve had addressed in their morning hymn (5.178), and the "mazes intricate" ally the angelic dance with the "mazy error" of the brooks in Eden.

"Evening now approached," continues Raphael, who adds in parentheses a comment implying a distinction between heaven and earth: "For we have also our evening and our morn, / We ours for change delectable, not need." But his very language suggests that we know more of the "sweet approach of even," the sweet "coming on / Of grateful evening mild" on earth than he does, and we have heard Eve testify that in Eden "all seasons and their change, all please alike." A few lines later he makes another parenthetical distinction—"the face of brightest heaven had changed / To grateful twilight (for night comes not there / In darker veil)" (5.644–46)—but we remember how, in Eden, the moon "unveiled her peerless light, / And o'er the dark her silver mantle threw" (4.609–10).

Raphael, had he wished, might have quibbled that the angels drink their nectar "in pearl, in diamond, and massy gold," Adam and Eve theirs in mere melon rinds. But the very brooks in Eden, we have been told, run nectar "on orient pearl and sands of gold." There is precious little to distinguish the angelic from the human pleasures. Angels repose, as Adam and Eve do, on flowers. And if they "quaff immortality and joy" (5.638), so do Adam and Eve reap "immortal fruits of joy and love" (3.67). Sleep itself comes to heaven and earth in the same guise:

> [Adam]   the timely dew of sleep
> Now falling with soft slumbrous weight inclines
> Our eyelids.
>
> (4.614–16)

> [Raphael]   And roseate dews disposed
> All but the unsleeping eyes of God to rest.
>
> (5.646–47)

Once asleep, the angels are "fanned with cool winds" accompanied by the sounds of "melodious hymns," while Adam and Eve sleep cooled by the waving of Love's "purple wings," "lulled by nightingales," and awakened, in the morning, by the sound of "Aurora's fan" (4.764, 771; 5.6).

One might argue that Raphael is merely accommodating the ineffable joys of heaven to the limited capacities of his human auditors—Adam, Eve, and the reader. But the very fact that he twice in this part of the narrative takes the trouble to make distinctions between heaven and earth, distinctions of a very minor sort, points in another direction. So numerous are the rough equivalences between heaven and earth that it seems more likely that Milton here, as elsewhere, is blurring the borders separating the three domains: heaven, Eden, and his own fallen world. Bliss and beauty are heavenly, harmony is divine, wherever they are experienced, seen, heard, or remembered. And they are fragile. As Adam and Eve's blissful evening in Eden becomes a night of disturbing dreams, so Raphael's solemn day turns quickly to rebellious night. Satan speaks to the sleeping Beelzebub and "infused / Bad influence into the unwary breast / Of his associate" (5.694–96) just as he had, at the end of Book 4, inspired "venom" into the ear of the sleeping Eve.

Leland Ryken has argued for the remoteness in Milton's epic of "the apocalyptic realm of transcendental, ideal experience" from "fallen reality,"[26] and for the existence of a "fundamental cleavage" between the two worlds. But sometimes the evidence he cites, such as Adam's expression of gratitude to Raphael for having revealed "great things, and full of wonder in our ears, / Far differing from this world" (7.70–71), undermines his thesis. There is an irony in Adam's words, for what has chiefly moved him to such wonder has been a very worldly, undignified, untranscendental sort of war in heaven, a story of

> things to their thought
> So unimaginable as hate in heaven,
> And war so near the peace of God in bliss
> With such confusion.
>
> (7.53–56)

Books 3 through 5 have exposed us to several different readings of the book of nature, descriptions of its splendor and variety, its almost confusing abundance, its simple, gentle beauty, its delicious and benignly tempting luxuriance, and its vital, organic wholeness.

In Book 6, however fervently Raphael may assure us that the rebel angels do not destroy but only disturb the peace in heaven, and however easily the Son restores to heaven "his wonted face" (6.783), we are left with a powerful impression of God's and nature's works turned upside down, misused, and violated. The war makes a mockery of creation. What we are reading about is that act, as Michael tells Satan, which "into nature brought / Misery, uncreated till the crime / Of [his] rebellion" (6.267–69).

Some of the work of connecting heavenly to earthly nature is done by the similes, not unlike those in Book 1, that Raphael uses to translate heavenly events for human ears. Satan recoils under Abdiel's assault "as if on earth / Winds under ground or waters forcing way / Sidelong, had pushed a mountain from his seat / Half sunk with all his pines" (6.195–98). The combat between Michael and Satan is,

> such as to set forth
> Great things by small, if nature's concord broke,
> Among the constellations war were sprung,
> Two planets rushing from aspect malign
> Of fiercest opposition in mid sky,
> Should combat, and their jarring spheres confound.
> (6.310–15)

Even the simile describing the barrels of the rebels' cannonry suggests the destruction and perversion of nature's works: "for like to pillars most they seemed / Or hollowed bodies made of oak or fir, / With branches lopped, in wood or mountain felled" (6.573–75).

But the similes are needed only for the unfallen Adam and Eve, and they are needed not because the events narrated are heavenly, but because they are more earthly than any the pair has witnessed. Milton had expressed his wonder at how "with one virtuous touch / The arch-chemic sun" produces deep in the earth "so many precious things / Of colour glorious and effect so rare" (3.608–12). And we have heard Adam's tribute to the "kindly heat" of the stars and to the "sun's more potent ray." Satan, in a passage that wonderfully begins with ten lines that sound like a similar, loving appreciation of nature's beauty, a meditation on the creatures that adopts the psalmist's stance ("When I beholde thine heavens..." [Ps. 8.3; Geneva Bible]), converts the underground elements of heaven—the "originals of nature," Raphael later calls them (6.511)—to explosive ends. The passage is quintessentially Satanic, moving, as we have come to expect, from wonder to destruction. It illustrates almost too well, too literally, the dangers of mentally penetrating, as Adam does, through the surfaces to the depths:

> Which of us who beholds the bright surface
> Of this ethereous mould whereon we stand,
> This continent of spacious heaven, adorned
> With plant, fruit, flower ambrosial, gems and gold,
> Whose eye so superficially surveys
> These things, as not to mind from whence they grow
> Deep under ground, materials dark and crude,
> Of spiritous and fiery spume, till touched
> With heaven's ray, and tempered they shoot forth
> So beauteous, opening to the ambient light.
> These in their dark nativity the deep
> Shall yield us pregnant with infernal flame,
> Which into hollow engines long and round
> Thick-rammed, at the other bore with touch of fire
> Dilated and infuriate shall send forth
> From far with thundering noise among our foes
> Such implements of mischief as shall dash
> To pieces, and o'erwhelm whatever stands
> Adverse.
>
> (6.472–90)

But this rape of nature's womb—which recalls Moloch's opening of the "spacious wound" to dig out sulphurous ore from the "womb" of a hill (1.670–91)—is not all. The grotesque climax of the nature-destroying violence comes when the loyal angels retaliate:

> Their arms away they threw, and to the hills...
> Light as the lightning glimpse they ran, they flew,
> From their foundations loosening to and fro
> They plucked the seated hills with all their load,
> Rocks, waters, woods, and by the shaggy tops
> Up lifting bore them in their hands.
>
> (6.639–46)

And the rebel angels retaliate in kind:

> The rest in imitation to like arms
> Betook them, and the neighbouring hills uptore;
> So hills amid the air encountered hills
> Hurled to and fro with jaculation dire.
>
> (6.662–65)

These passages constitute Milton's commentary on war, "hitherto the only argument / Heroic deemed," as he reminds us later. Observing the "jaculation dire," the Father comments, with telling understatement, "War wearied hath performed what war can do" (6.695).

By the end of Book 6 we have reached the midpoint of the poem. "Half yet remains unsung" (7.21). We will meet such war, such destruction, at the structurally appropriate moment at the end of Book 11. That war, equally grotesque, will be fought by human beings, and their self-destruction will bring forth the Flood. Mountains again will be moved. Nature and Paradise itself will be destroyed. (See 11.824–35)

Beginning with the Word

The war in heaven brings to a close that segment of the poem that began in Book 3 with the desire to behold the creation, and moved toward the fulfillment of that desire through the eyes of Satan, the narrator, Adam, Eve, and Satan. The reading of the book of nature that Raphael has given us in his account of that war is a lesson in its fragility. The pause between Books 6 and 7, like that between 11 and 12, is a pause between "the world destroyed and world restored" (12.3). Book 7 offers a new beginning to provide a powerful counterweight to the destruction we have witnessed. In it Raphael tells Adam and Eve how God "in a moment will create / another world" (7.154–55).

Whereas the invocation to Book 3 was addressed to "holy Light," that to Book 7 is addressed to Urania and her "voice divine." As Book 3 is devoted to vision, so Book 7 is devoted to voice, for it is the book of God's creative voice, the Word that "was in the beginning with God," the Word by whom "all things were made" (John 1:2–3). The book is a much-expanded paraphrase and gloss upon the account of the creation in Genesis 1:1–2:2, and within that paraphrase the first ten utterances attributed to God in Genesis are rendered in due order and with considerable literalness.[27] The two speeches which God spoke directly to man before the Fall (1:28–30 and 2:16–17) are presented, since Raphael is simply repeating and expounding upon what Adam and Eve have already heard, through indirect discourse.

Whereas in Book 3 the stress is on the Son as the visible face of the Father, the "divine similitude, / In whose conspicuous countenance, without cloud / Made visible, the almighty Father shines" (3.384–86), in Book 7 the stress is on the Son as God's Word. And as Book 3 sets forth the perfect example of filial obedience in the Son's response to the Father, so Book 7 presents another pattern of perfect obedience, starting with the obedience of Chaos itself, to the spoken Word:

> Silence, ye troubled waves, and thou deep, peace,
> Said then the omnific Word, your discord end:
> Nor stayed, but on the wings of cherubim
> Uplifted, in paternal glory rode
> Far into chaos, and the world unborn;
> For chaos heard his voice: him all his train
> Followed in bright procession to behold
> Creation, and the wonders of his might.
>
> (7.216–23)

Milton stresses all creation's obedience to the Word by transforming the first and second chapters of the Geneva and King James versions of Genesis. In those versions there are two ways in which God's creative commands, all beginning with the imperative "Let," are enacted. In the first instance, "God said, Let there be light: *and there was* light." In four instances the fulfillment of the command is announced with the clause *and it was so*. Elsewhere the command is followed by a clause asserting the act of making or creating; e.g., "Let there be a firmament... *and God made* the firmament;" "Let the waters bring forth abundantly the moving creature that hath life... *and God created* great whales." The effect of these formulations is wonderful in its own way, stressing both the sudden existence of what had not existed and the abstract immediacy of God's creative acts. But Milton changes the emphasis, picturing a universe in which the uncreated beings wait offstage, as it were, awaiting the call, ready to obey. Instead of "and there was light," we find:

> and forthwith light
> Ethereal, first of things, quintessence pure
> Sprung from the deep.
>
> (7.243–45)

Instead of "Let the dry land appear: and it was so," Milton gives us:

> Let dry land appear.
> Immediately the mountains huge appear
> Emergent, and their broad bare backs upheave
> Into the clouds, their tops ascend the sky.
>
> (7.285–87)

For the following verses—"And God said, Let the earth bring forth the living creature after his kind.... And God made the beast of the earth after his kind"—we have Milton's

> God said,
> Let the earth bring forth soul living in her kind,
> Cattle and creeping things, and beast of the earth,
> Each in their kind. *The earth obeyed,* and straight
> Opening her fertile womb teemed at a birth
> Innumerous living creatures.
>
> (7.450–55; my emphasis)

In Milton's story the light is waiting to spring; the mountains appear "emergent," rising from the waters in which they had been *sub*merged. In direct contrast to Satan's plundering of nature's womb to produce "implements of mischief," the earth, which had herself been waiting "in the womb...of waters" (276–77), now opens her own teeming womb and gives forth "innumerous living creatures." Instead of "And God made the beast of the earth," we find "Out of the ground up rose / As from his lair the wild beast" (456–57), as if not only the earth but the beast itself had ears to hear the Word and obeyed. Milton presents creation as the response of that which is as if already alive, embryonic, submerged, or dormant. He would seem to have infused the Genesis account with a reading of John 1:4 similar in spirit to that of the *New English Bible:* "All that came to be was alive with his [i.e., the Word's] life."[28] In the case of the creation of man, both Genesis and *Paradise Lost* depart from the patterns thus established. Milton follows Genesis in having God say "let us make man"—not let there be, or let the earth bring forth, but let us make. By so doing he highlights not the obedience of these creatures to the Word, but the Father's cooperative intervention in this special case and his intimate handiwork of forming and breathing:

> Let us make now man in our image, man
> In our similitude....
> This said, he formed thee, Adam, thee O man
> Dust of the ground, and in thy nostrils breathed
> The breath of life; in his own image he
> Created thee, in the image of God
> Express, and thou becamest a living soul.
>
> (7.519–28)

The passage parallels Adam's own account of God's creative surgery and the very physical fashioning of Eve: "The rib he formed and fashioned with his hands; / Under his forming hands a creature grew" (8.469–70). Adam and Eve were not, that is, the result of uncreation hearkening to the Creator's Word. Only *after* they were formed were the commandments uttered: "Be fruitful, multiply.... Of the tree / Which tasted works knowledge of good and evil, / Thou mayst not" (7.531, 542–44). Their obedience has yet to be tried.

CHAPTER 6

The Arts of Conversation

> forsakyng all other ... to live in a holy conversation with her
> —"The Form of Marriage"

Milton is faced in Book 9 with the challenge of rendering the Fall plausible even as he demonstrates that Adam and Eve were created "sufficient to have stood" (3.99). He must, in other words, show their understanding of their creaturely condition and of their relationship to each other and to their creator to be simultaneously beyond reproach yet vulnerable to assault. The conversation in which the couple engages on the morning of the Fall is beautifully designed to serve both purposes at once. For a reader who had in mind either the following injunction from the Puritan marriage service or the biblical passage on which it is based, the decision to separate for the morning would have seemed ominous indeed: "They that be thus coupled together by God cannot be severed, or put apart, unless it be for a season, with the consent of both parties, to the end to give themselves the more fervently to fasting and prayer, giving diligent heed in the mean time, that their too long being apart be not a snare to bring them into the danger of Satan through incontinency."[1] Yet the conversation moves steadily, as Eve's motive for separation changes, toward a fullness of understanding that we had not witnessed earlier.

That it is an intricate conversation is evident from the opposing interpretations critics have placed upon it, from Stein's view that once Adam has permitted Eve to work alone, "the eating of the apple is as good as done" and Adam himself "as good as fallen," to Beverly Sherry's claim that in the conversation "there is no false eloquence because there is no untruth. The argument is eminently reasonable: each person listens to the other, then proffers alternative arguments; Adam and Eve are well intentioned, both speak truth."[2] The conversation has been so variously interpreted perhaps because both Adam and Eve enunciate ideas that seem to echo Milton's, or the Father's, or those of Scripture itself, yet many readers wish to find, in their prelapsarian words and actions, causes for the Fall—what Fish called "an intelligible sequence of events" that will remove its mystery, its "incomprehensibility."[3] The conversation is dramatic because its course is dictated not entirely by logic, but also by feeling. Adam and Eve say both more and less than they intend, and their ways of taking each other's remarks are slightly, but very realistically, askew.

There is little to fault in the reasons Eve presents for her initial suggestion. God had told them to count the garden theirs "to till and keep" (8.319–20)—a "pleasant task enjoined," as Eve calls it (9.207). Adam himself had expressed a sense of urgency about their task when he earlier told her, "To morrow ere fresh morning streak the east / With first approach of light, we must be risen, / And at our pleasant labour" (4.623–25). Furthermore, as Mary Nyquist has pointed out, the narrator corroborates at least one strand of Eve's reasoning at the outset, introducing the dialogue by noting that "much their work outgrew / The hands' dispatch of two, gardening so wide" (9.202–3).[4]

Submerged feeling comes to the surface, however, when Adam, in his response to Eve's initial suggestion, introduces an issue that nothing in Eve's remarks could have prompted:

> But if much converse perhaps
> Thee satiate, to short absence I could yield.
> For solitude sometimes is best society,
> And short retirement urges sweet return.
>
> (9.247–50)

Seen from one point of view, it is a touching moment of diffidence, perfectly consistent with his earlier and charmingly expressed fear that his own "converse" may not entertain Raphael sufficiently to keep him from departing. Yet his little epigram also runs directly counter to his motives for seeking a mate in the first place. ("In solitude / What happiness?") Does it represent a momentary failure in Adam's proper self-esteem? Or worse, does it imply that he thinks Eve has not fully and honestly expressed her own motives? Because

Adam's doubt is so fleetingly expressed, we cannot quite be sure, though we can tell that more than horticulture is at stake. Like the initial question of how best to fulfill their assigned task in the garden, this one is dropped and does not reappear. Adam proceeds to express "other doubt": "lest harm / Befall thee severed from me." This doubt he expresses in terms that he surely intends as loving, courteous, and protective:

> leave not the faithful side
> That gave thee being, still shades thee and protects.
> The wife, where danger or dishonour lurks,
> Safest and seemliest by her husband stays,
> Who guards her, or with her the worst endures.
>
> (9.265–69)

What goes on in Eve's mind here we cannot know, and cannot guess at without imposing greater certainty on the dialogue than Milton wishes us to possess. What we know is simply that Eve construes Adam's remarks as an "unkindness," choosing not to hear the affection in his tone but to hear instead what is also, implicitly, there: the distrust that is the negative corollary of his insistent protectiveness:

> But that thou shouldst my firmness therefore doubt
> To God or thee, because we have a foe
> May tempt it, I expected not to hear....
> His fraud is then thy fear, which plain infers
> Thy equal fear that my firm faith and love
> Can by his fraud be shaken or seduced;
> Thoughts, which how found they harbour in thy breast
> Adam, misthought of her to thee so dear?
>
> (9.279–89)

It may be, as Sherry avers, that they both speak truth. But as the last line indicates, they do not both think that each speaks truth. And in presenting that inference Eve also expresses her sense of having been offended. Adam has, without meaning to, put her in a bind, and she has put him in another.

Instead of acknowledging, as he had earlier, that either of them could be shaken or seduced, Adam responds by trying to calm her anxiety about his doubt of her firmness. In doing so, he raises what seems to be a new and not altogether relevant issue:

> Not diffident of thee do I dissuade
> Thy absence from my sight, but to avoid
> The attempt it self, intended by our foe.
> For he who tempts, though in vain, at least asperses
> The tempted with dishonour foul, supposed
> Not incorruptible of faith, not proof
> Against temptation.
>
> (9.293–99)

Now it is possible to construe Adam's prior speech as meaning just that; he is not necessarily contradicting himself. But because the earlier speech does not specify the nature of the harm or danger feared, the effect of the new formulation is to diminish the threat, turning it into a question of dishonor coming from without rather than one of failure from within.

At this point Adam shifts the grounds of his argument (though Eve will return to the question of aspersion), urging Eve not to underestimate the "malice and false guile" of that very enemy "who could seduce / Angels." He acknowledges the strength he feels and would manifest in her presence, but concludes with a question that, though reasonable and just, may at the same time reveal some trepidation about the reciprocity of their love:

> Why shouldst not thou like sense within thee feel
> When I am present, and thy trial choose
> With me, best witness of thy virtue tried.
>
> (9.315–17)

Eve does not quite answer Adam's question. Instead she seems to distill her entire sense of Adam's variously expressed reasons for their remaining together into a series of powerful questions of her own, each of which has won wholehearted approval from some readers, and condemnation from others. Her questions, I would argue, are not only legitimate; they greatly elevate the discussion by directing it toward the central issue of the ultimate nature of their condition and the grounds on which their "happy state" depends. Her questions, in other words, recall, for the reader, the Father's Word, his own description of hers and Adam's nature and condition as set forth in his opening speech in Book 3:

> If this be our condition, thus to dwell
> In narrow circuit straitened by a foe,
> Subtle or violent, we not endued
> Single with like defence, wherever met,
> How are we happy, still in fear of harm?
> But harm precedes not sin: only our foe
> Tempting affronts us with his foul esteem
> Of our integrity: his foul esteem
> Sticks no dishonour on our front, but turns
> Foul on himself; then wherefore shunned or feared
> By us? Who rather double honour gain
> From his surmise proved false, find peace within,
> Favour from heaven, our witness from the event.
> And what is faith, love, virtue unassayed
> Alone, without exterior help sustained?
> Let us not then suspect our happy state
> Left so imperfect by the maker wise,
> As not secure to single or combined;
> Frail is our happiness, if this be so,
> And Eden were no Eden thus exposed.
>
> (322–41)

Dennis Burden claims that Eve's first question ("How are we happy, still in fear of harm?") "indicts God's providence."[5] As I see it, however, she would be indicting God's providence only if she agreed to the hypothetical description of their condition. But she does not. She is attributing the description to Adam, summarizing her sense (whether accurate or not) of his presentation of their condition. Her question is very much in the spirit of Augustine's when he argues that Adam and Eve could not have felt such emotions as fear in the happy state of Paradise: "For if they did feel any such, how were they happy in that never-to-be forgotten place of happiness called paradise? Who indeed can be called completely happy if he suffers fear or grief?"[6] As her subsequent lines indicate, Eve disputes what she considers to be an erroneous view of their Edenic situation. What she is asking, as I read her lines, is simply whether each of them, alone, is not "endued" with sufficient defense against the foe. If they are not—if, that is, they can only defend against the foe when together—*then* she would consider their condition unhappy. But she has clearly expressed her conviction that her own "faith and love" are firm enough to withstand shaking or seduction. It is possible, if one reads the word *like* in the phrase "we not endued / Single with like defence" as meaning equal or identical, to attribute to her a demand that there be no distinction whatsoever between their defenses. But such a wish has not surfaced before in the dialogue, and nothing in the poem suggests that her defenses are not sufficiently similar to Adam's to render her "sufficient to have stood." She is, God says to Adam, "thy likeness, thy fit help, thy other self" (8.450). The narrator calls her "virtue-proof" (5.384) when, naked, she greets the angel Raphael. She, like Adam, is free to fall, and like Adam she does fall. It is not that she cannot resist the temptation, but that she does not. That she is free—free to obey or disobey God or Adam, and free to regard or disregard their warnings—seems to me a fact on which the ensuing action, and indeed Milton's full justification of God's plan, clearly rests.[7]

Eve proceeds to remind Adam, in response to his claim that the foe's attempt itself would asperse her "with dishonour foul," that "harm precedes not sin." She need not fear harm provided she not sin. Her next question, as many readers have recognized, sounds very like Milton's own opinion as he expressed it in *Areopagitica:*

> And what is faith, love, virtue unassayed
> Alone, without exterior help sustained?
>
> (9.335–36)

As therefore the state of man now is; what wisdome can there be to choose, what continence to forbeare without the knowledge of evil? He that can apprehend and consider vice with all her baits and seeming pleasures, and yet abstain, and yet distinguish, and yet prefer that which is truly better, he is the true warfaring Christian. I cannot praise a fugitive and cloister'd virtue, unexercis'd & unbreath'd, that never sallies out and sees her adversary, but slinks out of the race, where that immortall garland is to be run for, not without dust and heat.[8]

Scholars have been at pains to dissociate Eve's thinking from Milton's, insisting that Milton was speaking of fallen man and that his remarks have no bearing on Adam and Eve in their innocence.[9] But this difference is not sufficient to repudiate Eve's question. Adam and Eve have already received the kind of knowledge of evil that Milton is referring to: the knowledge of what evil is and of how it can appear to be good. Both have experienced an inclination to sin. Both have been tempted, in their dreams, to eat of the fruit,[10] but, as Adam says, "evil [whether in Paradise or in our present state] may come and go, so unapproved, and leave / No spot or blame behind." In Eve's words, "harm precedes not sin." Just as Milton cannot praise a fugitive and cloistered virtue, so the Father asks—and his words apply to pre- as well as to postlapsarian man:

> Not free, what proof could they have given sincere
> Of true allegiance, constant faith or love,
> Where only what they needs must do, appeared,
> Not what they would? What *praise* could they receive?
> (3.103–6; my emphasis)

Eve is asking for a chance to give proof of her own "constant faith or love," or, as she puts it, her "firm faith and love" (9.286). God sees their freedom as necessary if they are to receive his praise for withstanding temptation. Eve, too, knows that their actions can obtain "favour from heaven, our witness from the event" only if they are performed "without exterior help"—that is, freely. And it should be added that in the last five lines of her speech, while she can conceive of the possibility of God's making an imperfect state for them (as Adam had done earlier), she does not think he has done so. The most troublesome interpretation one could put on her lines would be to suspect that by *secure* she means absolutely invulnerable, and that she may not see that their happiness *is* frail, even though she is sufficient in herself to stand.

Adam, in his answer to her, does not refute anything that Eve has said. Instead he clarifies the terms (like *secure*) that she has already used, and emphasizes, in perfect balance, both the nature of the danger and the nature of reason as their defence. In doing so he corrects his own earlier stress on danger from without. He does not for a minute suggest that Eve has not been given reason, a "like defense" to his, wherewith to distinguish between real and apparent good. His entire speech, as Fish has said, is "essentially an expansion of God's 'Sufficient to have stood, though free to fall.'"[11] I want to stress the word *entire* because Adam's last six lines are often read as a crucial failure on his part:

> But if thou think, trial unsought may find
> Us both securer than thus warned thou seem'st,
> Go; for thy stay, not free, absents thee more;
> Go in thy native innocence, rely
> On what thou hast of virtue, summon all,
> For God towards thee hath done his part, do thine.
>
> (9.370–75)

Here, Stein writes, Adam "approves her will though against his reason."[12] According to Burden, he is "overcome" by Eve's argument, and fails "to see through it." "For all his intelligence and shrewdness, he does let her go."[13] According to Joseph Summers, Adam

> suddenly dismisses reason, ignores his "better knowledge," abdicates his responsibility.... He sees the question of their separation ... as if it merely concerned whether she is "with him" at this moment.... Now he cares more for her immediate approval of him than he does for her ultimate safety; he prefers the risk of her destruction to the risk of her momentary resentment.[14]

But the similarity of Adam's last words ("God towards thee hath done his part, do thine") to Raphael's words to him ("Accuse not nature, she hath done her part; / Do thou but thine") should put us on guard against too hasty a dismissal of Adam's wisdom. He is, at this point in the action, simply accepting and fulfilling his appointed place in the hierarchy. As God (and Raphael) are to him, so is he to Eve. After warning her fully (as God had warned them both) he rightly insists upon her freedom. He is not "merely concerned" with whether she is with him, but with the terms on which her action rests. He does not "prefer the risk of her destruction to the risk of her momentary resentment." He prefers risking a challenge to her strength to forcing her to remain. His phrase "thy stay, not free, absents thee more" strikes me as a perfectly human, domestic version of the Father's "What praise could they receive? / What pleasure I from such obedience paid, / When will and reason...had served necessity, / Not me." (3.106–11). Adam, in his concluding words, finds "better knowledge," and does what we ought, but apparently do not, want him to do.

The entire scene, like Adam and Raphael's discussion of the effects of Eve's physical and spiritual beauty, dramatizes, illustrates, and describes the presence of thoughts and feelings that, if "approved," might result in disobedience. And, like the earlier scene, it simultaneously dramatizes their achievement of understanding and control. Adam and Eve together, as they explore the implications of Eve's initial suggestion, grow toward knowledge. Eve is no longer merely the poet of the two. To a far greater extent than in her earlier speeches, she reveals in this dialogue a capacity for rigorous argument, a capacity which throws into sharp relief the almost total silence Milton imposes on her in the company of Raphael, Michael, and her maker.[15]

That Adam is right to let Eve go, and that she falls, are facts that we must accept in conjunction if we are to do justice to the tragic nature of their fall and not reduce it to a simple exemplum (a warning to husbands to look well to their wives). Likewise we must recognize that Eve is right, even in her most fallen state, to reject Adam's locating the blame for their transgression in her "desire of wandering" (9.1136), though wrong when she immediately contradicts herself and blames him for permitting her to wander. And Adam is right when he answers:

> And am I now upbraided, as the cause
> Of thy transgressing? Not enough severe,
> It seems, in thy restraint: what could I more?
> I warned thee, I admonished thee, foretold
> The danger, and the lurking enemy
> That lay in wait; beyond this had been force,
> And force upon free will hath here no place.
>
> (9.1168–74)

What is wrong in their analyses here is that they reduce the complexity of the event, ignoring their own separate acts of disobedience to God ("neither self-condemning") and searching for earlier, easier explanations. When God later rebukes them, he refers not at all to their separating, but to their eating of "the tree / Whereof I gave thee charge thou shouldst not eat." (10.122–23).

And yet. And yet. In the earlier passage, when Eve relates her dream to Adam and he in turn kisses away her tears, Milton tells us unequivocally that "all was cleared" (5.136). Here, though Eve is fully within her rights, and though it is hard to imagine Adam being more persuasive without being coercive, this conversation leaves us with the sense that all has not been entirely cleared. If the separation is justified, it is nevertheless imprudent. It is a pivotal, delicately balanced conversation, prefiguring drastic discord without necessitating it. As Joan S. Bennett puts it, "they do not fall here, they do not sin; but they lose their balance ... and render themselves more vulnerable than usual to a push from the enemy."[16] Milton interjects between each speech brief comments that suggest the effort required to maintain courtesy and mutual understanding. To Eve's initial suggestion Adam returns a "mild" answer, but while the word may accurately describe his tone of voice, it hardly does justice to the feelings he expresses. His subsequent addresses are "healing," and then "fervent." Eve first replies "with sweet austere composure," a phrase that would be oxymoronic no matter what definition of *austere* we chose, but especially so in view of its earliest meaning, "sour or bitter and astringent." And her last speech is introduced as follows: "But Eve / Persisted, yet submiss, though last, replied" (9.376–77). The three turns in the brief sentence—but, yet, though—are representative of the conversation as a whole, of the need to qualify, to attempt to "compose" conflicting feelings and motives, to hear and to be heard. It is an improvised, arduous piece of counterpoint, decorum under stress.

Furthermore it is Eve, not Adam, who has the parting word, and as in earlier passages in the scene she has heard what she wants to hear:

> With thy permission then, and thus forwarned
> Chiefly by what thy own last reasoning words
> Touched only, that our trial, when least sought,
> May find us both perhaps far less prepared,
> The willinger I go, nor much expect
> A foe so proud will first the weaker seek;
> So bent, the more shall shame him his repulse.
>
> (9.378–84)

What Eve has chiefly in mind is in fact not Adam's warning at all, and not his "reasoning" words, but rather a concession to an idea *he* imputes to *her:*

> But if thou think, trial unsought may find
> Us both securer than thus warned thou seem'st,
> Go.
>
> (9.370–72)

As she leaves, Milton's description of her underscores both her innocence and her vulnerability. She is "a wood-nymph light," armed not, like Delia, with "bow and quiver," but with her gardening tools. She is likened to "Pomona when she fled / Vertumnus," and to "Ceres in her prime, / Yet virgin of Proserpina from Jove." The comparisons are not reassuring, for the qualifying phrases that insist on Pomona's and Ceres's virginity simultaneously make us look forward to Ceres's impregnation and to Vertumnus' successful seduction of Pomona. The word *fled* itself might lead us to call her motives into question.

Beguiling Eve

> But the woman being deceived
> was in the transgression.
>
> —1 Timothy 2:14

In the second chapter I suggested that the two actions that together constitute the Fall are best characterized as failures of memory, failures of the mind's inner ear. Indeed God so characterizes them. Adam and Eve are disobedient; Eve hearkens to Satan's voice, Adam to Eve's. Neither hearkens, at the very moment of crisis, to God's command, "sole daughter of his voice" (9.653). It is a sin against the Word. Yet so brief an account is bound to be reductive, even misleading. If Eve's words make their way into Adam's thinking, it is only after, not before, he makes up his mind. Furthermore, one can put the matter differently. As Georgia Christopher has said, "Satan invites Eve to measure God's words by human experience and human reason, rather than the other way round." "Eve's mistake is that she believes the words of a creature against those of the Creator."[17] In the terms of Paul's Letter to the Romans, Eve is engaging in idolatry.

The more fully one enters into the actual drama of Satan's dialogue with her, the more intertwined the ideas of nature and Scripture become. The God Adam and Eve sin against is both *maker* and *sayer*. At the heart of it, Eve is simply deceived. She believes that it is a serpent speaking to her, and that what it says is true, just as Uriel had thought that the visitor who asked him the way to the new creation was a well-intentioned "stripling cherub" (3.636). "For neither man nor angel can discern / Hypocrisy.... And oft though wisdom wake, suspicion sleeps / At wisdom's gate, and to simplicity / Resigns her charge, while goodness thinks no ill / Where no ill seems" (3.682–89).

Milton's little allegory has the unfortunate effect of excusing Uriel's (and, by implication, Eve's) failure, and of suggesting that it was inevitable. As an actual explanation, it is transparently insufficient. Eve does think ill; that is, she knows full well that Satan is urging her to disobey God's injunction. My own encounters with the extended conversation between Satan and Eve, and with its interpreters, have led me increasingly to doubt that Milton wanted the reader to be able to come up with an explanation that goes beyond the one afforded by Scripture: the woman was deceived. The story of Eve's fall (9.532–780) is long in the telling—roughly two and one-half times the length of the story of Adam's fall. It is a richly dramatic story, with a copiousness that makes the outcome plausible. Yet at every crucial turn its logic is debatable if not downright elusive. Like its counterpart in Genesis, it both provokes and resists interpretation.

Though eventually Satan will explicitly deny the truth of God's word, he works on Eve at first chiefly by contradicting what she has been taught, and what she believes, about the order of creation. With every new title he bestows upon her—"sovereign mistress," "sole wonder," "fairest resemblance of thy maker fair," "empress of this fair world," "sovereign of creatures, universal dame," "queen of this universe," "goddess humane"—he denies or inverts her relationship to Adam, and to God, as she herself has elsewhere described it.

Consider her response to Satan's initial flattering proem:

Into the heart of Eve his words made way,
Though at the voice much marvelling; at length
Not unamazed she thus in answer spake.
What may this mean? Language of man pronounced
By tongue of brute, and human sense expressed?

The first at least of these I thought denied
To beasts, whom God on their creation-day
Created mute to all articulate sound;
The latter I demur, for in their looks
Much reason, and in their actions oft appears.
Thee, serpent, subtlest beast of all the field
I knew, but not with human voice endued;
Redouble then this miracle, and say,
How camest thou speakable of mute, and how
To me so friendly grown above the rest
Of brutal kind, that daily are in sight?
Say, for such wonder claims attention due.

(9.550–66)

The placement of *though* at the beginning of the second line immediately deflects us away from an answer to the question of precisely which words made their way into Eve's heart and turns us instead toward the wonder or amazement she feels at the sheer fact of a brute, a beast, endued with human voice. Her repetition of *beast* and *brute* underscores the effort she is making to bring her present experience into line with what she thought she knew (and did know) about the scale of nature. The sense of wonder, to which Satan himself is so susceptible, leaves Eve off balance, teetering between belief and doubt. It leads naturally to curiosity, which in the present company is dangerous, as Nyquist has pointed out, because it invites rather than forecloses the continuation of the dialogue. "Unlike the purely reflective questions that open her speech, the questions that follow demand an answer."[18] It is only her last question—"How camest thou . . . to me so friendly grown?"—that hints that she may have paid more than skeptical attention to his flattery. Satan began his address to her by pleading, "Wonder not, sovereign mistress, if perhaps / Thou canst, who art sole wonder" (9.532–33), and it appears that when she says "such wonder claims attention due" it is his wonder at her that claims her attention rather than hers at him. He, at any rate, concludes his lengthy reply by answering her last question as if he had thus understood it:

But all that fair and good in thy divine
Semblance, and in thy beauty's heavenly ray
United I beheld; no fair to thine

> Equivalent or second, which compelled
> Me thus, though importune perhaps, to come
> And gaze, and worship thee of right declared
> Sovereign of creatures, universal dame.
>
> (9.606–12)

When they reach the tree, Satan tampers with the wording of the commandment.[19] God had said, "Of *every* tree that in the garden grows / Eat freely with glad heart.... But of the tree whose operation brings knowledge of good and ill...shun to taste" (8.321–27; my emphasis). Eve, after stressing in like fashion the variety and abundance of trees from which they are free to choose (9.618–24), uses a similar construction: "But of this tree we may not taste or touch" (9.651). Satan replies "guilefully," emphasizing not God's great generosity but his restrictiveness: "Indeed? Hath God then said that of the fruit / Of all these garden trees ye shall not eat, / Yet lord declared of all in earth or air?" (9.656–58). Eve's reply is such as to resist definitive commentary; it presents a literary example of the sorts of problems Milton perceived so clearly in the interpretation of Scripture:

> *Of the fruit*
> *Of each tree in the garden we may eat,*
> *But of the fruit* of this fair tree amidst
> The garden, God hath said, Ye shall not eat
> Thereof, nor shall ye touch it, lest ye die.
>
> (9.659–63)

The passage I have emphasized sets Satan's crooked version of the commandment absolutely straight. Is her phrase *this fair tree*, however, "a vague evasion," as Fowler would have it, "of the morally definitive 'tree of the knowledge of good and evil'"? Or worse, is it a sign of her attraction to it? But after all, as Diane McColley has pointed out,[20] the tree *is* fair—"pleasant to the eyes," according to the King James Version. Should we concur with Nyquist's assertion that "Eve's defense of the command is not so fervent or courageous as it should be," and that "the brevity of her speech signals a degree of acquiescence, a degree of surrender to the oppressive voice of doubt"?[21] Or is her very brevity an attempt to stick as close to the true

Word as she can, grasping it almost as a talisman? Consider, though the situation is very different, Adam's fervently self-serving nineteen-line amplification of Scripture when God asks him whether he has "eaten of the tree," and compare it with the brevity of Eve's verbatim rendering of Genesis 3:10, "The serpent me beguiled and I did eat" (10.125–43, 162). We accept the fact that Eve is "yet sinless." She has not yet broken the commandment. But beyond that Milton will not let us rest secure. His very supplementing of the Genesis account preserves the mystery at its core.

Eve is still sinless. But with one devastating speech (lines 679–732), fifty-three lines of choplogic, Satan erases her memory of God's words, making room for his own words—"reach then, and freely taste"—which "into her heart too easy entrance won." He begins, after his brief apostrophe to the tree, with his first direct and explicit contradiction of God's words: "Do not believe / Those rigid threats of death; ye shall not die." Then, like literary tempters before him,[22] he puts forward an argument that consists primarily of an accelerating tumble of suggestive but confused and confusing questions.

In her silent musings that follow, Eve adopts not only the thoughts but also the rhetoric and syntax that Satan has foisted upon her. Mimicking the serpent, she begins by addressing the tree itself: "Great are thy virtues, doubtless, best of fruits" (9.745). Her thinking, too, consists chiefly in the posing of questions. Satan had managed to suggest to her that there are no good reasons for not eating the fruit, and Eve reiterates his suggestions. Most of Satan's speech is dedicated to allaying Eve's fears of the consequences of eating the fruit, and some is dedicated to providing indirect evidence (the forbiddance itself) that the fruit must be desirable. A very few mysterious phrases ("It gives you life / To knowledge ... ye shall be as gods") suggest, but opaquely, why it might be desirable. Eve accepts the notion that "his forbidding / Commends thee more, while it infers the good / By thee communicated." But she has no idea of what that good might be, and she turns that very fact into a reason for yielding: "For good unknown, sure is not had, or had /And yet unknown, is as not had at all." Satan manages to call into question her correct assumption that she was created superior to the other creatures. "Shall that be shut to man," he asks, "which to the beast / Is open?" And the question becomes her own: "For us alone / Was death invented? Or to us denied / This intellectual food, for beasts reserved?" Eve's motive is in one sense oddly pure. She has no thought, before she eats, of trying to equal or surpass Adam in knowledge. She conveys no sense of having rankled under his domination. Nor does the idea of becoming "as the gods" seem to have taken a hold on her. She thinks that something good will happen to her if she eats, but she finds no positive terms for describing that good until the very end of her musings:

> Yet that one beast which first
> Hath tasted, envies not, but brings with joy
> The good befallen him, author unsuspect,
> Friendly to man, far from deceit or guile.
> What fear I then, rather what know to fear
> Under this ignorance of good and evil,
> Of God or death, of law or penalty?
> Here grows the cure of all, this fruit divine,
> Fair to the eye, inviting to the taste,
> Of virtue to make wise: what hinders then
> To reach, and feed at once both body and mind?
>
> (9.769–79)

Uriel failed to see through Satan's professed desire to praise the "universal maker" (3.676). Abdiel triumphed over Satan by denying his claim that the angels were "self begot" and subjecting it to scorn (5.809–95). At the heart of each episode is the relationship between the creature and the Creator. Eve confronts a similar challenge. Satan had presented God to her as a withholder of good, and he had questioned whether all, and especially the creatures of the earth, in fact proceed from the gods. Eve accepted the notion that God "forbids us good," and here, in her final sinless moment, she has her closest brush with blasphemy and the violation of the first commandment. She renames the serpent, whose titles include "author of all ill" and "author of evil" (2.381; 6.262)—renames him as the bringer, indeed the unenvying *author,* of good. The irony of her thinking of Satan as the author of her good redoubles when we put it side by side with Adam's expression of gratitude to God for the gift of Eve: "Giver of all things fair, but fairest this / Of all thy gifts, nor enviest" (8.493–94).[23]

For a brief moment ("What fear I then?") Eve seems sure of herself, but her dramatic qualification of the question reveals how totally

Satan has shaken her confidence and self-esteem. The effect of his hyperbolic flattery, which she recognizes as "overpraising" (9.615), has not been to flatter, but ultimately to insult and degrade her. Telling her that she has been kept "low and ignorant" (9.704), humiliating her with his unanswerable barrage of questions, he has made her indeed feel ignorant of everything that right now matters. Her ignorance of what to fear becomes the emptiness that only the forbidden fruit, she thinks, can fill. She will soon discover what she should have feared. At this point, however, her sense of deficiency is total, but pathetically vague, summed up in the generality of "here grows the cure of all." Milton takes from Genesis what appears to be the narrator's assessment of the tree—"And when the woman saw that the tree was good for food, and that it was pleasant to the eyes, and a tree to be desired to make one wise" (3:6)—and gives it to Eve. He thus casts doubt on the objectivity of the assessment and turns what in the Bible are reasons for eating the fruit into something more akin to rationalizations for risking an act the consequences of which she knows she does not know. Satan has led her, for now, to her wit's end.

No sooner does she eat than nature's works respond: "Earth felt the wound, and nature from her seat / Sighing through all her works gave signs of woe, / That all was lost" (9.782–84). Eve's first fallen words, spoken to herself, extend the idolatry already committed. In Paul's now familiar locution, she has "changed the truth of God into a lie," or better, in the Revised Standard Version, she has "*exchanged the truth about God for a lie*," and she is ready to worship and serve the creature more than the Creator (Rom. 1:25):

> O sovereign, virtuous, precious of all trees
> In Paradise . . .
>   henceforth my early care,
> Not without song, each morning, and due praise
> Shall tend thee.
>   (9.795–801)

Eve no sooner eats than she "knows" evil. She knows guilt ("And I perhaps am secret"), duplicity ("But to Adam in what sort / Shall I appear?"), and covetousness ("Shall I . . . keep the odds of knowledge in my power?"). She experiences an imagined or figurative death:

> Then I shall be no more,
> And Adam wedded to another Eve,
> Shall live with her enjoying, I extinct;
> A death to think.
>
> (9.827–30)

And she intends that Adam should die with her rather than live without her:

> Confirmed then I resolve,
> Adam shall share with me in bliss or woe:
> So dear I love him, that with him all deaths
> I could endure, without him live no life.
>
> (9.830–33)

No sooner does she so resolve than we see her violate once again the second commandment ("Thou shalt not bow down thyself to them, nor serve them" [Exod. 20:5]): "From the tree her step she turned, / But first low reverence done, as to the power / That dwelt within."

During her reflections before she plucked and ate the fruit, Eve used the first person plural pronouns—we, us, and our—no less than twelve times in sixteen lines. But they ring absolutely hollow, as if used out of habit. There is not a shred of evidence that she really thought of Adam at all. It is as if she had forgotten him, or assumed that she could speak for him, or had ceased to treat him as another individual whose conversation might be useful to her. It is only after she eats that she thinks of him and begins to wonder what "sort" she should choose in which to appear to him. And the sort she chooses is that of the good wife, one who did what she did "for thee / Chiefly," as she tells him. The words with which she salutes her spouse must be among the most transparently disingenuous in all literature: "Hast thou not wondered, Adam, at my stay? / Thee I have missed, and thought it long...."

Charming Adam

> And Adam was not deceived
>
> —1 Timothy 2:14

When Eve, "with liberal hand," offers the forbidden fruit to Adam, "he scrupled not to eat / Against his better knowledge, not deceived,

/ But fondly overcome with female charm" (9.997–99). However much of the complexity of the events leading to Adam's fall this concise analysis may omit, the contrast it states is clear enough. Adam disobeys God in order to be with Eve. He is not deceived. On the assumption that Milton took his scriptural source seriously, it behooves us to examine Adam's intellectual conduct just before the Fall with some care, especially in the light of the tendency of many readers to judge him guilty of almost every failure of reason imaginable.

I want to take seriously the possibility that Adam's knowledge did not fail him until he fell; until, that is, he ate the proffered fruit. It was Milton's view in *Christian Doctrine* that the sin—the eating of the fruit—brought about as one of its punitive effects "the loss or at least the extensive darkening of that right reason, whose function it was to discern the chief good, and which was, as it were, the life of the understanding." And this punishment took place "at the same moment as the fall of man, not merely on the same day."[24] It is after the fall, with the advent of "high passions, anger, hate, / Mistrust, suspicion, discord," that Milton tells us in the poem that "understanding ruled not, and the will / Heard not her lore" (9.1123–28).

Yet the doctrine is a hard one, for a poet if not for a philosopher, and like so much of what transpires in Book 9 it takes on an air of paradox. Eve, certainly, was deceived, her reason misled by "some fair appearing good" (9.354). It is difficult not to think that Adam, too, was deceived, by Eve or by himself, when he chose her (a fair appearing good) over God. But the poet tells us he was *not* deceived. We are to believe, that is, that Adam "discerned the chief good" even as he rejected it. How did Milton the poet grapple with the paradox?

Certainly we have seen Adam's "better knowledge" dramatized over and over again, in his conversations with Eve, with Raphael, and with God. At one point in his decorous but firm argument with his Creator over his need for a mate there is a suggestion that his intelligence is not unlike the Son's. The Almighty is pleased with Adam's exercise of his rational faculties, and he answers him—"I, ere thou spakest, / Knew it not good for man to be alone" (8.444–45)—in a spirit not unlike that of the Father's earlier answer to the Son's request that mercy be shown to mankind: "All hast thou spoken as my thoughts are, all / As my eternal purpose hath decreed" (3.171–72).

But clearly the most relevant knowledge Adam possesses pertains to his understanding of Eve herself and of his relationship to her. Before turning to his decision to join her in sin, we must pause to consider the conclusion of his discussion with Raphael, in which he raises his second question about the wisdom of God's and nature's works. He describes to the archangel the "change" that Eve works on his mind and tells him how he feels "here only weak / Against the charm of beauty's powerful glance":

> Or nature failed in me, and left some part
> Not proof enough such object to sustain,
> Or from my side subducting, took perhaps
> More than enough; at least on her bestowed
> Too much of ornament, in outward show
> Elaborate, of inward less exact.
>
> (8.534–39)

The exchange between Adam and Raphael has been variously interpreted, sometimes with an emphasis on its revelation of the nature and strength of Eve's power over Adam, sometimes with an emphasis on its revelation of Adam's knowledge of his weakness, and hence of his preparedness for whatever might ensue. It is important, I think, to see the interpretations as complementary, and to give each its full weight. Arnold Stein and Stanley Fish lay great stress on Adam's use of the word *seems* in the following passage:

> When I approach
> Her loveliness, so absolute she seems
> And in her self complete, so well to know
> Her own, that what she wills to do or say,
> Seems wisest, virtuousest, discreetest, best.
>
> (8.546–50)

According to Stein, Adam "presents his whole extravagant praise of Eve deliberately as an illusion, one that he presumes to control by his formal daylight knowledge of reality," but "the illusion that is enjoyed in spite of formal disapproval corrupts the control of reality."[25] For Stein it is as if Adam uses *seems* to give full play to his imaginings, acting out his fall before it occurs. For Fish, "Higher knowledge has *not* fallen degraded in Eve's presence, and, because the possibility has been noted, it is less likely to fall in the future. The delicacy (not frailty) of Adam's understanding is mirrored in the word 'seems,' a verbal extension of his will through which he controls the illusion of Eve's superiority by insisting on its status as illusion."[26]

But in fact it is only the syntax of those five lines of the passage that is governed by *seems*, after which Adam uses a forceful, unqualified declarative:

> All higher knowledge in her presence falls
> Degraded, wisdom in discourse with her
> Looses discountenanced, and like folly shows;
> Authority and reason on her wait,
> As one intended first, not after made
> Occasionally; and to consummate all,
> Greatness of mind and nobleness their seat
> Build in her loveliest, and create an awe
> About her, as a guard angelic placed.
>
> (8.551–59)

The word *seems* has dropped very far into the background. Adam, in his allegorizing of knowledge, wisdom, authority, and reason, speaks not of what has happened, or of what might happen or seems to happen, but of what does happen. He "well understands" that "in the prime end / Of nature" Eve is "the inferior" (8.540–41), and he knows that she was not intended first. But he also knows, nevertheless, that "wisdom in discourse with her / Looses discountenanced." It is this forceful presentation of what does happen to him against his better knowledge that justifies Raphael's stern warning:

> Accuse not nature, she hath done her part;
> Do thou but thine, and be not diffident
> Of wisdom, she deserts thee not, if thou
> Dismiss not her, when most thou need'st her nigh,
> By attributing overmuch to things
> Less excellent, as thou thy self perceiv'st.
>
> (8.561–66)

To say that Adam's higher knowledge has fallen, and does fall, degraded in Eve's presence is not to say that Adam has fallen, or that he is likely to. To fall is to disobey God's sole command. But Adam has demonstrated for us that he is capable of falling, and that he knows it. In his answer to Raphael, Adam correctly describes his own present moral state in terms that echo his earlier explanation of Eve's dream. To Raphael he says:

> I to thee disclose
> What inward thence I feel, not therefore foiled,
> Who meet with various objects, from the sense
> Variously *representing;* yet still free
> Approve the best, and follow what I *approve.*
>
> (8.607–11; my emphasis)

Whatever "external things" the "watchful senses *represent*" to us, he had said to Eve, "Evil into the mind of god or man / May come and go, so *unapproved,* and leave / No spot or blame behind" (5.103–4; 117–19; my emphasis). The tense simultaneity, at this point, of Adam's knowledge of his actual response to Eve and his knowledge of the response he ought to have could not be greater. It is a sign of the fullness of his knowledge. He has not done evil, but he has known and understood feelings within himself which, if approved and acted upon, could lead him to disobey God's command. And later, but only later, they do.

We arrive, then, at the point where Adam is confronted by an already fallen Eve, and if ever Adam needed help it is here. Milton has designed his response with extraordinary delicacy and care. Adam is not persuaded to join Eve in sin, nor does he persuade himself. Eve's arguments do not enter his thinking until after his decision has been firmly made. He simply wills, resolves, chooses, to join her. Given the fullness of that "better knowledge" we have seen him to possess, his willful choice is structurally similar to Macbeth's, in that scene where, after a twenty-eight line soliloquy in which *he* reveals his better knowledge, and with only the vaguest clues afforded us as to the psychological process involved, he flies in the face of that knowledge: "I am settled, and bend up / Each corporal agent to this terrible feat" (1.7). Adam's resolution is, if anything, more mysterious than Macbeth's because he remains more acutely aware of the nature and consequences of his act even as he determines upon it. And, from the reader's point of view, it is more complex because it is, to a degree we should not underestimate, an act of love. Macbeth, as distinct from Adam, never describes the good he seeks in positive terms.[27]

Adam's single, crucial mistake occurs in the very first words he utters to himself as he stands "speechless...and pale" before his fallen spouse. With absolute sincerity he describes Eve just as the archdeceiver had done minutes earlier:

> O *fairest of creation,* last and *best*
> *Of all God's works,* creature in whom excelled
> Whatever can to sight or thought be formed,
> Holy, divine, good, amiable or sweet!
>
> (9.896–99; my emphasis)

These lines contradict, explicitly and directly, the knowledge Adam had earlier expressed to Raphael: "For well I understand in the prime end / Of nature her the inferior" (8.540–41). They represent, in other words, a subversion of that placement of the man above the woman in the hierarchy which God (and Paul) had ordained and to which the Son later refers in censuring Adam:

> Thou didst resign thy manhood, and the place
> Wherein God set thee above her made of thee,
> And for thee, whose perfection far excelled
> Hers in all real dignity.
>
> (10.148–51)

Raphael had recommended "self esteem" to Adam (8.572), but Adam esteems Eve above himself, and that fact, while it defines his sin, has for countless readers colored his act with a decidedly romantic appeal.[28] He has not been, as Eve was, deceived by specious arguments. He knowingly chooses Eve against his better knowledge. He makes the choice unhesitatingly and in full knowledge that its consequence will be his ruin:

> How art thou lost, how on a sudden lost,
> Defaced, deflowered, and now to death devote?
> Rather how hast thou yielded to transgress
> The strict forbiddance, how to violate
> The sacred fruit forbidden! Some cursed fraud
> Of enemy hath beguiled thee, yet unknown,
> And me with thee hath ruined, for with thee
> Certain my resolution is to die.
>
> (9.900–907)

156 / MILTON'S WISDOM

Fish sees Adam in these lines as engaged in a subtle process of self-deception:

> At first his participles ("Defac't, deflow'r'd") make Eve the victim of an evil external to her; but Adam, who knows very well what must have happened, immediately corrects the distortion in his language with the word "rather," and returns the responsibility to her: "how hast *thou* yielded." Yet within three lines, Eve is again the object of the action ("beguil'd"), which ruins her and with her Adam, who enters into a conspiracy with himself by pretending to believe in his own linguistic sleight of hand. To protect himself from pain he has conferred on the act of disobedience a meaning he will feel comfortable with: Eve does not sin, she is undone by "some cursed fraud."[29]

But this hardly seems fair to Adam or true to the sense of amazement and astonishment that his lines convey and that makes elaborate pretense unlikely. His participles describe the appearance of Eve's face ("But in her cheek distemper flushing glowed") and do not in fact indicate whether the agent is external or internal. Furthermore, Eve has yielded *and* she has been beguiled by "some cursed fraud / Of enemy." Both attributions are true, and either alone would be incomplete. When God asks Eve what she has done, she answers, quoting Scripture, "The serpent me beguiled and I did eat" (10.162), and God does not say her nay. His own foreknowing words had been "man falls deceived / By the other first" (3.130–31). Adam, like Eve, needs two clauses to designate the two participating agents, and there is no indication that he suppresses either truth.

Adam proceeds to explain his decision to himself, and he does so in a moving restatement of his reasons for asking God for a companion "fit and meet" to end his solitude and partake with him of all the good that God's "hands so liberal" had provided:

> How can I live without thee, how forgo
> Thy sweet converse and love so dearly joined,
> To live again in these wild woods forlorn?
> Should God create another Eve, and I
> Another rib afford, yet loss of thee
> Would never from my heart; no no, I feel

> The link of nature draw me: flesh of flesh,
> Bone of my bone thou art, and from thy state
> Mine never shall be parted, bliss or woe.
>
> (9.908–16)

Like the words he utters when first he beholds the new-created Eve (8.494–99), this passage follows Genesis 2:23–24 closely, though each expands upon it in a direction that is consistent with the spiritual interpretation Milton gives to the words "bone of my bones, and flesh of my flesh" in *Tetrachordon* (see below). In the argument to Book 9 Milton wrote that Adam acted "through vehemence of love," and that seems right enough. "Sweet converse and love so dearly joined," and the refusal to live again forlorn, catch nicely Milton's often reiterated conception of the "prime and principall scope" of marriage: "a meet and happy conversation" and the "prevention of lonelinesse to the mind and spirit of man."[30]

Burden argued that Milton would have regarded Adam's desire for Eve's "sweet converse and love" as "absurd": his desire to join Eve "does not lead to love and amity for its outcome is death and despair. There can be no true society in sinfulness. The upshot of the Fall, Adam and Eve's quarrel and mutual recriminations, provides a logical and ironical end to what Adam is here calling their 'sweet Converse and Love.'"[31] But this is surely a narrow view of the upshot of the Fall. Adam's assessment of Eve in this regard receives full justification when, in Book 10, it is she whose sweet converse and love recover him from the depths of despair, anger, pride, and resentment into which he has fallen, and when, much later, he hears her final words and is "well pleased," as they join hands to leave Eden, solitary and together.

Fish simply finds Adam's "appropriation" of Genesis "irrelevant, an instance of the devil, or someone about to enter his service, quoting scripture."[32] Of course it may be so, but it may not. Adam's love is selfish—a version of his initial selfish request for companionship, but intensified by his experience and knowledge of just how sweet that companionship is. He does it clearly for himself, not for Eve. But it is selfless, too, in the sense that he is willing, knowing what he knows, to be ruined rather than to live without her. There is in Christian marriage an intimate connection between self-love and love for one's spouse. A man's love for his wife *is* self-love, and his love of himself is the pattern for love of his wife. As the marriage service, quoting Paul's Letter to the Ephesians, enjoins: "He that loveth his own wife, loveth himself.... let every one of you so love his own wife, even as himself." Milton intensifies the identification by having God present Eve to Adam as "thy other self" (8.450), and Adam sees Eve as "bone of my bone, flesh of my flesh, my self / Before me," foreseeing that the two of them "shall be one flesh, one heart, one soul" (8.495–99).

I see no way to do justice to the complexity of Adam's act, and of its consequences, other than with the aid of paradox: Adam does the wrong thing for good reasons.[33] The reasons do not make the act right, nor does the act make the reasons base. The result of the act will be the experiential knowledge of evil and death. It will also be the prospect of a paradise "happier far" and the promise, for the faithful, that they will be received "into bliss, / Whether in heaven or earth, for then the earth / Shall all be paradise, far happier place / Than this of Eden, and far happier days" (12.462–65).

To acquiesce in Milton's assertion that Adam fell "not deceived" we must take it in its narrow sense. He knows that he is doing wrong, and no one deceives him. At the same time, his description of Eve as "fairest of creation, last and best / Of all God's works" is, from God's and Raphael's point of view, inaccurate. His appraisal of her, as we have seen, is at odds with the hierarchy inscribed in the book of nature. But the balance is delicate. He appraises her, at the moment of his fall, according to his sense, based on experience rather than instruction, of her value to him. It is a misappraisal he has described to us, and one that we have almost heard him make before, though in tones so utterly winning that we pass over them without suspicion: "Best image of my self and dearer half" (5.95); "Sole Eve, associate sole, to me beyond / Compare above all living creatures dear" (9.227–28). Indeed the very first words we hear him utter to Eve seem, in retrospect, to sway on the balance: "Sole partner and sole part of all these joys, / Dearer thy self than all" (4.411–12). The difference is simple. In Book 9 the appraisal is transmuted into action.

But Adam is not mistaken on this one count alone. He does not know, or does not think of, everything he might. The narrator describes him as "submitting to what seemed remediless." He does not consider alternative courses of action. In the words of the marginal gloss on Genesis 3:7 in the Geneva Bible, "They soght not to God for remedie." And when, "in calm mood," he turns to speak to Eve, he acknowledges that her description of the effect of the fruit on the serpent may be accurate. Here, after having resolved to die, Adam seems to yield, indirectly, to Satan's deception:

> Yet so
> Perhaps thou shalt not die, perhaps the fact
> Is not so heinous now, foretasted fruit,
> Profaned first by the serpent, by him first
> Made common and unhallowed ere our taste;
> Nor yet on him found deadly, he yet lives,
> Lives, as thou saidst, and gains to live as man
> Higher degree of life, inducement strong
> To us, as likely tasting to attain
> Proportional ascent, which cannot be
> But to be gods, or angels demi-gods.
>
> (9.927–37)

Knowing Adam

Yet even here, I think, we must be careful not to oversimplify the state of Adam's knowledge by ignoring the sense in which his lines express truth. We can stress, if we wish, the sense in which they are only ironically true: he is not aware of their full implications. But we should also and equally stress their congruence with the divine plan according to which this is a fortunate fall. Anne Ferry sees ambition in the lines quoted above,[34] and she may be right, though merely naming something an inducement suggests an objectivity, a speculativeness, that *ambition* doesn't quite catch. Adam is attempting to place the happiest construction possible on the act he is determined to commit. In doing so he reveals an intuitive "better knowledge" than he can yet understand. He and Eve do, of course, become as gods ("O sons, like one of us man is become / To know both good and evil, since his taste / Of that defended fruit" [11.84–86]), though in a sense, and for a reason, that Adam cannot know. Nor can he understand, when he tells Eve "perhaps thou shalt not die," that they will and will not die. That is the hard lesson he will learn under Michael's tutelage. He does not know the full "remedy" God has in store:

> So death becomes
> His final remedy, and after life
> Tried in sharp tribulation, and refined
> By faith and faithful works, to second life,
> Waked in the renovation of the just,
> Resigns him up with heaven and earth renewed.
>
> (11.61–66)

But true to his intelligence, he will catch a glimmer of the promise even before Michael arrives to tell him that his Lord may "redeem [him] quite from Death's rapacious claim" (11.258). Aided by grace and prayer, he begins to suspect that "the bitterness of death / Is past, and we shall live" (11.157–58).

Beneath Adam's thinking, in other words, even as he persists in his determination to disobey God's command, there can be seen a continuing though twisted thread of faith in God's benevolence:

> Nor can I think that God, creator wise,
> Though threatening, will in earnest so destroy
> Us his prime creatures, dignified so high,
> Set over all his works, which in our fall,
> For us created, needs with us must fail,
> Dependent made; so God shall uncreate,
> Be frustrate, do, undo, and labour loose,
> Not well conceived of God, who though his power
> Creation could repeat, yet would be loth
> Us to abolish, lest the adversary
> Triumph and say; Fickle their state whom God
> Most favours, who can please him long; me first
> He ruined, now mankind; whom will he next?
> Matter of scorn, not to be given the foe.
>
> (9.938–51)

Here, all critics agree, Adam falls thoroughly apart. Ferry finds him guilty of blasphemy and "the absurd pride to think as Satan does that the fame of the Creator should depend upon the fate of the creature."[35] Stein agrees: "It is a full expression of Satan's mind, presuming to understand by reasoning from self."[36] But there are two problems with this analysis, if we keep the argument of the whole poem in view. The first is that Adam is, in large measure, right. The second is that his reasoning resembles very closely not Satan's but the Son's, when he urges his Father to be gracious to man:

> For should man finally be lost, should man
> Thy creature late so loved, thy youngest son
> Fall circumvented thus by fraud, though joined
> With his own folly? That be from thee far,
> That far be from thee, Father, who art judge
> Of all things made, and judgest only right.
> Or shall the adversary thus obtain
> His end, and frustrate thine, shall he fulfil
> His malice, and thy goodness bring to nought,
> Or proud return though to his heavier doom,
> Yet with revenge accomplished and to hell
> Draw after him the whole race of mankind,
> By him corrupted? Or wilt thou thy self
> Abolish thy creation, and unmake,
> For him, what for thy glory thou hast made?
> So should thy goodness and thy greatness both
> Be questioned and blasphemed without defence.
>
> (3.150–66)

As the Father's opening speech in Book 3 informed Eve's argument in the separation scene (see above, 137–39), so the Son's response to that speech informs Adam's. The fame of the Creator, it would seem, *does* depend upon the fate of the creature. Adam is reasoning from self, and reasoning strangely well, just as he had done when he asked God for a mate and later when he permitted Eve to work alone. Neither Adam nor the Son can believe that the Father in his wisdom would frustrate his ends or let the adversary triumph. Both recognize the importance of *this* creation—mankind—in God's plan. Both point to the criticism that would follow upon God's "uncreating" or "unmaking" his creation, as does Moses in the passage that has been cited as a likely source for the Son's speech—the passage where Moses argues with God to show mercy to his people:

> And Moses said unto the Lord, Then the Egyptians shall hear it (for thou broughtest up this people in thy might from among them;) and they will tell it to the inhabitants of this land.... Now if thou shalt kill all this people as one man, then the nations which

have heard the fame of thee will speak, saying, Because the Lord was not able to bring this people into the land which he sware unto them, therefore he hath slain them in the wilderness. And now, I beseech thee, let the power of my Lord be great, according as thou hast spoken, saying, The Lord is longsuffering, and of great mercy.[37]

There is, of course, the greatest possible difference between the situations of the Son and Adam. The Son, the "second Adam," is about to offer himself as a sacrifice for humankind, and Adam is about to commit the very sin that calls forth that sacrifice. On the basis of this fact, one might be tempted to speak of Adam's speech as an inadvertent parody of the Son's.[38] But the matter is not that simple. The former is, rather, an imperfect version of the latter. One might, for example, question whether Adam is right in calling himself and Eve God's prime creatures. There are, after all, the angels. But Adam is testifying to his sense of the great "dignity" God has bestowed upon them, and of how much their welfare must mean to him. And in describing the work of the sixth day Raphael had himself called Man "the master work, the end / Of all yet done ... chief / Of all his [God's] works" (7.505–16). Adam recognizes before he falls what Satan, with deep regret, remembers only after he falls: "My remembrance from what state / I fell, how glorious once above thy [the sun's] sphere" (4.38–39). As Adam cannot know the sense in which he and Eve both will and will not die, so he does not know that God will first "destroy" them and then through his grace give them the opportunity to recreate themselves. He will say to Eve before he falls, "If death / Consort with thee, death is to me as life" (9.953–54). He is willing to embrace death's bride as the only source of life to him. And he will come to know that she *is* the source of life, not for him alone but for all:

> Whence hail to thee,
> Eve rightly called, Mother of all Mankind,
> Mother of all things living, since by thee
> Man is to live, and all things live for man.
>
> (11.158–61)

For all the differences between the Son's speech and Adam's, then, Adam has within himself a knowledge of God's intentions beyond anything he has been told. He has not yet fallen, though he is fully resolved to fall. The knowledge he lacks—of death and second life, of destruction and renewal—is precisely the knowledge his subsequent experience, and Michael's teaching, will supply. What he now sees through a glass darkly will not be set in its true colors and light until Michael has "from Adam's eyes the film removed / Which that false fruit that promised clearer sight / Had bred" (11.412–14), an image that suggests not only how the false fruit blinds him but also how capable he was of seeing before he tasted it. What he lacks, which only grace can (and will) supply, is foresight; that is, providence. Nor does he, in his last words to Eve before he sins, let his speculations delude him into thinking they are immune from death:

> However I with thee have fixed my lot,
> Certain to undergo like doom, if death
> Consort with thee, death is to me as life;
> So forcible within my heart I feel
> The bond of nature draw me to my own,
> My own in thee, for what thou art is mine;
> Our state cannot be severed, we are one,
> One flesh; to lose thee were to lose my self.
>
> (9.952–59)

These lines reiterate the resolution, and the motive, expressed in his inward monologue and similarly recall his very first response to the sight of Eve. It seems to me that there can be little doubt that Adam is marrying Eve again: marrying her into fallen life, and into death, forgoing his Father for "bliss or woe"—a phrase they both use (9.831, 916)—or, in the words of the marriage ceremony, "in prosperity and adversity," "for better, for worse." If the marriage goes wrong, Eve will right it again and prove a fit help and comfort: "While yet we live ['til death us depart'], scarce one short hour perhaps, / Between us two let there be peace, both joining, / As joined in injuries" (10.923–25).

Critics who wish to see Adam as thoroughly fallen (and confused) before he falls argue that he is marrying for what Milton would have regarded as the wrong reason, as if the fact that Adam does not repeat in the last lines the idea of "sweet converse and love" indicates that his attraction is now degraded. Stein, for example, called Adam's choice a "choice of flesh": "When the crisis comes Adam's reactions are in terms of the 'Link of Nature'—the flesh of flesh and bone of bone. Individuality and love are reduced to the limits of the flesh and bone."[39] But in his prose writings Milton's interpretation of Adam's words "bone of my bones, and flesh of my flesh" as they occur in Genesis is unequivocal. In *Tetrachordon* he says that Adam spoke these words:

> in reference to those words which God pronounc't before; as if he had said, this is she by whose meet help and society I shall be no more alone; this is she who was made my image, ev'n as I the Image of God; not so much in body, as in unity of mind and heart. And he might as easily know what were the words of God, as he knew so readily what had bin don with his rib, while he slept so soundly.... *Adam* spake like *Adam* the words of flesh and bones, the shell and rinde of matrimony; but God spake like God, of love and solace and meet help, the soul both of *Adam's* words and of matrimony.[40]

Adam's words, that is, though on the surface they describe "the shell and rinde of matrimony," in fact mean what God meant, and refer to "the sweet and mild familiarity of love and solace and mutual fitness." Hence his concluding expression—"We are one, / One flesh; to lose thee were to lose my self"—need not be taken as a sign that he is joining Eve for the wrong reason, and in the absence of other evidence it probably should not be so taken. Adam uses, of course, two tantalizing phrases that occur neither in Genesis nor in *Tetrachordon*. They are "the link of nature," which Stein cites above, and "the bond of nature." Burden sees in these phrases a reference to "the sexual nature of Eve's appeal."[41] That the couple is about to be linked in sin is clear enough. The irony of Eve's reply to Adam's speech underlines that fact. Adam, she says, is "linked in love so dear, / To undergo with me one guilt, one crime" (9.970–71). But she is no more speaking of sexual attraction than Adam is. She hears Adam as speaking of a "union" of "one heart, one soul in both" (9.966–67). And to that extent she is right. It is a union of two souls who will sin as one. Carnal desire and lust are the results of man's first disobedience, not its cause.

Bond and *link* are not, of course, unusual terms to use in speaking of marriage. Milton himself speaks of "the sacred bond of mariage,"[42] and in *Christian Doctrine* he says that "when human nature was perfect, before the fall, God, in paradise, established marriage as an indissoluble bond [*indissolubile coniugium*]."[43] Richard Hooker speaks of the "bond of wedlock" as necessary in the light of the length of time human beings require to raise their offspring to perfection. "Man and woman being therefore to join themselves for such a purpose, they were of necessity to be linked with some strait and insoluble knot."[44] But these phrases fall short of the mark. What has troubled readers and led them to feel that there is something wrong in Adam's appeal to the bond and link *of nature*. William Madsen recognizes that "Adam does not always read the book of Nature correctly," and he regards Adam here as making "a specious appeal to Nature to justify his action."[45] Madsen may well be right. The link and bond of nature are drawing Adam toward Eve and, it would seem to follow, away from God. At the same time it is also possible that Milton had in mind some such idea as that implied by Augustine's "*copula naturalis*," which applies specifically to Adam and Eve. Augustine refers to it in the opening paragraph of his treatise *De Bono Conjugali*:

> Forasmuch as each man is a part of the human race, and human nature is something social, and hath for a great and natural good, the power also of friendship; on this account God willed to create all men out of one, in order that they might be held in their society not only by likeness of kind, but also by bond of kindred [*cognationis vinculo*]. Therefore the first natural bond [*copula naturalis*] of human society is man and wife. Nor did God create these each by himself, and join them together as alien by birth: but He created the one out of the other, setting a sign also of power of the union in the side, whence she was drawn, was formed. For they are joined one to another side by side, who walk together, and look together whither they walk.[46]

The passage strikes me as particularly apt because Milton would have approved of Augustine's emphasis here on society and friendship as the prime end of marriage. The idea expressed in the passage—that the first marriage was instituted between a man and a woman who were literally of one flesh as a sign of the strength of the social union of man and wife—recurs in similar contexts in *The City of God*. There Augustine writes, for example, that God's purpose in creating Eve from Adam's rib was to "bind them, through a bond of kinship, into a united concord based on the link of peace [*pacis vinculo*]."[47] Or again, his purpose was "to ensure that unity of fellowship itself and ties of harmony [*vinculum concordiae*] might be more strongly [*vehementius*] impressed on him, if men were bound to one another not only by their similar nature but also by their feeling of kinship."[48]

It is neither Augustine, however, nor Milton, who says best what it meant to Adam to have had Eve made from his rib. It is Adam who says it best and first:

> Return fair Eve,
> Whom fly'st thou? Whom thou fly'st, of him thou art,
> His flesh, his bone; to give thee being I lent
> Out of my side to thee, nearest my heart
> Substantial life, *to have thee by my side*
> *Henceforth an individual solace dear;*
> Part of my soul I seek thee, and thee claim
> My other half.
>
> (4.481–88; my emphasis)

Of course, we cannot know whether Milton had something like the Augustinian *copula naturalis* in mind, but it does afford a different way of reading Adam's lines, a way that is consistent with Milton's attributing Adam's decision to "vehemence of love" and with Adam's own reference to Eve's "sweet converse and love so dearly joined," his desire not to be forlorn. The link of nature that draws him to Eve draws him not to any woman (who might, after all, satisfy the needs of the flesh)—and not, indeed, to another woman made from his own side, could he "another rib afford"—but to this one woman.[49]

To stress the sense in which Adam's reasons for choosing to die with Eve have a kind of validity, and to note the degree to which even his rationalizations of his decision contain a degree of prophetic truth of which he is unaware, is by no means to exonerate him or to suggest that he is not tragically and deeply mistaken in choosing to disobey God's command. What the extent of Adam's better knowledge does suggest, I think, is the great care with which Milton approached an extraordinarily knotty problem, a problem theological in its origins but requiring a literary solution. Mankind is half-fallen when Eve comes to Adam with fruit in hand. Adam has not fallen, but is about to fall. And Milton must somehow dramatize both his sinful will and his as yet unfallen knowledge. It is easier said than done, easier named than shown. I think Milton shared Augustine's view of Adam's fall, and his desire to follow Scripture in seeing him as undeceived. Augustine's view is worth quoting at some length, both for the sympathetic tenderness of its tone, and for the ease with which the theologian, unburdened by the necessities of drama, can describe it:

> When we consider the situation of that first man and his woman, two fellow human beings all alone and married to each other, we must suppose that he was not led astray to transgress the law of God because he believed that she spoke the truth, but because he was brought to obey her by the close bond of their alliance [*sociali necessitudine*]. For the apostle was not speaking idly when he said: "And Adam was not deceived, but the woman was deceived." He must have meant that Eve had accepted what the serpent said to her as though it were true, while Adam refused to be separate from his sole companion even in a partnership of sin. Yet he was no less guilty if he sinned with knowledge and forethought.... The apostle meant us to understand the deceived as being those who do not think that what they do is sin. Adam, however, knew; otherwise, how can it be true to say: "Adam was not deceived"? But since he was not yet acquainted with the strict justice of God, he might have been mistaken in believing that his offence was pardonable.[50]

Even Augustine, as this passage makes clear, must struggle to create what is not, in fact, a very persuasive distinction between being deceived and being mistaken. Milton goes Augustine one better by casting Adam's ignorance of the severity of God's justice (Augustine calls him *inexpertus divinae severitatis*), his "mistake" about the verdict, in a hypothetical mode: "Perhaps thou shalt not die.... Nor can I think...." He has Adam act independent of those speculations: "However I with thee have fixt my lot...." The resolution, the choice made by the sinful will, is presented at the beginning of his response—unreasoned and hence, strictly speaking, undeceived—and reaffirmed at its conclusion. And the speculations that intervene contain hauntingly accurate premonitions, not unlike the Son's, of God's ultimately gracious plan. It is hard to conceive of a better literary solution to the problem posed by Scripture, or of a poetic tact that could do fuller justice to the tragic opposition and struggle inherent in the preposition: *against* his better knowledge, not deceived.

CHAPTER 7

Meditating on the Word

Adam and Eve before the Law

> If such pleasure be
> In things to us forbidden, it might be wished,
> For this one tree had been forbidden ten.
> —(*PL* 9.1024–26)

In narrating the Fall itself, Milton left very little out of the third chapter of Genesis, but he added a great deal to it, interpreting that spare account by supplying motives (in the form of expanded dialogue and interior monologue) and new events, such as Adam's and Eve's decision to work apart. He developed it into a story that included, as the Genesis story does not, a full-fledged acting out of the workings of grace and the process of redemption, showing how this "pagan" couple underwent conversion. For that reason, Paul's Letter to the Romans has a special relevance to Milton's dramatization of the Fall and its aftermath in Books 9 and 10, just as it does to his treatment of the topics of the Fall, of sin, regeneration, repentance, and saving faith in *Christian Doctrine*.

The opening chapters of the letter, though they make no mention of Adam or Eve, offer the most detailed analytical narrative account in the Bible of the dynamic progress of their sin as Milton presents it in *Paradise Lost*. They offer, too, Paul's strongest affirmation of the sinfulness of all men and of their subsequent need for grace, faith, and repentance. It is here that we find the clearest account of the spiritual state not only of those who lived, like Adam and Eve, before the Christian era but also of those who lived, again like Adam and Eve, in ignorance of or prior to the Mosaic law. In many ways the Letter to the Romans is the one best designed to show the justice of the ways of God to men—the justice of his all-encompassing severity and wrath and the sweetness of his unmerited grace.

Following the opening salutation and thanksgiving, Paul succinctly proclaims the "gospel of Christ" in a manner that expresses the central theme of the letter: "For I am not ashamed of the gospel of Christ: for it is the power of God unto salvation to every one that believeth; to the Jew first, and also to the Greek. For therein is the righteousness of God revealed from faith to faith: as it is written, the just shall live by faith" (Rom. 1:16–17). Jew and Greek and Gentile, he will go on to argue, are justified by faith, not by knowledge of the law. Faith, and knowledge of God, are available to all, "because that which may be known of God is manifest in them; for God hath shewed it unto them. For the invisible things of him from the creation of the world are clearly seen, being understood by the things that are made, even his eternal power and Godhead; so that they are without excuse" (Rom. 1:19–20). No one, in other words, can plead ignorance of the law, for God's power and Godhead are manifested to us, as we have seen them to be manifested to Adam and Eve before the Fall, by and in his works.

Paul's subsequent description of the sinfulness of the "unrighteous" Gentiles, though it was not so intended, reads like a gloss on Milton's account of Adam and Eve's experience of sin:

> They are without excuse: because that, when they knew God, they glorified him not as God, neither were thankful; but became vain in their imaginations, and their foolish heart was darkened. Professing themselves to be wise, they became fools, and changed the glory of the uncorruptible God into an image made like to corruptible man, and to birds, and fourfooted beasts, and creeping things. Wherefore God also gave them up to uncleanness through the lusts of their own hearts, to dishonour their own bodies between themselves: Who changed the truth of God into a lie, and worshipped and served the creature more than the Creator, who is blessed for ever. Amen. For this cause God gave them up unto vile affections.... And even as they did not like to retain God in their knowledge, God gave them over to a reprobate mind, to do those things which are not convenient. (Rom. 1:20–28)

Adam and Eve knew God but ceased to glorify him. Eve first, and then both together, are filled with numerous "vain imaginations," of which the following two may be cited if only because they are explicitly labeled so:

> For Eve
> Intent now wholly on her taste, naught else
> Regarded, such delight till then, as seemed,
> In fruit she never tasted, whether true
> Or *fancied* so, through expectation high
> Of knowledge, nor was godhead from her thought.
> (9.785–90; my emphasis)

> They swim in mirth, and *fancy* that they feel
> Divinity within them breeding wings
> Wherewith to scorn the earth.
> (9.1009–11; my emphasis)

Both Adam and Eve foolishly profess themselves to be wise, and Eve transforms the tree, and Adam Eve, into idols to be worshiped and served "more than the Creator." God gives them up to lust—"in lust they burn" (9.1015)—a phrase Milton took from the two verses, omitted above, in which Paul tells how "the men, leaving the natural use of the woman, burned in their lust one toward another." Through their disobedience they "dishonour their own bodies between themselves," as Paul would have it. The fruit of their new knowledge, as Adam says, leaves them

> naked thus, of honour void,
> Of innocence, of faith, of purity,
> Our wonted ornaments now soiled and stained,
> And in our faces evident the signs
> Of foul concupiscence.
> (9.1074–78)

Paul's narrative concludes with a long list of the crimes that accompany unrighteousness, and like the similar list that Milton gives in *Christian Doctrine* of the crimes contained within the original sin,[1] it may be applied to Adam and Eve's behavior in Book 9. The unrighteous are guilty of "fornication, wickedness, covetousness, maliciousness; full of envy, murder, debate, deceit, malignity: whisperers, backbiters, haters of God, despiteful, proud, boasters, inventors of evil things, disobedient to parents, without understanding, covenant-breakers, without natural affection, implacable, unmerciful: who knowing the judgment of God, that they which commit such things are worthy of death, not only do the same, but have pleasure in them that do them" (Rom. 1:29–32).

That Adam and Eve's lustful lovemaking is fornication is suggested by Milton's comparing them to the "harlot" Dalilah and her lover Samson (9.1060). Murderers of themselves and of their progeny, boasters (Eve "boasts" herself sprung from Adam's side [9.965]), disobedient to their sole parent, they are, like Paul's unrighteous Gentiles, filled with "vile affections"—"anger, hate, / Mistrust, suspicion, discord"—and they are without understanding:

> For understanding ruled not, and the will
> Heard not her lore, both in subjection now
> To sensual appetite.
>
> (9.1127–29)

Paul's intent in the second chapter of the letter is to diminish, if not entirely erase, the distinction between Jew and Gentile by showing that because all men have the law written in their hearts, the mere possession of the (Mosaic) law gives the Jew no advantage over the Gentile. The argument is double-edged: it both justifies God's punishment of those who never heard of Moses and shows the Jews' "boast of the law" to be vain. The elements of Paul's argument helped Milton define Adam and Eve's spiritual condition both before the Fall and during the hours of "mutual accusation" they spend on the day after the Fall. The central passage, perhaps, is that in which Paul defines the position of the Gentiles:

> For there is no respect of persons with God. For as many as have sinned without law shall also perish without law: and as many as have sinned in the law shall be judged by the law; (For not the hearers of the law are just before God, but the doers of the law shall be justified. For when the Gentiles, which have not the law, do by nature the things contained in the law, these, having not the law, are *a law unto themselves:* which shew the work of the law written in their hearts, their conscience also bearing witness, and

their thoughts the mean while *accusing or else excusing one another*). (Rom. 2:11–15; my emphasis)

Before the Fall, in *Paradise Lost,* Adam and Eve "do by nature the things contained in the law." Having not ten commandments to obey but only one, they are, in large measure, a law unto themselves. As Eve rightly tells Satan:

But of this tree we may not taste nor touch;
God so commanded, and left that command
Sole daughter of his voice; the rest, we live
Law to our selves, our reason is our law.

(9.651–54)

The couple's heated quarrel following the Fall illustrates, I believe, "the work of the law written in their hearts, their conscience also bearing witness," as they accuse each other and excuse themselves. This text is one that Milton cites frequently in *Christian Doctrine* as proof that even in fallen man "some traces of the divine image still remain in us, which are not wholly extinguished by this spiritual death" in spite of the "loss of that divine grace and innate righteousness by which, in the beginning, man lived with God."[2] When Milton describes the fallen pair as spending fruitless hours in "mutual accusation," he is giving a direct rendering of the Junius-Tremellius translation that he cites in *Christian Doctrine,* where Romans 2:15, quoted above in the King James Version, reads: "Ut qui ostendant opus Legis scriptum in cordibus suis, una testimonium reddente ipsorum conscientia & cogitationibus sese *mutuo accusantibus* aut etiam defendentibus" (my emphasis).[3]

The text was most often interpreted as describing a mental dialogue, an internal debate that is evidence of the workings of conscience,[4] but given Milton's steady insistence on the image of Adam and Eve as "one soul" both before and after the Fall,[5] it would seem that he has simply externalized the debate, dramatizing it in the accusations and self-excusings of the fallen couple. When they awake on the following morning, Adam's moral sense has returned. By that I mean that he expresses a strikingly accurate understanding of what has happened to them, an accuracy underscored by the congruity, both verbal and conceptual, between his assessment and Milton's, which precedes it. In Adam's words:

> O Eve, in evil hour thou didst give ear
> To that false worm, of whomsoever taught
> To counterfeit man's voice, true in our fall,
> False in our promised rising; since our eyes
> Opened we find indeed, and find we know
> Both good and evil, good lost, and evil got,
> Bad fruit of knowledge, if this be to know.
>
> (9.1067–73)

From this point on until the end of Book 9, Adam and Eve blame each other and try to excuse themselves. They ignore their respective acts of disobedience to God's command and return to their earlier conversation—Eve's request to work apart and Adam's allowing her to do so—as the easier occasion for pinning blame on each other. And indeed the present conversation sounds much like an angrier and more explosive replay of that one. Adam initiates the quarrel with a self-righteous expression of feigned incredulity, well calculated, with its sting in its tail, to hurt rather than heal. His wish is understandable, but he is altogether too sure of his own imperviousness to temptation:

> Would thou hadst hearkened to my words, and stayed
> With me, as I besought thee, when that strange
> Desire of wandering this unhappy morn,
> I know not whence possessed thee. . . .
>
> (9.1134–37)

Eve's reply is, at first, perhaps just, but her tone, as self-righteously shocked as Adam's, is all wrong:

> What words have passed thy lips, Adam severe,
> Imput'st thou that to my default, or will
> Of wandering, as thou call'st it, which who knows
> But might as ill have happened thou being by,
> Or to thyself perhaps.
>
> (9.1144–48)

She then proceeds to pile contradiction upon contradiction. Adam could/couldn't have resisted the serpent. She was right to want to leave/Adam was wrong to let her leave:

> Hadst thou been there,
> Or here the attempt, thou couldst not have discerned
> Fraud in the serpent....
> Was I to have never parted from thy side?
> As good have grown there still a lifeless rib.
> Being as I am, why didst not thou the head
> Command me absolutely not to go,
> Going into such danger as thou saidst?...
> Hadst thou been firm and fixed in thy dissent,
> Neither had I transgressed, nor thou with me.
>
> (9.1148–61)

If Eve here presents herself as more helpless than she has been, or than she will become, Adam goes on ("incensed") to present himself, quite blindly, as less in need of Eve than he earlier claimed to be, and than in fact he is, radically distorting the feelings that had governed his decision to die with her, as if he had then imagined a possible bliss without her, but chose nevertheless to sacrifice it for her sake:

> Is this the love, is this the recompense
> Of mine to thee, ingrateful Eve, expressed
> Immutable when thou wert lost, not I,
> Who might have lived and joyed immortal bliss,
> Yet willingly chose rather death with thee.
>
> (9.1163–67)

What had been before the Fall an admirably straightforward capacity to explain and instruct when his opinion was required has now become a preachy and pompous inclination toward generalizing and moralizing, stupidly condescending both to Eve and to her sex:

> Thus it shall befall
> Him who to worth in women overtrusting
> Lets her will rule; restraint she will not brook
> And left to her self, if evil thence ensue,
> She first his weak indulgence will accuse.
>
> (9.1182–86)

Milton summarizes the episode:

> Thus they in mutual accusation spent
> The fruitless hours, but neither self-condemning
> And of their vain contest appeared no end.
>
> (9.1187–89)

One may have to strain to see a sign in Adam and Eve's quarreling, their "mutual admiration," that all is not irrevocably lost, but quarreling, as C. S. Lewis explains at a particularly Pauline moment, "means trying to show that the other man is in the wrong. And there would be no sense in trying to do that unless you and he had some sort of agreement as to what Right and Wrong are."[6] Adam and Eve are both firmly convinced that there are standards by which actions can be judged. To that their quarreling bears witness. Yet if Milton's use of Romans 2 indicates that Adam and Eve's very antagonism toward each other reveals those "traces of the divine image" which still remain in them, it also indicates very clearly how far they are, "neither self-condemning," from understanding and from righteousness: "Therefore thou art inexcusable, O man, whosoever thou art that judgest: for wherein thou judgest another, thou condemnest thyself; for thou that judgest doest the same things.... And thinkest thou this, O man, that judgest them which do such things, and doest the same, that thou shalt escape the judgment of God?" (2:1, 3). Adam and Eve, as Book 9 closes, are, in Paul's words, "contentious, and do not obey the truth, but obey unrighteousness." Unto such, God renders "indignation and wrath, tribulation and anguish" (Rom. 2:8–9). They have yet to acquire what Milton calls "the better fortitude / Of patience" (9.31–32). They have yet to learn, in Paul's words, that to those who repent and "who by patient continuance in well doing seek for glory and honour and immortality" he will render "eternal life" (2:7–9).

The Work of Salvation

In his Letter to the Philippians Paul wrote: "Work out your own salvation with fear and trembling. For it is God which worketh in you both to will and to do of his good pleasure" (2:12–13). The instruction is, if not paradoxical, at least delicately poised. Whose work is the work of salvation? Is it man's work, or God's? Since the subject of the following pages is Milton's dramatization of man and woman working out their own salvation with fear and trembling in Book 10 of *Paradise Lost,* and since the opening lines of Book 11 attribute Adam and Eve's regeneration to "prevenient grace descending" (3), Milton's treatment of the subject of grace and of "faithful works" merits some review.

Milton's answer to the question "Whose work?" would be, on the evidence of both *Christian Doctrine* and *Paradise Lost,* "God's first, and then man's." In his prose treatise Milton is unequivocal in his insistence that man is "brought to" a state of grace, that repentance is "the gift of God," and that saving faith is "implanted in us by the gift of God." At the same time he repeatedly insists on fallen man's freedom to choose—to hear or not to hear the call, to believe or not to believe, to act or not to act—as in his comment on the passage from Philippians: "What can this mean but that God gives us the power to act freely, which we have not been able to do since the fall unless called and restored? We cannot be given the gift of will unless we are also given freedom of action, because that is what free will means." "Renovation," for Milton, is "the restoration of the will to its former liberty"; a "regenerate will" is a "freed will."[7]

On the question of grace, as Dennis Danielson has pointed out, Milton sided with Arminius, who, "in contrast to orthodox Calvinists, ... claims that grace is resistible rather than irresistible."[8] C. A. Patrides, who explored the Pauline paradox in Milton's writings and in the Protestant tradition, analyzes the Father's speech in Book 3 of *Paradise Lost* (lines 173–202) to show how "the absolute primacy of grace is established absolutely," and yet how "Milton ensures the proper balance with strategically placed words. Grace ... is 'offer'd,' it 'invites,' it can even be 'neglected.'"[9] Throughout the poem the importance of human agency is assumed and reiterated. Fallen man's "endeavor" and "sincere intent" and "persistence" matter (3.192, 197). God himself utters his decrees in the conditional mood. Before the Fall, but speaking of fallen man, he says, "I will place within them as a guide / My umpire conscience, whom *if* they will hear, / Light after light well used they shall attain, / And to the end persisting, safe arrive" (3.194–97; my emphasis). "*If* patiently thy bidding they obey," he tells Michael, "dismiss them not disconsolate" (11.112–13; my emphasis). Adam in turn gains the faith that if he and Eve pray, God's ear will hear, his heart incline to pity (10.1061). They do pray, and their prayer has the desired effect.

It is sometimes argued, nonetheless, that Milton would have placed all the emphasis on the second half of Paul's instruction ("it is God which worketh in you") and none on the first ("work out your own salvation"), as if, to cite John Spencer Hill, "man's good works are efficacious before the Fall but not after it; human merit is purely a prelapsarian phenomenon."[10] I would argue, however, that Adam and Eve's condition with respect to grace, free will, merit, and the efficacy of works after the Fall is scarcely to be distinguished from their condition prior to the Fall. Adam gladly acknowledges in the first words we hear him utter that he and Eve "have nothing merited, nor can perform / Aught whereof he [God] hath need" (4.418–19). It is a strong statement, reflecting one of Milton's most deeply held convictions. (Cf. sonnet 19, "God doth not need / Either man's work or his own gifts.") It applies to both unfallen and to fallen man, as does Adam's much later recognition that his happiness before the Fall was "of [God's] grace" (10.767). God *needs* nothing from man, but he *requires* service and obedience.

Milton believed, as the following passage makes clear, that at the Fall man became "forfeit and enthralled / By sin to foul exorbitant desires." Grace, then, is not merely a matter of restoring free will. It involves as well a kind of continuing spiritual support, "strength added from above" (11.138), a partial release from enthrallment, for those who endeavor "with sincere intent" to "pray, repent, and bring obedience due" (3.190–92):

> Man shall not quite be lost, but saved who will,
> Yet not of will in him, but grace in me
> Freely vouchsafed; once more I will renew
> His lapsed powers, though forfeit and enthralled
> By sin to foul exorbitant desires;
> Upheld by me, *yet once more* he shall stand
> On even ground against his mortal foe,
> By me upheld, that he may know how frail
> His fallen condition is, and to me owe
> All his deliverance, and to none but me.
>
> (3.173–82; my emphasis)

The first two lines are a beautiful instance of what Patrides calls Milton's "premeditated inexactness."[11] Without spelling out the precise relationship between the two, they nevertheless give a distinct edge to grace while letting human will run a close second. They suggest that salvation is within our reach if we will reach for it, and that it is within our reach only because we are in God's hands. "Upheld by me" does not mean that God will do all that is necessary for our salvation. It means, rather, that he gives us another chance, a fresh start: "Yet once more he shall stand / On even ground against his mortal foe"—precisely as Adam and Eve stood "on even ground against [their] mortal foe" (3.179) before the Fall. (The Father explains that before the Fall man's free will was left "to her own inclining... in even scale" [10.46–47].) Of course, those who are delivered owe their deliverance to God, for it is he who gives them the opportunity, standing on even ground, freely to stand or fall. We owe him all our deliverance because it is his grace that allows us to deliver ourselves.

Grace in *Paradise Lost* connotes, among many other things, a period of time, God's "day of grace" (3.198), in which the sinner is given a chance to change his ways. Michael's first words to Adam develop the idea:

> Adam, heaven's high behest no preface needs:
> Sufficient that thy prayers are heard, and Death,
> Then due by sentence when thou didst transgress,
> Defeated of his seizure many days
> Given thee of grace, wherein thou mayst repent,
> And one bad act with many deeds well done
> Mayst cover: well may then thy Lord appeased
> Redeem thee quite from Death's rapacious claim.
>
> (11.251–58)

As Michael's legal metaphor makes clear, grace does not bring good works about. It defers a penalty so that the transgressor can cover or repay the debt he has incurred with deeds well done. Good works are efficacious for fallen man. Indeed Michael's entire mission assumes that man has the capacity to learn, to choose, and to do "faithful works" (11.64). He speaks of Joseph's "worthy deeds" (12.161), of the apostles' "race well run" (12.505). If such achievements do not have merit in the same sense that the Son has merit (i.e., righteousness deriving from his perfectly sinless nature and his sacrifice), they are nevertheless meritorious in that they deserve reward. The sinner is not raised to heaven, as Hill would have it, only because Christ's merit is, by legal fiction, imputed to him.[12] What Christ's merit does is to perfect man's good works (11.35). Christ's merit has to have some works to work with. Enoch, for "daring single to be just, / And utter odious truth," is exempted from death "to walk with God / High in salvation and the climes of bliss"—a story Michael tells Adam to show him "what reward /Awaits the good" (11.703–10). For Milton the rewards and punishments meted out at the last judgment presume moral categories—the good men and the bad, the just and the unjust, the faithful and the unfaithful, those who have earned salvation and those who have not.[13] Such categories are not arbitrary. They depend on actions, deeds, or works arising out of choices freely made by men and women. As Milton argued in *Christian Doctrine,* if God "turns man's will to moral good or evil just as he likes, and then rewards the good and punishes the wicked, it will cause an outcry against divine justice from all sides."[14]

Adam's Soliloquy and Protestant Meditation

As the foregoing account suggests, Adam and Eve are no more constrained to repent after the Fall than they were constrained, in the state of innocence, to fall. Stanley Fish suggested that Milton postpones the reference to "prevenient grace descending" to allow "the illusion of independent action on the human level." But we might with equal reason say that he postponed the reference to let us experience fully Adam and Eve's recovery of each other and of God as the human achievement—the "truly heroic" achievement, Fish later calls it—that it is.[15] Their achievement is dependent on the gift of grace, but certainly not necessitated by it. The descent of grace took place when the Son "descended" as "man's friend, his mediator" and "gracious judge," establishing the covenant of grace, "though in mysterious terms," through the curse he lets fall on the serpent ("her seed shall bruise thy head" [10.175–81]), clothing Adam and Eve's "inward nakedness ... with his robe of righteousness" (10.221–22), and providing them with an unexpected period of grace ("all the days of thy life"). Adam dimly perceives the significance of that moment when later he remembers the "gracious temper" with which the Son judged them and the "favor, grace, and mercy" that then shone in his face

(10.1047, 1096). From that moment on, they are free to work out their own salvation with fear and trembling—if they will.

Milton stresses the role of human endeavor in the working out of one's salvation more forcefully than most of his predecessors, but among English Puritans—especially the "spiritual brotherhood" that William Haller has described and that had such strong ties to Cambridge and to Milton's own college there—it was not a new idea.[16] Even William Perkins, whom Arminius attacked for his Calvinist views on predestination, had distinguished between passive and active conversion, the second being that sort "whereby man being converted by God, doth further turne and convert himselfe to God, in all his thoughts, words, and deeds." Spelling out the Pauline formulation in a way Milton would have approved, he goes on to say that "this conversion is not onely of grace, nor onely of will.... For being first turned by grace, we then can move and turne our selves. And thus there is a cooperation of mans will with Gods grace."[17]

Adam and Eve's own conversion follows the classic Puritan pattern described by Edmund Morgan. Beginning with what Morgan calls "attendance on the ministry of the word," the sinner is led to a profound "conviction of sin"—not only a conviction that one is a sinner, but a convicting of the self in a quasi-legal sense. (Richard Sibbes, who was Master of St. Catherine's Hall during Milton's years at Cambridge, was only making explicit a commonplace metaphor when he wrote that "God hath set up a court in mans heart, wherein the conscience hath the office, both of *Informer, accuser, witnesse*, and *Judge*."[18]) One might attain such conviction of sin and never move beyond it, or, recognizing one's own total inability to save oneself and consequently the need for divine assistance, one may discover within oneself, Morgan writes, a reminder of the promise of salvation, a "spark of faith" that may produce "a feeling of 'assurance' and persuasion of mercy." And if the struggle against doubt and despair is successful, one may find the strength to pray, to "cry for pardon and sorrow for sin."[19]

The key to Adam and Eve's faltering but persistent steps toward atonement can be found in Paul's Letter to the Romans: "The word is nigh thee, even in thy mouth, and in thy heart: that is, the word of faith, which we preach.... So then faith cometh by hearing, and hearing by the word of God" (10:8, 17). And it can be found as well in Psalm 119: "Wherewithal shall a young man cleanse his way? by taking heed thereto according to thy word.... I prevented the dawning of the morning, and cried: I hoped in thy word. Mine eyes prevent the night watches, that I might meditate in thy word" (119:9, 111, 147–48). Adam's soliloquy, with which the process of conversion begins, has all the earmarks of the sort of meditation suggested by the psalmist and recommended by those Puritan divines who believed that by meditating on the Word, and applying it to one's sins, one could soften or break the heart, preparing it for the workings of grace.[20] Protestant writers, as Barbara Lewalski has pointed out, stressed the intense application of the subject matter to the self. "The Word was... to be made flesh... in the self of the meditator."[21] The starting point, in other words, is not a "composition of place," or vivid imagining of a scene from the life of Christ, but a doctrine, command, law, or promise drawn from Scripture.

The Puritan treatises on meditation referred time and time again to two scriptural passages: the seventeenth verse of the central penitential text, Psalm 51 ("The sacrifices of God are a broken spirit: a broken and a contrite heart, O God, thou wilt not despise"), and the Letter to the Hebrews ("The word of God is quick, and powerful, and sharper than any two-edged sword, piercing even to the dividing asunder of soul and spirit, and of the joints and marrow, and is a discerner of the thoughts and intents of the heart" [4:12]). As Thomas Hooker wrote, "There must be a broken heart, before there can be faith, or before Christ will dwell in our hearts to our comfort."[22] According to Hooker, who pictured the process of self-conviction with a more vivid ferocity than any of his fellows, "Meditation exacts and slayeth the soule of a poor sinner." "It leadeth as it were an army of arguments, an army of curses, and miseries, and judgments, against the soule.... Meditation makes all a mans sins, and any truth belonging therunto, more powerfully and plainly to be brought home unto the heart: It is the action of the understanding, when a man doth gather all reasons, and musters up force of arguments, and labours to presse the soule, and lay them heavy upon the heart, and bring it under the power of the truth."[23]

Though the goal of such self-searching is to lay a sure foundation for the workings of grace within us, the road toward that destination is a road through terror and despair. The sinner must not only recognize, but also feel, his utter helplessness. "Hee must," Perkins writes, "with heavinesse of heart as a judge upon the bench give sentence against himselfe, acknowledging that he is worthy of everlasting hell, death, and damnation."[24]

To the question "What ought a man to do, that he may be translated out of a state of sin, into the state of grace?" William Ames answers:

> It is first required, that a man seriously look into the law of God, and make an examination of his life, and state.... It is required, secondly, that upon that comparing of our state with Gods Law, there do follow a conviction of Conscience.... Thirdly, after this conviction of Conscience, there must follow, a despare of Salvation, both in respect, of all strength of our owne, and of any helpe which is to be had from the creatures. Fourthly, after all these; there must follow, a true humiliation of heart, which consists in griefe and fear because of sin, and doth bring forth confession.

Though Ames numbers the stages through which a penitent must pass, as if he were giving systematic instructions, he is describing not a series of things to do, but a series of emotional states that must be suffered: "The first affection arising from the accusation and condemnation of Conscience," he writes, is "*Shame.*" The second is "*Sadnesse,* or Sorrow, whereby the heart is troubled, because of the evil that is come upon it." The third is "*Feare.*" The fourth is "*Despaire,* whereby the soul casts away all hope of escaping." And the fifth and last is "*Anguish* and *vexation of spirit,* because of the misery, which lyeth on it."[25]

In setting forth "how a man should apply aright the Word of God to his owne soule," Perkins, too, suggests that the sinner should meditate first on "the Law, because it is the ministery of death." "Looke now onely upon the Law of God, apply it to thy selfe, examine thy thoughts, thy words, thy deedes by it." Only much later, after such application, are we ready for the second step. "When by these meanes thou art feared, and thy minde is disquieted in respect of God's judgment for thy sinne: have recourse to the promises of mercie contained in the old and New Testament." "The Gospel containing the bountifull promises of God in Christ," he writes, "is as oyle, to poure into our wounds, and as the water of life to quench our thirsty soules."[26]

Arthur Hildersam's advice on the best time and place to engage in meditation is, not surprisingly, directly relevant to Adam. We should choose, he says, "a solitary, and secret place." And "the first fit time to work our hearts to godly sorrow, is presently after some fall we have received, some grosse sinne we have slipped into."[27] At such a time and place, and "in a troubled sea of passion tossed," Adam begins his "sad complaint":

> O miserable of happy! Is this the end
> Of this new glorious world, and me so late
> The glory of that glory, who now become
> Accurst of blessed, hide me from the face
> Of God, whom to behold was then my highth
> Of happiness: yet well, if here would end
> The misery, I deserved it, and would bear
> My own deservings; but this will not serve;
> All that I eat or drink, or shall beget,
> Is propagated curse. O voice once heard
> Delightfully, *Increase and multiply,*
> Now death to hear! For what can I increase
> Or multiply, but curses on my head?
> Who of all ages to succeed, but feeling
> The evil on him brought by me, will curse
> My head, Ill fare our ancestor impure,
> For this we may thank Adam; but his thanks
> Shall be the execration; so besides
> Mine own that bide upon me, all from me
> Shall with a fierce reflux on me redound,
> On me as on their natural centre light
> Heavy, though in their place. O fleeting joys
> Of Paradise, dear bought with lasting woes!
>
> (10.720–42)

As Richard Rogers urged the meditator: "Thou must applie that which is set downe (generally to all Christians) to the selfe, as if it were spoken only to thee."[28] That is easy enough for Adam to do, since the Word on which he chiefly meditates was that commandment, "be fruitful, multiply," which God had given to Adam and Eve on the sixth day of the creation (7.531). Adam does not begin his meditation with the Word, but his misery and sense of shame quickly lead him to it, and through it to a recognition of how his sin has corrupted his entire progeny. The ideas of procreation and progeny, of creating and being created, along with their opposites, destruction and death, dominate and motivate the entire meditation.

Adam's first wish is to be hidden from the face of God, an image which signifies over and over again in Scripture the condition of loss or separation from God through sin. It is the condition of Cain: "And Cain said unto the Lord, My punishment is greater than I can bear. Behold, thou hast driven me out this day from the face of the earth; and from thy face shall I be hid" (Gen. 4:13-14). It is the condition that Job bemoans—"Wherefore hidest thou thy face and holdest me for thine enemy?" (Job 13:24)—and which, for a different reason than Adam's, David seeks: "Hide thy face from my sins, and blot out all mine iniquities" (Ps. 51:9). The "voice once heard / Delightfully" is "now death to hear!" ("And the commandment, which was ordained to life, I found to be unto death" [Rom. 7:10].) Adam's figurative use of *death* here—a word whose meaning had puzzled him before the Fall (4.425)—suggests that he is learning through experience what Milton called in *Christian Doctrine* the first degree of death: "everything which seems to lead to destruction."[29] He feels contaminated. He knows that he deserves punishment, and he is pained by the thought that he has brought about woes that shall extend to all ages. But at this point in the meditation what haunts him most, as his imagination conjures up the feelings of his offspring, is the perpetual curses they will level at their "ancestor impure." Like Job, Adam desires "to reason with God" (Job 13:3), and, turning from thoughts of his offspring to thoughts of his own Creator, he initiates a colloquy with him, a colloquy that begins in bitter complaint:

> Did I request thee, Maker, from my clay
> To mould me man, did I solicit thee
> From darkness to promote me, or here place
> In this delicious garden? As my will
> Concurred not to my being, it were but right
> And equal to reduce me to my dust,
> Desirous to resign, and render back
> All I received, unable to perform
> Thy terms too hard, by which I was to hold
> The good I sought not. To the loss of that,
> Sufficient penalty, why hast thou added

The sense of endless woes? Inexplicable
Thy justice seems.

(10.743-55)

But Adam, again like Job, and in the spirit of Paul's rebuke to the Romans—"Nay but, O man, who art thou that repliest against God? Shall the thing formed say to him that formed it, Why hast thou made me thus?" (Rom. 9:20)[30]—quickly reins himself in, and provides God's answer, first in debate with himself, and then by imagining his own son speaking to him. He brings what we might think of as the first stage of his meditation to its conclusion, ending with another remembered "word," in this case God's judgment on him: "For dust thou art, and shalt to dust return" (10.208):

Yet to say truth, too late,
I thus contest; then should have been refused
Those terms whatever, when they were proposed:
Thou didst accept them; wilt thou enjoy the good,
Then cavil the conditions? And though God
Made thee without thy leave, what if thy son
Prove disobedient, and reproved, retort,
Wherefore didst thou beget me? I sought it not:
Wouldst thou admit for his contempt of thee
That proud excuse? Yet him not thy election,
But natural necessity begot.
God made thee of choice his own, and of his own
To serve him, thy reward was of his grace,
Thy punishment then justly is at his will.
Be it so, for I submit, his doom is fair,
That dust I am, and shall to dust return.

(10.755-71)

Throughout these passages Adam employs his reason and his memory—as the treatises on meditation recommend—to understand his present fallen state, and time and time again he adequately counters his own evasions and his complaints. On the basis of what he knows and remembers, he reasons flawlessly, reaching precisely the only conclusions possible in the absence of faith.[31] He is a testimony to the fact that the Word is not of "profit" when it is "not being mixed with faith in them that heard it" (Heb. 4:2), a fact that may explain the greater passion of his utterances when he returns in Books 11 and 12 to the questions raised in the meditation. Throughout the meditation he is oppressed by his anticipation of "lasting woes" (10.742), "endless misery" (10.810), and a generalized sense of "endless woes" (10.754). He is suffering the misery defined by Rogers: "To be utterly darkened and destitute of the true knowledge of God and of the life to come (the knowledge whereof is the beautie of the world) and to be hastning to endlesse woe, and yet not to understand it: what part of miserie can be greater in this world?"[32] The phrase takes us back to the equally generalized "all our woe" of the third line of the poem, which is corrected by "*till* one greater man...." And it looks forward to God's explanation:

> I at first with two fair gifts
> Created him endowed, with happiness
> And immortality: that fondly lost,
> This other served but to *eternize woe;*
> *Till* I provided death; so death becomes
> His final remedy, and after life
> Tried in sharp tribulation, and refined
> By faith and faithful works, to second life....
>
> (11.57–64; my emphasis)

Adam cannot, as yet, provide the *till*'s. But his mind, taking off from "and shall to dust return," does turn toward death. And again, though Job is convinced of his innocence, Adam of his guilt, it is Job he most resembles:

> Why delays
> His hand to execute what his decree
> Fixed on this day? Why do I overlive,
> Why am I mocked with death, and lengthened out
> To deathless pain? How gladly would I meet
> Mortality my sentence, and be earth
> Insensible, how glad would lay me down
> As in my mother's lap? There I should rest
> And sleep secure; his dreadful voice no more
> Would thunder in my ears, no fear of worse
> To me and to my offspring would torment me
> With cruel expectation.
>
> (10.771–82)

> Why died I not from the womb? why did I not give up the ghost when I came out of the belly?... For now should I have lain still and been quiet, I should have slept: then had I been at rest.... Oh that I might have my request; and that God would grant me the thing that I long for! Even that it would please God to destroy me; that he would let loose his hand, and cut me off! (Job 3:11, 13; 6:8–9)

But Adam's hope for death as a remedy gives way to his fear of it, whatever form it takes. He is afraid, first, that death may be of the body only, that "the spirit of man" will live on in the grave (782–89), but argues, much as Milton had argued in *Christian Doctrine*, that since it was the "breath [i.e., spirit] / Of life that sinned... All of me then shall die" (789–92).[33] The questions that follow—"For though the Lord of all be infinite, / Is his wrath also?... Will he draw out, / For anger's sake, finite to infinite / In punished man, to satisfy his rigour / Satisfied never?" (794–95; 801–4)—are an extreme extension of Paul's question: "What if God, willing to shew his wrath, and to make his power known, endured with much longsuffering the vessels of wrath fitted to destruction?" (Rom. 9:22). He is led, at last, to the fear that death may not be "one stroke... bereaving sense," but "endless misery" that will last "to perpetuity" (809–12), and the word *perpetuity* brings his meditation back to his offspring. But with a difference. His feelings for his "sons" are more selfless, more compassionately paternal than before, and his sense of his own corruption and guilt more intense:

> Nor I on my part single, in me all
> Posterity stands cursed: fair patrimony
> That I must leave ye, sons; O were I able
> To waste it all my self, and leave ye none!
> So disinherited how would ye bless
> Me now your curse! Ah, why should all mankind
> For one man's fault thus guiltless be condemned,
> If guiltless? But from me what can proceed,
> But all corrupt, both mind and will depraved,
> Not to do only, but to will the same
> With me? How can they then acquitted stand
> In sight of God? Him after all disputes
> Forced I absolve: all my evasions vain,

> And reasonings, though through mazes, lead me still
> But to my own conviction: first and last
> On me, me only, as the source and spring
> Of all corruption, all the blame lights due.
>
> (10.817–33)

It is Adam's role as source and spring ("increaser and multiplier") of all corruption that most grieves him. It is as if he were living through the sort of meditation recommended by Hildersam, who urged his reader to consider "how thou hast by thy sinne corrupted others": "Must it needs be a heartbreaking to thee, whensoever thou dost seriously thinke of it all the dayes of thy life.... If thou hadst beene the mean to undo another in his outward estate, much more if thou hadst taken away his life, it would be a just cause of heavinesse to thee, how much more cause of humbling is it that thou hast beene a meane of destroying the soul of any."[34] Adam knows that he cannot support, even with Eve's help, "that burden heavier than the earth to bear," just as David knows: "Mine iniquities are gone over mine head: as an heavy burden they are too heavy for me" (Ps. 38:4). But while the psalmist turns repeatedly to God as his "hope" and "refuge,"[35] Adam feels that all such hope has been destroyed:

> Thus what thou desirest
> And what thou fear'st, alike destroys all hope
> Of refuge, and concludes thee miserable
> Beyond all past example and future,
> To Satan only like both crime and doom.
> O conscience! into what abyss of fears
> And horrors hast thou driven me; out of which
> I find no way, from deep to deeper plunged!
>
> (10.837–44)

Adam's lament does not end here, and indeed it could not. Milton interrupts it, but indicates clearly that it continues, going back through the same mazes of thought and feeling, working him ever further into his "abyss of fears and horrors." Because Adam's logic is unaided by faith in God's mercy, it leads him always and only, "though through mazes," to his "own conviction" (10.831). "Our heart," Greenham wrote, "is a wandering thing, it is like the mill, that is ever grinding, still setting us a work with more commaundments, then ever God gave us. If we follow Gods way, there is some end, but if we follow our owne way there is an endlesse maze."[36] Adam has followed his own way. In one sense the purpose of meditation has been accomplished. He has come, in Greenham's words, "to quake and tremble for fear of God's judgments."[37] He has found himself, to use Paul's phrase yet again, "a being without excuse," and has achieved (though the word is a strange one in this context) a deep despair of salvation.

Though Adam has succeeded, in Ames's words, in "casting away all hope of escaping," the extent of the danger he is in, and the utter insufficiency of his meditation, are brought home by the event that follows hard upon it. When Eve approaches and tries to apply "soft words to his fierce passion," he immediately throws to the wind even that conviction of his own guilt that he had achieved and twists the events of Eve's and his own history around a core of self-righteous hatred. His heart appears to be as hardened toward Eve as Satan's had been toward God:

> Out of my sight, thou serpent, that name best
> Befits thee with him leagued, thy self as false
> And hateful; nothings wants, but that thy shape,
> Like his, and colour serpentine may show
> Thy inward fraud, to warn all creatures from thee
> Henceforth; lest that too heavenly form, pretended
> To hellish falsehood, snare them. But for thee
> I had persisted happy....
>
> (10.867–74)

Adam reveals the tendency he manifested so clearly in Book 8, though now out of control, to call God's wisdom and the perfection of nature into question: "O why did God, / Creator wise, that peopled highest heaven / With spirits masculine, create at last... this fair defect of nature...?" (10.888–92). Before the Fall he had Raphael and God to set him straight. Here he has Eve.

Piecing Scripture Together

"How much more is it needfull now against all the sorrows and casualties of this life," Milton noted, "to have an intimate and speaking help, a ready and reviving associate in marriage."³⁸ When Adam's despair turns into anger, it is Eve, as critic after critic has noted, whose words calm his anger and whose presence is necessary to restore hope in him. Nothing reveals more clearly the difference between Spenser's allegorical and Milton's dramatic modes of writing than the contrast between Una's rescue of the Redcrosse Knight from the cave of Despaire in Book 1 of *The Faerie Queene* and Eve's rescue of Adam. Redcrosse enters the cave, threatens to slay Despaire, who counters with some nine and one-half stanzas of arguments in behalf of suicide, interrupted only once by a brief and feeble rejoinder from Redcrosse. The encounter is brought to its fortunate conclusion when Una "snatcht the cursed knife" from her knight's hand, reminds him that he has a part in "heavenly mercies" and that "where justice growes, there grows eke greater grace," and commands him to arise and "leave this cursed place."³⁹ For Adam and Eve, on the other hand, despair is within, and it is conquered only gradually, through a series of mutually achieved insights as they grope together toward further recollection and partial understanding of the Word as it has been delivered to them: the redemption that God promised them even before he judged them and pronounced their sentence. What Fidelia and Speranza give to Redcrosse at the "house of Holiness"— namely, the faith and hope necessary to read and remember the "sacred Booke" aright—Adam and Eve begin to acquire on their own, prior to the additional, more formal schooling Adam will receive in Books 11 and 12.

The notion that Adam and Eve's dialogue in Book 10 is in a sense a meditation of two is consistent with the Puritan writings on meditation. Greenham advised that after meditating on the Scriptures, "the next thing is conference. In naturall things man standeth in neede of helpe, then much more in spiritual things he standeth in need of others."⁴⁰ In *The Spiritual Watch* Thomas Gataker underscores the same point with a quotation from Ecclesiastes 4:9–10: "*Two*, saith the Wiseman, *are better than one. For if the one of them fall, the other is at hand to helpe him up againe. But woe be to him that is alone. For if he fall he hath none to helpe to raise him againe.*"⁴¹ Sibbes cites 1 Peter 3:7 as testimony to the importance of "cheer[ing] up one another by word and example":

> St *Peter* knew this well, and therefore he willeth, that there should be *quietnesse and peace betwixt husband and wife, that their prayers be not*

hindered; Insinuating that their prayers are hindered by family breaches. For by that meanes, those two (that should be one flesh and spirit) are divided, and so made two, and when they should minde duty, their minde is taken up with wrongs done by the one to the other.

There is nothing more required for the performing of holy duties than uniting of spirits; and therefore God would not have the sacrifice brought to the Altar, before reconciliation with our brother. He esteems peace so highly, that hee will have his owne service stay for it.[42]

Adam's mind, one might say, has been taken up with the wrongs Eve has done him, and it is Eve who heals the family breach. Peter's letter was a crucial text for defining the wife's role in marriage. Quoted at length in the Church of England marriage service, it is a letter preaching submission, subjection, and patient suffering: the submission of all Christians to civil ordinances and rulers, of servants to their masters, wives to their husbands, and the young to their elders. Throughout the letter, Christ is held up as the model of subjection and patient suffering:

For what glory is it, if, when ye be buffeted for your faults, ye shall take it patiently? but if, when ye do well, and suffer for it, ye take it patiently, this is acceptable with God. For even hereunto were ye called: because Christ also suffered for us, leaving us an example, that ye should follow his steps: who did no sin, neither was guile found in his mouth: who, when he was reviled, reviled not again; when he suffered, he threatened not; but committed himself to him that judgeth righteously. (1 Pet. 2:20–23)

Peter instructs wives to subject themselves to their husbands not, as Paul did, because "the husband is the head of the wife" (Eph. 5:23), but because, by so subjecting themselves, they may win their husbands back to the faith. "Be in subjection to your own husbands; that, if any obey not the word, they also may without the word be won by the conversation of the wives; While they behold your chaste conversation coupled with fear" (1 Pet. 3:1–2). This passage assigns a ministrative function to the wife similar to that assumed by Eve, who, like Christ, when she "was reviled, reviled not again," and thereby "won" her husband—with, it should be added, the help of her memory of the Word. Following Adam's vilification of her he "from her turned."

> But Eve
> Not so repulsed, with tears that ceased not flowing,
> And tresses all disordered, at his feet
> Fell humble, and embracing them, besought
> His peace, and thus proceeded in her plaint.
>
> (10.909–13)

Eve's tears here are a far, far cry from those she "let drop" from their crystal sluices when first she felt remorse. Her behavior is indeed exemplary, figuring not only what the wife should be, but also what the husband should become. Joan Mallory Webber has argued that in *Paradise Lost* "what women have always stood for, the apparent passivity of their patience and heroic fortitude, has become an essential attribute of the hero. The feminine principle, necessary to creation, is also necessary to the acceptance of mortality and the continuation of life."[43] We may catch in the description of Eve, and in her subsequent speech, echoes of various biblical pleaders and penitents: of Abigail, for example, pleading with David that she might bear the blame for her husband's folly. She "fell before David on her face, and bowed herself to the ground, and fell at his feet and said, Upon me, my lord, upon me let this iniquity be" (1 Sam. 25:23–24). In Eve's fear of being forlorn ("Bereave me not.... Forlorn of thee, / Whither shall I betake me?"), we may hear overtones of Ruth weeping before Naomi and saying, "Intreat me not to leave thee, or to return from following after thee: for whither thou goest, I will go.... Where thou diest, will I die" (Ruth 1:16–17). Or, as one requesting and receiving peace, we may feel in Eve the presence of Mary Magdalene, who "stood at [Jesus'] feet behind him weeping, and began to wash his feet with tears, and did wipe them with the hairs of her head," and to whom Jesus replies, "Thy faith hath saved thee, go in peace" (Luke 7:38, 50):

> Forsake me not thus, Adam, witness heaven
> What love sincere, and reverence in my heart
> I bear thee, and unweeting have offended,
> Unhappily deceived; thy suppliant

> I beg, and clasp thy knees; bereave me not,
> Whereon I live, thy gentle looks, thy aid,
> Thy counsel in this uttermost distress,
> My only strength and stay: forlorn of thee,
> Whither shall I betake me, where subsist?
> While yet we live, scarce one short hour perhaps,
> Between us two let there be peace, both joining,
> As joined in injuries, one enmity
> Against a foe by doom express assigned us,
> That cruel serpent: on me exercise not
> Thy hatred for this misery befallen
> On me already lost, me than thy self
> More miserable; both have sinned, but thou
> Against God only, I against God and thee,
> And to the place of judgment will return,
> There with my cries importune heaven, that all
> The sentence from thy head removed may light
> On me, sole cause to thee of all this woe,
> Me me only just object of his ire.
>
> (10.914–36)

If Eve's supplicating posture in Book 10 has much in common with Abigail's and Mary's, her supplicating voice is most like David's in the psalms. The spirit of the passage is not unlike that of Psalm 38, which also found its way into Adam's soliloquy: "O Lord, rebuke me not in thy wrath: neither chasten me in thy hot displeasure.... Forsake me not, O Lord: O my God, be not far from me." By having her address Adam as her "strength and stay," Milton calls to mind a stock Old Testament formula for addressing God (e.g., "our refuge and strength," "my strength and my redeemer," "my help and stay," "my strength and stay").[44] When she says to Adam, "Both have sinned, but thou / Against God only, I against God and thee," she is out-Daviding David's confession to God in Psalm 51: "Against thee, thee only have I sinned." By so addressing Adam, she has reestablished her appointed relationship to him, turning to him ("He for God only, she for God in him") in a manner that eventually leads to their mutual turning to God. And in the last few lines of her speech, we move, as it were, from the shadowy type, David, to the truth, for it is here, as Joseph Summers and others after him have pointed out,[45] that Eve speaks in what is, in *Paradise Lost*, the "voice of the redeemer": "Behold me then, me for him, life for life / I offer, on me let thine anger fall" (3.236–37).

In her reply to Adam the lyrical rhythms and graceful balanced repetitions of Eve's earlier poetry are gone. There is little order, as her fears and desires issue forth, with many pauses and in phrases of irregular length, as if in the process of speaking she spontaneously feels the insufficiency of each phrase and the need to supplement and intensify, as in "on me . . . on me already lost, me than thyself / More miserable." "Love sincere" is strengthened to "reverence," "unweeting" to "unhappily deceived." "While yet we live" becomes "one short hour." "A Foe" becomes "that cruel serpent." The effect is one of forceful, passionate insistence, especially as she moves from what at first appears to be a desire to escape punishment ("On me exercise not / Thy hatred") to a determination to take all the responsibility and punishment on herself alone.

Eve's pleas are successful because she persists in her softness, subjecting herself not because she has learned to do so, but out of need and love. Her "soft words" (10.865), as the proverb promises, finally do turn away wrath ("His anger all he lost" [10.945]), and with her own creative fiat—"let there be peace"—she carries the process of renewal forward. Eve, as we know, was formed not only for softness, but for "sweet attractive grace," and here God's grace appears to be working through her to soften Adam's heart, which "soon . . . relented" (10.940). Whereas Adam's solitary meditation had suggested to him no course of action, Eve's recollection of the Word helps her to redefine her relationship with Adam positively, as that of mutual opposition to an adversary. It is she who first recalls God's words to the serpent—"Between thee and the woman I will put / Enmity" (10.179–80)—a passage that she beautifully interprets as "one enmity / Against a foe assigned *us*" (my emphasis). By putting it that way, she gently counters Adam's accusation that she is leagued with the serpent, as well as Satan's earlier and ominous stage whisper, "League with you I seek" (4.375). She wishes to be joined to Adam "while yet [they] live" ("so long as you both shall live," as the marriage service has it). "Joined in injuries," just as Satan and Beelzebub had been "joined . . . in equal ruin" (1.90–91), the couple will now join against the foe assigned them. Furthermore, it is she who first feels an impulse to return to the place where they had been judged and "importune heaven." Throughout this and her following speech, what rings through her lines is a belief in their ability to choose a course of action, a belief that had been wanting.

Adam's initial response to Eve's words of reconciliation must strike the reader as more than a little ungenerous. He faults her for having born his "displeasure" so ill (10.952), as if that were an adequate description of the hatred and abusive contempt with which he had rejected her. But he soon begins, in lines that clearly echo Paul's entreaties to his followers, to advance toward the goal she had suggested:

> But rise, let us no more contend, nor blame
> Each other, blamed enough elsewhere, but strive
> In offices of love, how we may lighten
> Each other's burden in our share of woe.
>
> (10.958–61)

Let us not therefore judge one another any more. . . . Let us therefore follow after the things which make for peace, and things wherewith one may edify another. . . . Bear ye one another's burdens, and so fulfil the law of Christ. (Rom. 14:13, 19; Gal. 6:2)

The actions that Eve proposes return us to the Word—"increase and multiply"—from which Adam's meditation had begun. Sensing that what had perplexed her husband most was "care of our descent . . . which must be born to certain woe, devoured / By death at last," she proposes sexual abstinence, then suicide. Her motives are decidedly unselfish:

> And miserable it is
> To be to others cause of misery,
> Our own begotten, and of our loins to bring
> Into this cursed world a woeful race,
> That after wretched life must be at last
> Food for so foul a monster. . . .
>
> (10.981–86)

She envisions their deaths as a means to destroy Death itself, "destruction with destruction to destroy" (10.1006). Her proposals are misguided, in ways that Adam is characteristically quick to point out, but we should remember that the abolishing or unmaking of the creation had seemed to the Son a sufficiently plausible solution to the problem presented by the Fall to warrant his dissuading his Father from considering it (3.162–66). The vivid terms in which Eve expresses the sacrifices she is willing to make suggest, after all, a skewed parallel to the Son's offer to die in order to defeat death:

> So death shall be deceived his glut, and with us two
> Be forced to satisfy his ravenous maw.
>
> (10.990–91)

> On me let Death wreak all his rage....
> While by thee raised I ruin all my foes,
> Death last, and with his carcass glut the grave.
>
> (3.241, 258–59)

Eve's is the human remedy for their predicament—perfectly rational, selfless, but void of faith—a remedy, as Adam says, that "cuts us off from hope" (10.1043). And indeed, once she expresses her determination "destruction with destruction to destroy, ... she ended here, or vehement despair / Broke off the rest" (10.1006–8).

For a meditation to move beyond despair, the meditator must, as we have seen, turn outward from himself to God, and from a recognition of his own sinfulness and helplessness to a recognition of God's mercy. Rogers urges the penitent, for example, to meditate not only on the Word but also on

> any part ... of God himself, his wisdom, power; his mercie, or of the infinite varietie of good things which we receive of his free bountie.... or of our mortalitie, of the changes of this world, of our deliverance from sinne, and death: of the manifold afflictions of this life, and how we may in best manner beare and goe through them, and the benefit thereof, and the manifold and great priviledges which we enjoy daily through the inestimable kindnesse of God towards us; but specially of those things which we haue most speciall need of.[46]

Adam does reflect on all these things: on how they escaped the immediate death they had expected, on the mildness of the curses placed upon them, on how to bear, and to benefit from, the afflictions brought upon them by the changes in their world, and on how to seek "remedy or cure" for the evils their misdeeds have wrought (10.1048–85). Above all he reflects on God's mercy and kindness. He uses his memory and his intelligence to discover grounds for hope and faith. He builds on Eve's partial, incomplete recollection of the curse upon the serpent by remembering, and then interpreting, its conclusion:

> Then let us seek
> Some safer resolution, which methinks
> I have in view, calling to mind with heed
> Part of our sentence, that thy seed shall bruise
> The serpent's head; piteous amends, unless
> Be meant, whom I conjecture, our grand foe
> Satan, who in the serpent hath contrived
> Against us this deceit.
>
> (10.1028–35)

Though he does not make the connection explicit, we can see that Adam has reinterpreted the words that had been death to hear—"increase and multiply"—by placing them in the context of those other, closely related words—"Her seed shall bruise [the serpent's] head." Hence he can foresee procreation as the source and spring of joy as well as woe, a joy that he expresses with an assurance that hints, with its echoes of the Gospels of Luke and John,[47] at both the birth and resurrection of Jesus:

> when lo, to thee
> Pains only in child-bearing were foretold,
> And bringing forth, soon recompensed with joy,
> Fruit of thy womb.
>
> (10.1050–53)

During their life before the Fall, Adam and Eve had meditated often, and fruitfully, on the creatures, and come to an understanding of God's nature by observing his wondrous works. In Book 10 they meditate on his wondrous words. Their turn toward Scripture after the Fall is nicely glossed by Greenham's observation, cited earlier, that "our father *Adam* had nothing to leade him by, but the great booke of the creatures, which when by sinne it was blotted, the Lord supplied this want by the word."⁴⁸ The word in this case is threefold: "Be fruitful, and multiply" (Gen. 1:28); "Dust thou art, and unto dust shalt thou return" (Gen. 3:19); "And I will put enmity between thee and the woman, and between thy seed and her seed; it shall bruise thy head, and thou shalt bruise his heel" (Gen. 3:15). Raphael has taught Adam and Eve the first chapter of Genesis, and the couple has lived through the second chapter and all but the very end of the third. These three verses in particular, each of which they have heard God speak, lead them into, and then out of, despair. Though their understanding of them is still, at this point, incomplete, they construct on them a hope for the future. The poetry enacts that process whereby one passage of Scripture reinterprets another, providing a different perspective on it. Adam and Eve's groping first steps in exegesis are an expansive version of the tense dialectic operating in Milton's meditative sonnet 19, "When I consider how my life is spent," in which the anxieties induced in the octave by Milton's application of the parable of the talents and John 9:4 ("I must work the works of him that sent me, while it is day") to his own life are calmed by the voice of patience, who draws on other scriptural passages, such as Lamentations 3:2–27, to place the earlier ones in a new perspective.

Nothing could be more characteristic of the Protestant habit of mind than the fortuitous movement of the memory by which one passage of Scripture leads to another and to another. That movement is the subject, for example, of the second of George Herbert's sonnets entitled "The Holy Scriptures," which not only reveals a preference for Scripture over the book of the creatures, but also constitutes a fine gloss on Adam and Eve's "reading" in Book 10. Addressing Scripture itself, Herbert wrote:

> Oh that I knew how all thy lights combine,
>   And the configurations of their glorie!
>   Seeing not onely how each verse doth shine,
> But all the constellations of the storie.
> *This verse marks that, and both do make a motion*
>   *Unto a third, that ten leaves off doth lie:*
>   Then as dispersed herbs do [make] a potion,
> These three make up some Christian's destinie.
> Such are thy secrets, which my life makes good,
>   And comments on thee: for in ev'ry thing

>   Thy words do finde me out, and parallels bring,
>   And in another make me understood.
>   Starres are poore books, and oftentimes do misse;
>   This book of starres lights to eternall blisse.⁴⁹

"Faith," Paul wrote, "cometh by hearing, and hearing by the word of God" (Rom. 10:17). The penitent, soul-searching Adam has this advantage over most of his fallen progeny: though he has no written text to recall, he can draw on his memory of the Word as interpreted by voice and face, the Word as heard from divine presence itself:

>   Remember with what mild
> And gracious temper he both heard and judged
> Without wrath or reviling.
>
>   (10.1046–48)

> Undoubtedly he will relent and turn
> From his displeasure; in whose look serene,
> When angry most he seemed and most severe,
> What else but favour, grace, and mercy shone?
>
>   (10.1093–96)

One of Adam's descendants who was thought to have had a similar advantage was the disciple Peter, whose remorse over his denial of Christ was a model frequently held out to the would-be penitent. According to Hildersam, "It was not the crowing of the Cock twice, that made *Peters* heart melt, but the gracious looke that Christ cast upon him."⁵⁰

With full faith, now, in God's graciousness and pity, Adam also (or therefore) has faith in the efficacy of prayer:

> How much more, if we pray him, will his ear
> Be open, and his heart to pity incline.
>
>   (10.1060–61)

> What better can we do, than to the place
> Repairing where he judged us, prostrate fall
> Before him reverent, and there confess
> Humbly our faults, and pardon beg, with tears
> Watering the ground, and with our sighs the air
> Frequenting, sent from hearts contrite, in sign

Of sorrow unfeigned, and humiliation meek.
                                        (10.1086–92)

And the narrator, as if in antiphonal, assenting response, describes their prayer in Adam's very words:

> They forthwith to the place
> Repairing where he judged them prostrate fell
> Before him reverent, and both confessed
> Humbly their faults, and pardon begged, with tears
> Watering the ground, and with their sighs the air
> Frequenting, sent from hearts contrite, in sign
> Of sorrow unfeigned, and humiliation meek.
>   (10.1098–1104)

The "end" of the fallen couple's meditation, in both senses of the word, has been achieved. Grace has allowed them, to recall Morgan's terms, "to cry for pardon and sorrow for sin." These passages strongly convey a sense of closure, the completion of a significant episode, the fulfillment of promises heard by the reader long before. Adam's language ("his heart to pity incline") refers back to repetitions in the angelic hymn to the Father and Son in Book 3, where the Father is twice described as "much more to pity inclined" (3.402, 405). And Milton's seven-line, all-but-verbatim repetition of Adam's language is an expanded fulfillment of the Father's own self-repetition:

> For I will clear their senses dark,
> What may suffice, and soften stony hearts
> *To pray, repent, and bring obedience due.*
> *To prayer, repentance, and obedience due,*
> Though but endeavoured with sincere intent,
> Mine ear shall not be slow, mine eye not shut....
>   (3.188–93; my emphasis)

And those repeated lines are like the first half of a parenthesis that the Father himself closes when he sees the couple at prayer: "He [man] sorrows now, repents, and prays contrite" (11.90).

Two of Milton's most astute readers, Stanley Fish and Arnold Stein, have offered diametrically opposed assessments of the conclusion of Book 10. Fish suggests that the repetitions we have been observing "indicate stylistically that prayers will hereafter be patterned, and not, as they had been in Eden, spontaneous." "The easy and various expression of praise will be replaced by the rigidity of ritual."[51] Stein, on the other hand, argues that the penitential prayer "is to be understood as expressing... a sincerity beyond words. Its eloquence, we are made to understand, exceeds that of the prayer which took the form of a hymn of praise in Book V."[52]

Fish is surely right in directing our attention toward ritual. Adam's exhortation to prayer is similar in spirit, and to some extent in language, to the minister's call in the Prayer Book's "Commination against Sinners":

> Let us... return unto our Lord God, with all contrition and meekness of heart, bewailing and lamenting our sinful life, [ac]knowledging and confessing our offenses, and seeking to bring forth worthy fruits of penance.... Let us therefore return unto him, who is the merciful receiver of all true penitent sinners, assuring ourself that he is ready to receive us, and most willing to pardon us, if we come to him with faithful repentance....

The morning hymn of Book 5, however, is not only sung in unison. It is patterned, as we have noted, on ritual, that is, the canticle set for morning prayer. The crucial difference between the two prayers is that we hear the first "pronounced or sung" (5.148), whereas the second, as Stein points out, is described rather than rendered. The second is "breathed" in "sighs... unutterable" (11.5–6), like the "groanings which cannot be uttered" of Romans 8:26. It is anything but rigid. Because they have an advocate in the Son, who can "interpret" for them (11.33), they can feel, in effect, what David felt: "Lord, all my desire is before thee; and my groaning is not hid from thee.... For in thee, O Lord, do I hope: thou wilt hear, O Lord my God" (Ps. 38:9, 15).

The question of which prayer is the more eloquent is perhaps neither answerable nor important to answer. Their purposes and occasions are different, and both are acceptable. The ritual-like repetitions at the end of Book 10 place a seal of approval on the spirit of Adam and Eve's unvoiced but eloquent prayer.[53] At the same time, the penitential prayer is not, like the earlier one, "unmeditated" (5.149). It is, as we have seen, the hard-won result of meditation. It is meditated not in the sense of its language having been worked out in advance. Far from it. The meditation has not prepared their lips to speak but their hearts to sigh. Adam and Eve have had to learn to pray because they need a new sort of prayer, a prayer that requires hearts prepared by meditating on the Word, leading to conviction of sin, to mutual forgiveness, and to the discovery of hope.

CHAPTER 8

Wisdom and the Loss of Paradise

In the second of his four early drafts for a tragedy or morality play on the subject of the loss of Paradise, Milton listed Justice, Mercy, and Wisdom among the "persons" of the drama, and if the third draft had been executed, act 1 would have included a scene in which the same three figures would have appeared "debating what should become of man if he fall."[1] In *Paradise Lost,* we might say, the dialogue between the Father and the Son in Book 3 represents Justice and Mercy debating that very question, though *debate* is too severe a word for the Son's affirmation of what the Father had intended all along. As we have already noted, furthermore, the Son discerns the "strife" between "mercy and justice" in the Father's very face, and it is the desire to end that strife and bring peace and joy back into his face that chiefly inspires the Son to offer to die "for man's offence."

What, then, has become of the figure of Wisdom? She plays, I think, a more prominent role in Milton's epic than has been recognized. In our consideration of the Fall we have focused on the drama of Adam and Eve's conversations with each other, with themselves, and with Satan. But the verbal and conceptual setting within which the drama is played out is such as to complicate and enrich our understanding of it in many ways. In this chapter I want to explore a previously unnoticed aspect of that setting—an aspect richly colored by Milton's extensive use of the biblical Wisdom literature. Though analogues for many of the attitudes toward wisdom and knowledge dramatized in the poem can be found in classical, patristic, and seventeenth-century authors, it was chiefly the thought and language of the Scriptures that he incorporated in his epic.[2] They inspired, too, some of the most moving and poignant dramatizations of just what it is that most distinguishes life in Paradise from life after the Fall.

Wisdom's absence as a single, speaking, participating character in

Paradise Lost is no doubt the product of Milton's having moved so far away, in the epic, from the allegorical conception implied in his early drafts. It may owe something, too, to Wisdom's protean nature in Scripture. In Proverbs alone, for example, she is known by the company she keeps (she dwells with Prudence, and Understanding is her kinswoman, and she will be our sister or bride if we will so name her), and she is also known by the treasures she holds in store for us, the fruits she offers, and the counsel she gives, which ranges from knowledge of the mysteries and secrets of God on the one hand to practical advice on how to keep friends and manage social and financial affairs on the other. Milton would no more have been inclined to fix Wisdom's identity as a single "person" than he was to do so in the case of the Holy Spirit.[3] Nevertheless, we can readily discern a loose cluster of associations that are present both in Scripture and in Milton's poem. We have already noted Wisdom's association with the creation of the world, with the Logos, and with the Son, whom the Father, echoing 1 Corinthians 1:24, calls "my word, my wisdom, and effectual might" (3.170). To this cluster we can add yet another term. Wisdom is the Son and the creative Word and also light, "the true Light, which lighteth every man that cometh into the world" (John 1:9). The prologue to Book 3 is the blind poet's prayer, "wisdom at one entrance" having been "quite shut out," for the "celestial Light" to "shine inward" (3.50–52). It is, in fact, a prayer for prophetic wisdom. As James Sims and others have noted,[4] the Neoplatonic imagery of the invocation to Book 3 is reminiscent of Solomon's celebration of Wisdom as both light and prior to light, the maker of all things new, and the source of such prophetic inspiration as Milton is calling upon:

> She [Wisdom] is the breath of the power of God, and a pure influence flowing from the glory of the Almighty.... For she is the brightness of the everlasting light, the unspotted mirror of the power of God, and the image of his goodness. And being but one, she can do all things: and remaining in herself, she maketh all things new: and in all ages entering into holy souls, she maketh them friends of God, and prophets. For God loveth none but him that dwelleth with wisdom. For she is more beautiful than the sun, and above all the order of stars: being compared with the light, she is found before it. (Wisd. 7:25–29)

Closer to home, wisdom is God's gift to man, a virtue as well as a body of doctrine, something man can both possess and acquire. Adam and Eve were created by wisdom, and they were also created wise. "Wisdom" shines in their "looks divine;" and the first thing that Eve learns—namely, that "beauty is excelled by manly grace / And wisdom, which alone is truly fair" (4.490–91)—is, waiving the term "manly," very much a part of the tradition. Solomon loved Wisdom "above health and beauty, and chose to have her instead of light" (Wisd. 7:10). The virtuous wife described in Proverbs 31, whose mouth speaks "wisdom," and who is clothed in "strength and honor" just as Adam and Eve are "with native honour clad" (4.289), recognizes that "beauty is vain." Given these manifold referents for wisdom, then, it is perhaps no wonder that Milton rejected his earlier plan to embody wisdom in a single character. She is, nonetheless, a very real presence in the poem.

Wisdom and Forbidden Knowledge

Late in his dialogue with Michael, Adam refers to himself as one "who sought / Forbidden knowledge by forbidden means" (12.278–79). It is an odd formulation in many ways, not least because elsewhere in the poem only Satan, and Eve when she is under his deceiving spell, speak of the knowledge that the forbidden tree purportedly affords as "forbidden" (4.515; 9.758–59), and when they do so they are clearly distorting the meaning of the prohibition, which forbids only the tasting of the fruit of the tree. Eve herself sought wisdom by forbidden (and ineffectual) means, though as we have seen, she had only the haziest sense of the nature of the knowledge she desired, and it is not clear that the sort of wisdom she sought was forbidden. As for Adam, he is never deceived, before the Fall, into thinking that God had forbidden them knowledge.

Yet earlier in the epic Milton dramatizes the danger of intellectual pride arising in Adam just as surely as he dramatizes Eve's pride in her own beauty and her delight in being the object of others' gazes. If it is misleading to describe Adam as one who fell because he "sought forbidden knowledge," it is nevertheless apparent that Milton was deeply concerned, throughout much of the poem, with the uses of knowledge, with the nature of wisdom, and with the means of attaining it. If the connection between these concerns and the Fall itself is tenuous, it is nevertheless important to try to grasp it.

Proverbs, The Wisdom of Solomon, and Ecclesiasticus all show the effects, and often retain the formal characteristics, of an Hebraic tradition of instruction and discipline. All three books portray the sincere desire for instruction and discipline as the beginning of wisdom,[5] and it seems likely that Milton saw Raphael, the "divine instructor" (5.546), and Michael, the "heavenly instructor" (11.871), as fulfilling a role with respect to Adam and Eve like that of the Jewish teacher. Like Wisdom herself, they mediate between God and man. They embody wisdom and reveal precisely the knowledge which Wisdom is said to bestow on those who seek her out.

Over one quarter of the lines in *Paradise Lost* are spoken by these two archangels, whose different pedagogical styles have been described by Kathleen Swaim.[6] If one adds to them Eve's and Adam's replies, and includes as well the descriptions of the visions Michael reveals to Adam, a third of the poem begins to look like a story of formal instruction, an educational supplement to what Adam and Eve learn from each other and from observing the world around them. The wisdom with which the couple is endowed at the creation intuitively governs their relationships toward each other and toward God. Perhaps, in a world less complicated, less free, than the one into which they are born, it would have sufficed. But Milton clearly perceived them as needing an education. Or rather two educations: one to assure their sufficiency to withstand temptation, and another to prepare them for life in the fallen world.

The notion that Wisdom served such a function for Adam was itself traditional. Richard Hooker commented that "Wisdom was Adam's instructor in Paradise; wisdom endued the fathers who lived before the law with the knowledge of holy things."[7] In so saying he was drawing on The Wisdom of Solomon, where we learn that "[Wisdom] preserved the first formed father of the world, that was created alone, and brought him out of his fall," and that she gave his offspring "knowledge of holy things" (Wisd. 10:1, 10).

Raphael, in order to "preserve" Adam and Eve, instructs them in many things, including the major events that took place before they were created. He tells them about the war in heaven, the angelic hierarchy, and the creation of the world. He gives them a detailed version of the knowledge that Solomon claimed to have received from

Wisdom herself: "certain knowledge of the things that are, namely, to know how the world was made, and the operation of the elements: The beginning, ending, and midst of the times: the alterations of the turning of the sun, and the change of seasons: The circuits of years, and the positions of stars" (Wisd. 7:17–19). In addition, Raphael gives them moral instruction: instruction about their duties to themselves and to their Creator.

Before Raphael's arrival in Paradise, however, and indeed before we meet Adam and Eve, Milton introduces us to the problematic nature of wisdom and of the search for it. As early as Book 2 he dismisses the "vain wisdom ... and false philosophy," the "pleasing sorcery," of the fallen angels who pass their time in hell in "sweet" and "charming" discourse:

> and reasoned high
> Of providence, foreknowledge, will and fate,
> Fixed fate, free will, foreknowledge absolute,
> And found no end, in wandering mazes lost.
> Of good and evil much they argued then,
> Of happiness and final misery,
> Passion and apathy, and glory and shame. . . .
>
> (2.558–64)

Whatever combination of Schoolmen, Stoics, and Epicureans Milton may be mocking, theirs are the "enticing words," the "philosophy and vain deceit, after the tradition of men" against which Paul warned the Colossians, urging them instead "to the acknowledgment of the mystery of God, and of the Father, and of Christ; In whom are hid all the treasures of wisdom and knowledge" (Col. 2:2–8). Void of faith, and relying on reason alone, the fallen angels "found no end, in wandering mazes lost"—phrases that foreshadow both the fruitless hours that the fallen Adam and Eve spend following the Fall ("And of their vain contest appeared no end" [9.1189]) and Adam's private "evasions vain, / And reasonings ... through mazes" (10.829–30).

Raphael is persistently diffident in his instruction, and Adam in turn is sensitive to the need for diffidence and exhibits precisely the right attitude. The need for diffidence arises from the infinite nature of God's wisdom and also, perhaps, from the illicit nature of aspects of that wisdom, though on this latter point Raphael is careful to hedge. His "secrets of another world" are *"perhaps* / Not lawful to reveal" (5.569–70; my emphasis). The criterion of lawfulness quickly yields to the criterion of moral and practical utility. He teaches them, as Adam gratefully acknowledges, things "which human knowledge could not reach . . . things above earthly thought, which yet concerned / Our knowing, as to highest wisdom seemed" (7.75, 82–83). In the words of Solomon, Raphael has shown Adam and Eve "the kingdom of God, and given [them] knowledge of angels" (Wisd. 10:10; Geneva Bible). He is carefully explicit about the purpose and scope of his undertaking. His discourse on angelic diet is designed to set forth how, if men be found obedient, their "bodies may at last turn all to spirit, / Improved by tract of time, and winged ascend / Ethereal" (5.497–99). He tells them of the war in heaven as a warning: "Let it profit thee to have heard / By terrible example the reward / Of disobedience" (6.909–11). What he tells them, he tells them for their own good.

Uriel had assured the inquisitive Satan that the desire "to know / The works of God, thereby to glorify / The great work-master" (3.694–96) is a praiseworthy desire, just as Solomon instructs us to "acknowledge the workmaster . . . for by the greatness and beauty of the creatures . . . the maker of them is seen" (Wisd. 13:1, 5). When Adam asks for an account of the creation, he does so in terms of which Uriel would have approved: "We, not to explore the secrets ask / Of his eternal empire, but the more / To magnify his works, the more we know" (7.95–97), and this indeed is Raphael's intent. He will give them such knowledge as "best may serve / To glorify the maker, and infer / Thee also happier" (7.115–17). From this point of view one might regard Raphael's entire narration as an expansion of the description in Ecclesiasticus of "how God created and furnished man in the beginning": "Withal he filled them with the knowledge of understanding, and shewed them good and evil. He set his eye upon their hearts, that he might shew them the greatness of his works. He gave them to glory in his marvellous acts for ever, that they might declare his works with understanding" (17:7–9).

The problem is, as Wisdom herself declares, "They that drink me shall yet be thirsty" (Ecclus. 24:21). Adam, after he hears of the war in heaven, is "as one whose drouth / Yet scarce allayed still eyes the current stream, / Whose liquid murmur heard new thirst excites"

(7.66–68). And though the story of the creation, he later says, "largely hast allayed / The thirst I had of knowledge," "something yet of doubt remains" (8.7–8, 13). Since wisdom is irresistably sweet, the more Adam learns, the more he wants to know. His subsequent question about the stars "that seem to roll / Spaces incomprehensible . . . merely to officiate light / Round this opacous earth . . . in all their vast survey / Useless besides" (8.19–25) is in fact a questioning of that wisdom that was present at the creation and assumes that what he regards as disproportions are in fact disproportions:

> Reasoning I oft admire,
> How nature wise and frugal could commit
> Such disproportions, with superfluous hand
> So many nobler bodies to create,
> Greater so manifold to this one use, . . .
>
> (8.25–29)

It would appear that Adam is teetering on the edge of intellectual pride, as he goes on to offer his own theory of how things might have been better arranged. Raphael, however, does not pick him up on this point, and he does not regard Adam's question as blameworthy. In fact the only idea Adam had put forth that Raphael explicitly challenges is the notion that the bright stars are more noble than the earth and serve the earth. Raphael answers, first, that "bright infers not excellence" (8.91) and, second, that "those bright luminaries" do not serve the earth, but rather "thee earth's habitant" (8.98–99). There is a nice irony, if we assume that Eve's dream embodied her thoughts about how the world could have been better made, in the fact that she envisioned a world where the stars served her ("with ravishment," to be sure), while Raphael must *teach* Adam that the stars serve him. Raphael, in contrast to Adam, stresses the importance of man on the one hand, while on the other he places human glory in the context of God's greater glory "above the heavens":

> And for the heaven's wide circuit, let it speak
> The maker's high magnificence, who built
> So spacious, and his line stretched out so far;
> That man may know he dwells not in his own;
> An edifice too large for him to fill,

Lodged in a small partition, and the rest
Ordained for uses to his Lord best known.

(8.100–106)

It is the Lord's uses, or, in Uriel's term, his causes, not all of which are human centered, that must remain known only to him. Though Raphael in no sense rebukes Adam, his lengthy and involved reply to Adam's question is nevertheless well calculated to make Adam think twice before venturing again upon such lofty speculations. Raphael does not even deny the possibility that there may be disproportions. Human conjecture and opinion about the heavens, he seems to imply, are not so much forbidden as they are "quaint" (8.78). And he later adds:

God to remove his ways from human sense,
Placed heaven from earth so far, that earthly sight,
If it presume, might err in things too high,
And no advantage gain.

(8.119–22)

Solomon has similar ideas:

The thoughts of mortal men are miserable, and our devices are but uncertain. For the corruptible body presseth down the soul, and the earthly tabernacle weigheth down the mind that museth [as Adam's surely does!] upon many things. And hardly do we guess aright at things that are upon earth, and with labour do we find the things that are before us: but the things that are in heaven who hath searched out? (Wisd. 9:14–16)

Raphael's primary point has been all along that the search for knowledge or wisdom should be directed always by a closely related cluster of principles. We should seek knowledge that shows us how "happy" or fortunate we are, knowledge that leads us to magnify the Creator, and knowledge that offers us moral instruction for our good. And so here, in Book 8, he concludes:

Solicit not thy thoughts with matters hid,
Leave them to God above, him serve and fear . . .
           joy thou

> In what he gives to thee, this Paradise
> And thy fair Eve; Heaven is for thee too high
> To know what passes there; be lowly wise:
> Think only what concerns thee and thy being.
>
> (8.167–74)

And Adam hears him well, acknowledging that the "prime wisdom" is

> ... Not to know at large of things remote
> From use, obscure and subtle, but to know
> That which before us lies in daily life.
>
> (8.191–93)

Raphael's advice and Adam's reply have very close analogues in classical and Christian as well as Hebrew writers. Cicero, who was a contemporary of the author of The Wisdom of Solomon, spoke approvingly of our "desire to know the secrets or wonders of creation" insofar as they are "indispensable to a happy life," but he warned against devoting "too much industry and too deep study to matters that are obscure and difficult and useless as well." For him too, astronomy was a prime example of potentially useless knowledge, and he praised Socrates as "the first to call philosophy down from the heavens and set her in the cities of men and bring her also into their homes and compel her to ask questions about life and morality and things good and evil."[8] And Augustine had written:

> We ought not to suppose that it concerns our attainment of felicity that we should know the causes of the great corporal movements in the universe, such as are hid at the most secret bounds of nature.... But the causes of good things and evil it is our duty to know, and that to the extent to which it is granted to man, in this life, full of errors and distresses, to know them for the avoidance of these same errors and distresses.... How clear it is with what patience we should bear our ignorance of that which is hidden from us concerning the secrets of heaven and earth.[9]

But Raphael, before he departs, places his entire discourse in a different perspective, the perspective of the single obligation under which Adam and Eve live:

> Be strong, live happy, and love, but first of all
> Him whom to love is to obey, *and keep*
> *His great command.*
>
> (8.633–35; my emphasis)

For this wisdom—the most crucial wisdom Adam can receive in his situation—the closest analogue is in Ecclesiasticus: "Seek not out the things that are too hard for thee, neither search the things that are above thy strength. *But what is commanded thee*, think thereupon with reverence, for it is not needful for thee to see with thine eyes the things that are in secret. Be not curious in unnecessary matters" (3:21–23; my emphasis).

These parting words of wisdom have an obvious and direct relevance to Adam's fall, or, in Adam's words, to "that which before us lies in daily life." Yet there is a curious disproportion between the great care Raphael takes in instructing Adam in the purposes of inquiry—particularly in view of the fact that Adam is so apt a pupil—and the slight bearing that instruction has on the latter's reasons or motives for disobeying God. On the one hand, Howard Schultz was no doubt correct when he argued that "Milton, writing of Adam, had no choice but to write of curiosity,"[10] and he reinterpreted that traditional notion in the light of the Wisdom literature. On the other, he was perfectly aware that there is no reference in Scripture to Adam's having sought forbidden knowledge. Indeed from Raphael's account it is far more certain that some kinds of knowledge are unattainable than that they are forbidden. What is clear is that the most directly pertinent practical and moral instruction Raphael gives to Adam comes, like the injunction to keep his great command, in response to Adam's account of the effect Eve has on him. That instruction, too, comes partly from the Wisdom literature, as we shall see when we explore Milton's use of that literature in his account of the Fall.

Eve and the Savour of Wisdom

The Genesis account of Eve's and Adam's reasons for eating of the fruit of the tree of knowledge is nothing if not succinct: "And when the woman saw that the tree was good for food, and that it was pleasant to the eyes, and a tree to be desired to make one wise, she took of the fruit thereof, and did eat, and gave also unto her husband with her; and he did eat" (3:6). The text ascribes to the man no reason whatsoever for eating the fruit. To the woman it ascribes three positive reasons, and Milton develops each of them in presenting Eve's fall, adding, however, an insistent stress on the inviting odor of the tree and its fruit, as if to underscore the shared etymology of *savour* and *sapience*. When Eve recounts to Adam the dream in which she is first tempted, she says that "the pleasant savoury smell / So quickened appetite, that I, methought, / Could not but taste" (5.84–86). Satan's feigned and Eve's actual encounters with the tree are presented in very similar terms:

> I nearer drew to gaze;
> When from the boughs *a savoury odour blown*,
> Grateful to appetite, more pleased my sense
> Than smell of sweetest fennel or the teats
> Of ewe or goat dropping with milk at even,
> Unsucked of lamb or kid, that tend their play.
> To satisfy the sharp desire I had
> Of tasting those fair apples, I resolved
> Not to defer; hunger and thirst at once,
> Powerful persuaders, *quickened at the scent*
> *Of that alluring fruit*, urged me so keen.
>
> (9.578–88; my emphasis)

> Mean while the hour of noon drew on, and waked
> An eager appetite, *raised by the smell*
> *So savoury of that fruit*, which the desire,
> Inclinable now grown to touch or taste,
> Solicited her longing eye....
>
> (9.739–43; my emphasis)

Eve mistakes the "tree of knowledge of good and evil" for a tree whose fruit affords wisdom, and it is perhaps no wonder, in hindsight, that she does so, for Milton has described his tree of knowledge in such a way that one might readily confuse it, in this one respect, with what we might call the tree of true Wisdom, who describes herself in Ecclesiasticus through a series of similes as enticing to the sense of smell as the forbidden fruit itself:

> I was exalted like a palm tree in En-Gaddi, and as a rose plant in Jericho, as a fair olive tree in a pleasant field, and grew up as a

plane tree by the water. I gave a sweet smell like cinnamon and aspalathus, and I yielded a pleasant odour like the best myrrh.... As the vine brought I forth pleasant savour, and my flowers are the fruit of honour and riches. I am the mother of fair love, and fear, and knowledge, and holy hope.... Come unto me, all ye that be desirous of me, and fill yourselves with my fruits. For my memorial is sweeter than honey, and mine inheritance than the honeycomb. They that eat me shall yet be hungry, and they that drink me shall yet be thirsty. (Ecclus. 24:14–21)

Milton presents the forbidden fruit, in other words, as a parody of the fruit of Wisdom. There was, in fact, a tradition that associated the tree of life with Wisdom. For Augustine, as for Isidore of Seville after him, the tree of life signified both Christ and "wisdom herself, the mother of all good." Within that framework one might say that Satan is deceiving Eve by attributing the qualities of the tree of life to the tree of knowledge.[11] Those who eat the fruit of Wisdom's tree, according to the passage from Ecclesiasticus, "shall yet be hungry," and those who drink "shall yet be thirsty," but Satan is "sated," Eve "satiate at length" (9.598, 792). Satan calls the tree of knowledge the "Mother of science" (9.680), while Wisdom is the mother of love and fear and knowledge and hope. Wisdom, according to Proverbs, "is a *tree of life* to them that lay hold upon her" (3:18; my emphasis), while Eve, although she knew it not, was "eating death" (9.792).

Satan tantalizes Eve with a suggestively vague apostrophe to the tree, an apostrophe that directly contradicts the assertion that he had heard from Uriel to the effect that wisdom brought forth the works of God, "but hid their causes deep" (3.707):

> O sacred, wise, and wisdom-giving plant,
> Mother of science, now I feel thy power
> Within me clear, not only to discern
> Things in their causes, but to trace the ways
> Of highest agents, deemed however wise.
>
> (9.679–83)

Eve, as we have seen, has only a dim, confused sense of what sort of wisdom or knowledge she hopes to attain, though she is certain that the fruit must be "of virtue to make wise." Forgetting that she *was* made wise, and that Raphael has already taught her about "the ways of highest agents," and drawing from the fact that God forbids the fruit the false inference that he "forbids us to be wise," "she plucked, she ate," and "all was lost."

No sooner does Eve eat than she proceeds to demonstrate her fallen nature by violating two of the most frequently reiterated warnings in the Wisdom literature. The first, which we have glanced at, is the warning against the evils of idol-worship, to which Solomon devotes several chapters: "For the worshipping of idols not to be named is the beginning, the cause, and the end, of all evil" (Wisd. 14:27). The second is the warning against deluding oneself into thinking that one's unrighteous deeds may escape God's notice: "Say not thou, 'I will hide myself from the Lord: shall any remember me from above? I shall not be remembered among so many people: for what is my soul among such an infinite number of creatures?' ... [The] ways [of the unrighteous] are ever before him, and shall not be hid from his eyes" (Ecclus. 16:17; 17:15). Eve addresses the tree and promises, as if having dispensed with the sort of morning hymn in praise of God that she was wont to sing with Adam, "Henceforth my early care, / Not without song, each morning, and due praise / Shall tend thee." Then, reflecting that wisdom is "secret," the word triggers the promptings of shame:

> And I perhaps am secret; heaven is high,
> High and remote to see from thence distinct
> Each thing on earth; and other care perhaps
> May have diverted from continual watch
> Our great forbidder, safe with all his spies
> About him.
>
> (9.811–16)

Adam and the Strange Woman

The case with Adam is very different. Milton conceived of him not as seeking Wisdom, but as forsaking her. During Adam's candid, moving account of the effect of Eve's loveliness upon him he confesses to Raphael that "all higher knowledge in her presence falls / Degraded, wisdom in discourse with her / Looses discountenanced, and like folly shows" (8.551–53). His incipient personification of wisdom gently hints at the competition in Proverbs between Wisdom and "the strange woman," the "harlot," for the affections of the young man being instructed—the strange woman "which flattereth with her words; which forsaketh the guide of her youth, and forgetteth the covenant of her God," whose lips "drop as an honeycomb, and her mouth is smoother than oil" (2:16–17, 5:3). Whoever finds Wisdom "findeth life, and shall obtain favour of the Lord" (8:35), but the strange woman's "house is the way to hell, going down to the chambers of death" (7:27). The young man's instructor advises him to turn away from the false temptress and "get wisdom.... Forsake her not, and she shall preserve thee: love her, and she shall keep thee" (4:5–6). Or, in Raphael's words to Adam:

> Be not diffident
> Of wisdom, she deserts thee not, if thou
> Dismiss not her, when most thou need'st her nigh.
>
> (8.562–64)

Adam, if we follow the logic of this personification, falls because he dismisses Wisdom, and she in turn temporarily deserts him. He chooses a different woman. Raphael warns him that Eve merits his cherishing, his honoring, and his love, but not his subjection (8.561–70). It is counsel that the Wisdom books, which are not noted for their celebration of equality between the sexes, insist upon repeatedly: "Give not thy soul unto a woman to set her foot upon thy substance" (Ecclus. 9:2). "Stumble not at the beauty of a woman, and desire her not for pleasure" (Ecclus. 25:21). "Give not thy strength unto women" (Prov. 31:3). Adam gives his strength to a woman, overcome with female charm.

The first words that Adam utters after eating the fruit, which again recall that *sapere*—to taste—is the root of both *savour* and *sapience*, are designed to remind us that Adam's innate wisdom, like Eve's, has been strangely warped: "Eve, now I see thou art exact of taste, / And elegant, of sapience no small part" (9.1017–18). It is no wonder that the couple's lustful dalliance, though its setting remains innocently pastoral, is presented in terms derived in part from the more exotic account in Proverbs of the harlot's seduction of the young man who has deserted Wisdom and hence is "void of understanding":

>   Flowers were the couch,
> Pansies, and violets, and asphodel,
> And hyacinth, earth's freshest softest lap.
> There they their fill of love and love's disport
> Took largely, of their mutual guilt the seal,
> The solace of their sin. . . .
>
> (9.1039–44)

I have decked my bed [says the harlot] with coverings of tapestry, with carved works, with fine linen of Egypt. I have perfumed my bed with myrrh, aloes, and cinnamon. Come, let us take our fill of love until the morning: let us solace ourselves with loves. (7:16–18)

One might assume from these passages that Eve is being cast unequivocally in the role of harlot. Mary Nyquist, however, has pointed to numerous problems that follow from that assumption. There is no reason to believe that it was Eve who decked this particular couch, and it was Adam, not Eve, who extended the harlot's invitation, "Come, so well refreshed, now let us play" (9.1027). Though Milton's appropriation of the episode from Proverbs might have led him toward picturing Eve as the destroying temptress, or Adam as Samson waking "from the harlot-lap / Of Philistean Dalilah... shorn of his strength" (9.1060–62), he resists, to a considerable degree, the logic of his imagery. Speaking of the extended simile of lines 1051–63, Nyquist points out that "on the level of syntax alone it is patently obvious that *both* Adam and Eve are being compared with Samson."[12] Following their postcoital slumber:

>   Up *they* rose
> As from unrest, and each the other viewing,
> Soon found their eyes how opened, and their minds
> How darkened; innocence, that as a veil
> Had shadowed them from knowing ill, was gone,
> Just confidence, and native righteousness
> And honour from about them, naked left
> To guilty shame he covered, but his robe
> Uncovered more, *so rose the Danite strong*
> Herculean Samson from the harlot-lap
> Of Philistean Dalilah, and waked

> Shorn of his strength, *they* destitute and bare
> Of all their virtue.
>
> (9.1051–63; my emphasis)

If we move beyond syntax, however, the matter is not quite so clear. The specific reference to Adam immediately prior to the second half of the simile ("he covered, but his robe / Uncovered more") encourages the Adam/Samson connection. It seems likely that Milton's use of both the Samson story and the passage from Proverbs will remain unsettled and unsettling.

The Delights of Wisdom

We have considered Raphael's role as a divine instructor, a messenger from God who imparts to Adam and Eve such wisdom as is required to render them "sufficient to have stood." But his pedagogical role constitutes only half the story of his relationship to the Hebrew Wisdom tradition. The more affective half of the story has to do not so much with knowledge as with friendship, or what one might almost call intellectual camaraderie, between the human and the divine—between Adam and Eve and Raphael, Adam and God, and, of course, between Milton and his muse. Behind this idea, I believe, stands, once again, the figure of Wisdom, whom we encounter directly and explicitly in *Paradise Lost* only in the invocation to Book 7. The opening fifteen lines of that invocation present two wonderfully different but congruent pictures of social relationships, or of what Milton might have called conversations. The first is his own finely deferential relationship to Urania herself, whose "guest" in heaven he has been and who in turn, almost as lover, visits his slumbers nightly. The second is the playful, casual relationship conveyed by the picture of Urania conversing with her sister, eternal Wisdom, playing and singing in the presence of the Father. I want to treat these lines and their scriptural source as the originating metaphor for one of the epic's central themes, a metaphor that will place in a new light Milton's understanding of both the nature of Paradise and the significance of its loss.

> Descend from heaven Urania, by that name
> If rightly thou art called, whose voice divine
> Following, above the Olympian hill I soar,
> Above the flight of Pegasean wing.

> The meaning, not the name I call: for thou
> Nor of the Muses nine, nor on the top
> Of old Olympus dwell'st, but heavenly born,
> Before the hills appeared, or fountain flowed,
> Thou with eternal Wisdom didst converse,
> Wisdom thy sister, and with her didst play
> In presence of the almighty Father, pleased
> With thy celestial song. Up led by thee
> Into the heaven of heavens I have presumed,
> An earthly guest, and drawn empyreal air,
> Thy tempering....
>
> (7.1–15)

As is well known, the passage contains echoes of verses 22–31 of the eighth chapter of Proverbs, where Wisdom speaks:

> The Lord possessed me in the beginning of his way, before his works of old. I was set up from everlasting, from the beginning, or ever the earth was. When there were no depths, I was brought forth; *when there were no fountains abounding with water.* Before the mountains were settled, *before the hills was I brought forth:* While as yet he had not made the earth, nor the fields, nor the highest part of the dust of the world. When he prepared the heavens, I was there: when he set a compass upon the face of the depth: when he established the clouds above: when he strengthened the fountains of the deep: when he gave the sea his decree, that the waters should not pass his commandment: when he appointed the foundations of the earth: Then I was by him, as one brought up with him: *and I was daily his delight, rejoicing* [Vulgate: *ludens*, playing] *always before him;* rejoicing in the habitable part of his earth; and my delights were with the sons of men.

It is only the phrases I have emphasized that Milton came close to quoting in the invocation, but the entire passage, stressing Wisdom's presence prior to and during the creation, is obviously appropriate to the hexameral subject matter of Book 7. Appropriate too are the images of Wisdom "rejoicing in the habitable part of [God's] earth," and confessing the delights she enjoys "with the sons of men." As if in tribute to these images, the new-created earth, habitable but as yet uninhabited, is described as "a seat where gods might dwell, / Or wander with delight, and love to haunt / Her sacred shades" (7.329–31). After the creation of man, we learn that "God will deign / To visit oft the dwellings of just men / Delighted, and with frequent intercourse / Thither will send his winged messengers / On errands of supernal grace" (7.569–73). Both Milton's invocation, then, and Wisdom's account of herself in Proverbs, suggest the possibility of sociable intercourse between human and divine beings. Milton himself has been led up by Urania "into the heaven of heavens" as "an earthly guest," "rapt above the pole."

Du Bartas's Urania, like Milton's, transports humankind "above the *Poles*," "teaching their hands to touch, and eyes to see / All th' entercourse of the *Celestial Court*."[13] The idea of such intercourse or friendship is commonplace in both the classical and biblical Wisdom traditions. In *De Officiis* Cicero wrote: "That wisdom which I have given the foremost place is the knowledge of things human and divine, which is concerned also with the bonds of union between gods and men and the relations of man to man."[14] According to The Wisdom of Solomon, those who attain wisdom "become the friends of God" (7:14). Time and time again, as if he were amplifying the phrase "and my delights were with the sons of men," the author describes Wisdom's accessibility and testifies to the pleasure he finds in her company. She is "a loving spirit," "easily seen of them that love her, and found of such as seek her. She preventeth them that desire her, in making herself first known unto them" (Wisd. 1:6; 6:12–13). Above all, Wisdom is conversant with both God and man:

> I loved her, and sought her out from my youth, I desired to make her my spouse, and I was a lover of her beauty. In that she is conversant with God, she magnifieth her nobility: yea, the Lord of all things himself loved her. For she is privy to the mysteries of the knowledge of God, and a lover of his works.... After I am come into mine house, I will repose myself with her: for her conversation hath no bitterness; and to live with her hath no sorrow, but mirth and joy. (Wisd. 8:2–4, 16)

There are instances in the Old Testament of God visiting man, or speaking directly to him, as when the Lord speaks to Moses "face to face, as a man speaketh unto his friend" (Exod. 33:11). Behind Adam's willingness to argue with Raphael and with God lies not only

Abraham's and Moses' successful attempts to persuade the Lord to a particular course of action (Gen. 18; Exod. 4, 32; Num. 14) but also Solomon's prayer for an understanding heart. "And the speech pleased the Lord, that Solomon had asked this thing" (1 Kings 3:10). Behind Adam's awed and rather nervous excitement at his first glimpse of Raphael, and Eve's preparation of a perfect meal to please their guest, there lies the equally domestic and high-spirited scene in which the Lord, in the company of two angels, visited Abraham and Sarah, and Abraham "hastened into the tent unto Sarah" and ordered her to prepare food for their visitors (Gen. 18:1–15).

None of these passages, however, conveys so charmingly the possibility of delight and pleasure in the intimate fellowship between gods and men as these passages from Proverbs and The Wisdom of Solomon. Such literature, I suggest, may have authorized for Milton his stress on the sheer delight Adam takes in Raphael, whom God sends down to converse with him "as friend with friend" (5.229–30). In the New Testament, as we have seen, James, perhaps echoing Solomon, describes "the wisdom that is from above" as "peaceable, gentle, and easy to be intreated" (James 3:17). The description fits Raphael, "the sociable spirit" (5.221), to a "T." Adam addresses him as a "favourable spirit, propitious guest" (5.507). He is the "gentle" archangel (8.648), and above all he is "affable" (7.41; 8.648)—that is, the archangel with whom it is easy to converse.[15]

Milton contrasts Adam's first greeting of Raphael with "the tedious pomp that waits / On princes": "Adam though not awed, / Yet with submiss approach and reverence meek, / As to a superior nature, bowing low...." (5.354–60). The angel is reassuring, even to the point of stressing that he has the afternoon off and can accept Adam's luncheon invitation:

> Adam, I therefore came, nor art thou such
> Created, or such place hast here to dwell,
> As may not oft invite, though spirits of heaven
> To visit thee; lead on then where thy bower
> O'ershades; for these mid-hours, till evening rise
> I have at will.
>
> (5.372–77)

More remarkable than Adam's decorousness, though, is his playfulness and ingratiating sense of humor that so clearly expresses the pleasure he finds in Raphael's company. After Raphael's account of the war in heaven, and well aware that the afternoon is drawing toward its close, Adam devises a most pleasant series of conceits to persuade Raphael that sufficient time remains for yet another story:

> And the great light of day yet wants to run
> Much of his race though steep, suspense in heaven
> Held by thy voice, thy potent voice he hears,
> And longer will delay to hear thee tell
> His generation, and the rising birth
> Of nature from the unapparent deep:
> Or if the star of evening and the moon
> Haste to thy audience, night with her will bring
> Silence, and sleep listening to thee will watch,
> Or we can bid his absence, till thy song
> End, and dismiss thee ere the morning shine.
>
> (7.98–108)

There is nothing naive or literal-minded about Adam's witty personification of the sun, the moon, night, silence, and sleep, as can be seen by contrasting these lines with those in which he is being dead serious about the movements of the heavenly bodies (4.660–88; 8:12–38). He plays delightfully, too, with the root meaning of *suspense* (hung aloft) and the more common meaning dear to the storyteller, and slyly implies that (like all children and most adults) the sun would be especially pleased to hear a story about himself. He hedges his bets carefully; just in case the sun does not stand still, night will bring silence, and if sleep cannot be trusted to remain attentive and watch without dozing, they can at least bid his absence.

Adam's entreaties are ingratiating in part because of his candidness about his own motives. His deference is not self-deprecating, but he engages Raphael, and us, by his willingness to see himself in a slightly comic light, thus assuring that his expressions of gratitude and praise will bear no trace of flattery. The story of the creation having been told, what can he do more to keep his new friend with him a while longer?

> Thee I have heard relating what was done
> Ere my remembrance: now hear me relate
> My story, which perhaps thou hast not heard;

> And day is yet not spent; till then thou seest
> How subtly to detain thee I devise,
> Inviting thee to hear while I relate,
> Fond, were it not in hope of thy reply:
> For while I sit with thee, I seem in heaven,
> And sweeter thy discourse is to my ear
> Than fruits of palm-tree pleasantest to thirst
> And hunger both, from labour, at the hour
> Of sweet repast; they satiate, and soon fill,
> Though pleasant, but thy words with grace divine
> Imbued, bring to their sweetness no satiety.
>
> (8.203–16)

As the last six lines suggest, Raphael's discourse to Adam fulfills Wisdom's own promise in Ecclesiasticus: "I was exalted like a palm tree.... Come unto me, all ye that be desirous of me, and fill yourselves with my fruits. For my memorial is sweeter than honey, and mine inheritance than the honeycomb. They that eat me shall yet be hungry, and they that drink me shall yet be thirsty" (Ecclus. 24:14, 19–21). Raphael, we must feel, is right when he answers, "Nor are thy lips ungraceful, sire of men, / Nor tongue ineloquent."

Raphael himself is less charming, and certainly less playful, than Adam. But God atones for Raphael's straitlacedness in his own response to Adam's persistent but tactful request for a "human consort" to provide him with "fellowship... fit to participate / All rational delight" (8.389–92). In a colloquy so sublime that it eventually leaves Adam thoroughly "dazzled and spent," there is more than a touch of high comedy,[16] as in God's teasing of our first parent:

> A nice and subtle happiness I see
> Thou to thy self proposest, in the choice
> Of thy associates, Adam, and wilt taste
> No pleasure, though in pleasure, solitary.
> What think'st thou then of me, and this my state,
> Seem I to thee sufficiently possessed
> Of happiness, or not?
>
> (8.399–405)

God has come down to earth here in more ways than one, and Adam strikes the right colloquial note when, at the sight of the newly created

Eve, he cannot forbear expressing his joy aloud: "This turn," he says—this subtle device, this change from your apparent intention, this act of good will—"hath made amends" (8.491).

When Raphael must at last depart, Adam bids him farewell. As Addison, who no doubt was more sensitive than we in such matters, observed, the speech "has in it a Deference and Gratitude agreeable to an Inferior Nature, and at the same time a certain Dignity and Greatness, suitable to the Father of Mankind in his State of Innocence."[17] It also rings with deeply poignant irony:

> Since to part,
> Go heavenly guest, ethereal messenger,
> Sent from whose sovereign goodness I adore.
> Gentle to me and affable hath been
> Thy condescension, and shall be honoured ever
> With grateful memory: thou to mankind
> Be good and friendly still, and oft return.
>
> (8.645–51)

With these lines Book 8 comes to an end, and with them the easy fellowship between this affable embodiment of God's wisdom and the father of mankind. Book 9 sounds the tragic note by focusing precisely on the effect of the Fall that will most grieve Adam. All that is offered by the picture of relaxed and sociable intercourse between gods and men in the opening lines of Book 7 is taken away:

> No more of talk where God or angel guest
> With man, as with his friend, familiar used
> To sit indulgent, and with him partake
> Rural repast, permitting him the while
> Venial discourse unblamed.
>
> (9.1–5)

If Raphael has been Adam's heavenly guest on earth, so Milton, led by Urania, had been an earthly guest in heaven, and she in turn "condescends" to him. She is not Wisdom precisely, but as the "voice divine," she is so closely akin to her as to make them one. Milton doubtless felt deeply the parallel between his relationship with his muse and Adam's with Raphael. He would have shared, I think, Du Bartas's account of his own relationship with his muse, which he described as "the type of th'vpper Paradice; / Where *Adam* had (O wondrous strange) discourse / With God himselfe, with Angels intercourse." He would have agreed, too, with Joshua Sylvester's marginal comment on this passage, in which he calls such intercourse "Edens principall, and most excellent beauty."[18] It is appropriate that, following Raphael's departure from Adam, Milton never again speaks directly to his muse.

When we ask, as the title of the epic invites us to ask, what is lost when Paradise is lost, we may be tempted to answer in the terms of the judgment the Son pronounces on Adam and Eve (10.193–208). What is lost, we gather, is childbearing without sorrow or pain, an abundance of food easily harvested, and eternal life, adding to these the perfectly temperate climate of perpetually mingled spring and fall. And that is no doubt true. But Adam and Eve learn to live with the judgment rather easily. Adam regards it as a mild judgment, and even, perhaps, as an invigorating challenge (10.1050–59). Though he wrestles hard with the thought of death, sometimes fearing it and sometimes desiring it, with Michael's aid he learns first to regard it with detachment, with more concern for living well than for the length of life, and then, at the last, to recognize it as, for the faithful, the "gate of life."

Or we may think of the loss as an impairment of reason or will, a greater proclivity to sin, or the loss of the intuitive capacity to call things by their right names, or the loss of an innocent language. And while Milton might have agreed that the Fall entailed all this, he did very little by way of dramatizing it in the action of the poem. What we see instead, following the disastrous and discordant scenes at the end of Book 9 and in the middle of 10, is a process of regeneration that shifts the situation in a way that makes it difficult if not impossible to weigh loss against gain on a single pair of scales. Though we know that their offspring will sin and sin again through history, we do not witness in Adam and Eve themselves a greater tendency toward sin. And if Michael has to keep interpreting the visions of history for Adam, adjusting his initial perception, it is not clear whether Michael's efforts are necessary because Adam's reason has been impaired or, what seems more likely, because new experience will necessitate new forms of understanding. Adam has much to learn, and he proves himself a ready learner. As for their language, there is no essential difference between the language they speak before the Fall and the language they speak after it. If, in Books 9 and 10, they misuse their language for purposes of manipulation, excoriation, deceit, and self-excuse, Eve, as Anne Ferry has shown, leads them back toward a cooperative harmony of dialogue at least as impressive as any they had enjoyed before.[19]

If we were to put the question to Adam, however, and ask him what the loss of Paradise meant to him, he would answer the question in far other terms, terms that ally him with Milton's loss of the human face divine and his precarious relationship with his muse's "voice divine." Given what we saw earlier of the extraordinary delight Adam took in conversing with and listening to Raphael, who is Wisdom in her most accessible guise, this fact should come as no surprise. In Paradise he had only to call on God and God would visit him (8.299). When Michael tells him that they must depart "this happy place," Adam says:

> This most afflicts me, that departing hence,
> As from his *face* I shall be hid, deprived
> His blessed *countenance;* here I could frequent,
> With worship, place by place where he vouchsafed
> *Presence divine,* and to my sons relate;
> On this mount he *appeared;* under this tree
> Stood *visible,* among these pines *his voice*
> *I heard,* here with him at this fountain *talked.*
>
> (11.315–22; my emphasis)

Like God, Michael will insist, when he explains the miseries of fallen human life to Adam, that the suffering and loss men will experience is self-inflicted ("by themselves defaced"). Adam's separation from God's face and voice, "presence divine," and from Raphael, is a separation he brings upon himself by deserting the wisdom Raphael had bestowed upon him. The condition he seeks following the Fall echoes the condition that the fallen poet experiences and fears in the prologues to Books 3 and 7, a life of savage solitude, cut off from the sight of the human face divine and from light itself:

> How shall I behold the face
> Henceforth of God or angel, erst with joy
> And rapture so oft beheld? Those heavenly shapes
> Will dazzle now this earthly, with their blaze

> Insufferably bright. O might I here
> In solitude live savage, in some glade
> Obscured, where highest woods impenetrable
> To star or sunlight, spread their umbrage broad
> And brown as evening: cover me ye pines,
> Ye cedars, with innumerable boughs
> Hide me, where I may never see them more.
>
> (9.1080–90)

Adam, that is, initially desires his punishment. It is the desire for hiddenness that arises from shame, and it precedes the official judgment. When that judgment comes, Milton builds wonderfully on the haunting sentence from the King James translation of Genesis 3:8, "And they heard the voice of the Lord God walking in the garden in the cool of the day." Milton expands Genesis by having God's first rebuke (the Lord is not above using their old intimacy to make Adam squirm) directed at Adam's lack of courtesy—that quality of which he had been so fully possessed before the Fall:

> Where art thou Adam, wont with joy to meet
> My coming seen far off? I miss thee here,
> Not pleased, thus entertained with solitude,
> Where obvious duty erewhile appeared unsought:
> Or come I less conspicuous, or what change
> Absents thee, or what chance detains? Come forth.
>
> (10.103–8)

It is, appropriately, their faces, "discountenanced" and "discomposed," that give them away, for they have taken on a Satanic multiplicity of conflicting feelings, none of them good: "Love was not in their looks, either to God / Or to each other, but apparent guilt, / And shame, and perturbation, and despair, / Anger, and obstinacy, and hate, and guile" (10.112–14). Later, at the beginning of his anguished soliloquy, Adam will call down upon himself the very loss he will later most regret: "Hide me from the face / Of God, whom to behold was then my highth / Of happiness" (10.723–25).

Self-exiles, then, from Raphael's conversation, and from direct access to God's face and voice, Adam and Eve must substitute for "presence divine" the memory of his face and of his words. They must replace the knowledge of things seen with faith in things unseen, acquiring new skills in the reading of the book of the creatures and, more crucial still, an understanding of and a reliance on Scripture. What they need, in short, is a further education in "the sum of wisdom," an education that they themselves will initiate, and that Michael, the "heavenly instructor," will complete.

CHAPTER 9

The Sum of Wisdom

> That their hearts might be comforted, being knit together in love, and unto all riches of the full assurance of understanding, to the acknowledgement of the mystery of God, and of the Father, and of Christ; in whom are hid all the treasures of wisdom and knowledge.
>
> —(Colossians 2:2–3)

Adam's new situation as a fallen man calls for new instruction and new wisdom. Educated by Raphael to the recognition that "the prime wisdom" is "to know / That which before us lies in daily life" (8.192–94), Adam now enters a world where what lies before him might seem downright unbearable. We have seen, however, that according to Solomon, Wisdom not only "preserved the first formed father of the world, that was created alone;" she "brought him out of his fall" as well (Wisd. 10:1). In *Paradise Lost* our first father is brought out of his fall by Michael, to whom God says:

> If patiently thy bidding they obey,
> Dismiss them not disconsolate; reveal
> To Adam what shall come in future days,
> As I shall thee enlighten, intermix
> My Covenant in the woman's seed renewed;
> So send them forth, though sorrowing, yet in peace.
>
> (11.112–17)

While there are precedents for ending epic poems with surveys of "what shall come in future days,"[1] it is hardly surprising, given the importance that The Wisdom of Solomon and Ecclesiasticus had for Milton, that this epic, like those two works, should conclude with narratives of the history of Israel, and of her few righteous men. The tenth chapter of The Wisdom of Solomon contains a brief celebration of Wisdom's just dealings with Adam, Cain, Noah, Abraham, Lot, Jacob, Joseph, and Moses. The rest of the book seeks to demonstrate God's mercy, mildness, and justice toward Israel, detailing the extraordinary severity of his punishment of Egypt, and attributing the sins of the heathen to their ignorance of God as manifested in their worship of beasts and man-made idols. Ecclesiasticus concludes (chaps. 44–50) by praising the deeds and faith of the patriarchs, kings, and prophets through whom God's covenant was kept alive.

Milton is indebted very little to these historical sections of the Wisdom books for particular details,[2] though they share with Books 11 and 12 an insistent didacticism. If Michael explains to Adam the translation of Enoch in order "to show [him] what reward / Awaits the good, the rest what punishment" (11.709–10), Sirach offers Enoch as "an example of repentance to all generations" (Ecclus. 44:16). Solomon, in a spirit closer to Milton's, pictures him as a bitter lesson for the unrighteous, who, when God has "cast them down headlong" and punished them, shall see Enoch, and "they shall be troubled with terrible fear, and shall be amazed at the strangeness of his salvation, so far beyond all that they looked for" (Wisd. 4:19–5:2). Sirach's is an encomiastic and unsophisticated history, beginning "Let us now praise famous men, and our fathers that begat us. The Lord hath wrought great glory by them through his great power from the beginning" (Ecclus. 44:1–2). These men, he assures us, in what constitutes his sole general commentary on the series of deeds he will relate:

> were honoured in their generations, and were the glory of their times.... With their seed shall continually remain a good inheritance, and their children are within the covenant.... Their bodies are buried in peace; but their name liveth for evermore. The people will tell of their wisdom, and the congregation will shew forth their praise.
> (Ecclus. 44:7–15)

The Wisdom of Solomon embodies a considerably more complex view of history than Ecclesiasticus, a view much closer to Milton's own. It is an attempt to justify God's ways by showing not only that the punishments God brought upon Israel's enemies were deserved and appropriate (e.g., 11:15–20), but also that he tempers his justice with mercy, chastening offenders "little by little" so that they may come to believe in him and repent (Wisd. 12). It is a providential history, both on a national and an individual scale, fully in accord with Hamlet's oft-quoted comment, after returning safely from his sea voyage, that "there's a divinity that shapes our ends, / Rough-hew them how we will." In a section on the foolishness of putting our trust in false idols, for example, the author tells us:

> One preparing himself to sail, and about to pass through the raging waves, calleth upon a piece of wood more rotten than the vessel that carrieth him. For verily desire of gain devised that, and the workman built it by his skill. But thy providence, O Father, governeth it: for thou hast made a way in the sea, and a safe path in the waves; shewing that thou canst save from all danger: yea, though a man went to sea without art. (14:1–4)

If Solomon's God is at times mightily wrathful, he is also a God of great mercy and love:

> For thou canst shew thy great strength at all times when thou wilt; and who may withstand the power of thine arm? . . . But thou hast mercy upon all; for thou canst do all things, and winkest at the sins of men, because they should amend. For thou lovest all the things that are, and abhorrest nothing which thou hast made: for never wouldest thou have made any thing, if thou hadst hated it. And how could any thing have endured, if it had not been thy will? or been preserved, if not called by thee? But thou sparest all: for they are thine, O Lord, thou lover of souls. (Wisd. 11:21–26)

The Sign Language of the Creatures

Michael's vision of Jewish history, however, is not only providential but teleological. Because his aim, finally, is to demonstrate to Adam the need for the Messiah—to make him, indeed, yearn for a savior—his story is far more bleak than either Solomon's or Ben Sira's. Books 11 and 12 are a testimony to Satan's, and to Sin's and Death's, temporary though long-enduring victory, an enactment of those times foretold in Book 1 when Satan with his followers

> By falsities and lies the greatest part
> Of mankind they corrupted to forsake

> God their creator, and the invisible
> Glory of him that made them, to transform
> Oft to the image of a brute, adorned
> With gay religions full of pomp and gold,
> And devils to adore for deities.
>
> (1.367–73)

What Michael offers Adam is an education in patience. His are not the secrets of the kingdom of God and the life of the angels, but a homelier wisdom concerning how to live in a world less just than that pictured in the Wisdom books, a world in which God's mercy is seen but seldom and his justice is chiefly punitive. To match such a vision one would have to turn to those other and notoriously heterodox Wisdom books, Job and Ecclesiastes, and listen to Job's complaints: "Wherefore do the wicked live, become old, yea, are mighty in power?" (21:7), or to the Preacher telling us, "All things have I seen in the days of my vanity: there is a just man that perisheth in his righteousness, and there is a wicked man that prolongeth his life in his wickedness" (7:15).

The loss of Paradise, as we saw in chapter 5, entailed the loss of the actual, physical presence of God, the loss of that world "where God or angel guest / With man, as with his friend, familiar used / To sit indulgent." Face to face "venial discourse" gave way to "sighs and prayers." One aspect of Michael's task in Books 11 and 12 is to provide Adam and Eve with such recompense as he can, consistent with divine justice, for this loss. Even before Michael's arrival, however, Adam's faith had grown, and he had experienced the efficacy of prayer as providing a kind of presence and a kind of discourse:

> For since I sought
> By prayer the offended Deity to appease,
> Kneeled and before him humbled all my heart,
> Methought I saw him placable and mild,
> Bending his ear.
>
> (11.148–52)

The word *methought* strikes a nicely tentative balance between uncertainty and knowledge, and, by implication, between the sense in which God is absent (I am not *sure* I saw him) and the sense in which he is present (but I *think* I saw him). Prayer begins to close the gap between Adam and God not only visually, but also verbally, by recovering and renewing the Word pronounced long before:

> Persuasion in me grew
> That I was heard with favour; peace returned
> Home to my breast, and to my memory
> His promise, that thy seed shall bruise our foe;
> Which then not minded in dismay, yet now
> Assures me that the bitterness of death
> Is past, and we shall live.
>
> (11.152–58)

Although Adam is essentially correct, his sense of relief is premature. No sooner does Eve express her own sense that all is as well as it can be ("Here let us live, though in fallen state, content" [11.180]) than Michael appears to remove and send them from the garden (11.260–61). From the very beginning of their conversation it is clear that Michael is going to instruct the pair in a radically new way of thinking. He responds to Eve's dismay at having to leave the "native soil" of her garden by instructing her that, wherever she and Adam abide in the fallen world, she should "think there [her] native soil" (11.290–92). Adam recovers from his state of shock and tells the archangel, "This most afflicts me, that departing hence, / As from his face I shall be hid, deprived / His blessed countenance." Michael reassures him that God's "omnipresence fills / Land, sea, and air," that "his presence" is not "to these narrow bounds confined / Of Paradise or Eden" (11.336–42). This is not quite the notion of presence that had been in Adam's mind when he recalled God standing "visible" under a particular tree or talking with him at a particular fountain (11.320–22). But it will have to do. It is a presence that will have to be inferred, a presence in which Adam will have to believe though he cannot quite see it:

> Yet doubt not but in valley and plain
> God is *as* here, and will be found *alike*
> Present, and of his presence many a sign
> Still following thee, still compassing thee round
> With goodness and paternal love, his face
> Express, and of his steps the track divine.
>
> (11.349–54; my emphasis)

Michael's language is carefully vague. Adam must believe that God is *as* here, or, as Adam himself later puts it, he must learn "to walk / As in his presence" (12.562–63). The phrasing stops just short of, but puts us in mind of, *as if*. *Alike* carries both its meanings. God will be present in the same manner as before; he will be present in a similar (and hence different) manner. Has nothing changed? Or everything? The signs of God's presence are "his face / Express," the track left by his steps. The primary meaning of *express* here is no doubt "exactly resembling," a meaning that, according to the OED, is used "chiefly with reminiscence of *Heb*. i.3," where the Son is called "the express image of [God's] person." In the poem Adam is said to have been made "in the image of God / Express" (7.527–28), but an equally relevant passage is that which relates how the Father "on his Son with rays direct / Shone full, he all his Father full expressed / Ineffably into his face received" (6.719–21). The implication is that the signs of God's presence in the fallen world are "his face," just as the Son is his Father's face, though it is precisely the Son whom Adam had twice seen, and will never, at least in the same sense, see again. To believe, wherever he goes and whatever he experiences, that "God is as here," Adam will have to learn to read signs that he has not confronted before, and it is partly to instruct him in that skill that Michael has been sent to him.

Structurally, as I suggested in chapter 3, Books 11 and 12 recapitulate the transition from seeing the creatures to hearing the Word that occurs between Books 1 and 2 and again between Books 6 and 7. Milton introduces the theme of seeing the creatures early in Book 11. At the very moment when Adam and Eve are expressing their hope that, at least within certain limits, all may be well, "nature first gave signs, impressed / On bird, beast, air, air suddenly eclipsed / After short blush of morn" (182–84). Adam, thinking aloud, proceeds to read these signs, and the accuracy of his rather tentative inferences is affirmed by the narrator:

> O Eve, some further change awaits us nigh,
> Which heaven by these mute signs in nature shows
> Forerunners of his purpose, or to warn
> Us haply too secure of our discharge
> From penalty, because from death released
> Some days; how long, and what till then our life,

> Who knows, or more than this, that we are dust,
> And thither must return and be no more.
> Why else this double object in our sight
> Of flight pursued in the air and o'er the ground
> One way the self-same hour? Why in the east
> Darkness ere day's mid-course, and morning light
> More orient in yon western cloud that draws
> O'er the blue firmament a radiant white,
> And slow descends, with something heavenly fraught.
>   He erred not....
>   (11.193–208)

Adam is still adept at reading divine purpose in the disruptions of the familiar world of Eden. But that familiarity has hardly prepared him for the creatures he will confront in the world that now lies before him. The description of Michael's healing of Adam's "blindness," removing the "film" from his eyes, "purging" the "visual nerve," instilling drops from the well of life that "pierced, / Even to the inmost seat of mental sight" (11.412–18), vividly recalls, in its physiological particularity, the poet's futile search for light's "piercing ray," his description of his own blindness, and his prayer that the "celestial Light / Shine inward, and the mind through all her powers / Irradiate, there plant eyes, all mist from thence / Purge and disperse" (3.51–54). In Book 11 Adam, led by Michael, ascends "in the visions of God" (377). From that vantage point, like the Father in Book 3, he looks down upon the course of human history, "his own works and their works at once to view" (3.59). Like the Father, he looks into the future. Adam's own works are his offspring, and *their* works the effects of his and of Eve's disobedience. What Adam first sees, however, are not visions of heaven, but sights "of terror, foul and ugly to behold" (11.464), sights of human death, disease, and deformity, the chief of nature's works engaged in acts of destruction and self-destruction.

Reading accurately these "blotted" pages from the book of the human creatures is not easy, and as many critics have observed, much of Book 11 is devoted to Michael's correcting or modifying of Adam's interpretations of the visions he is shown.[3] When he beholds Cain smiting the life out of Abel, he can see with his eyes that Abel was one who sacrificed well, and he asks the right question: "Is piety thus and pure devotion paid?" (452). But he cannot see beyond what he can see to the future, when "the bloody fact / Will be avenged, and the other's faith approved / Lose no reward" (457–59). Like a child, Adam mistakes this, the first death he sees, for Death itself, the type of all deaths (462), and Michael takes pains to enlarge and educate his conceptions of and attitudes toward "the many shapes of death." Then Adam misjudges the amorous and festive pleasures of the "tents / Of wickedness" as "portend[ing] ... hope / Of peaceful days" (599–600). Such sights continue to distress him through Book 11 until at last the Flood abates and the rainbow appears—one of those natural signs that "God is as here ... still compassing thee round, / With goodness and paternal love, his face / Express, and of his steps the track divine." It is a leaf from the book of nature that Adam reads well:

> But say, what mean those coloured streaks in heaven,
> Distended as the brow of God appeased,
> Or serve they as a flowery verge to bind
> The fluid skirts of that same watery cloud,
> Lest it again dissolve and shower the earth?
> To whom the archangel. Dextrously thou aim'st.
>
> (11.879–84)

Book 11 concludes as Michael translates Adam's metaphorical interpretation of the rainbow as the brow of God's face in literal terms and gives him a lesson on how such signs should be read in the future, a brief instruction in meditating on fallen nature's works. What Michael teaches is a new way of reading: not simply the inferring of God's immediate purpose or state of mind from the observed phenomenon, but the recognition of the phenomenon as an arbitrarily stipulated reference to an historical event with enduring significance. The rainbow is a conventional as well as a natural sign, and hence a sign whose meaning Adam must be taught, just as he must be taught the meaning of the olive leaf as a "pacific sign" (11.860) and of baptism as the "sign" of being cleansed of "guilt of sin" (12.442–43). Michael explains:

> When he brings
> Over the earth a cloud, [God] will therein set

His triple-coloured bow, whereon to look
And call to mind his Covenant: day and night,
Seed time and harvest, heat and hoary frost
Shall hold their course, till fire purge all things new,
Both heaven and earth, wherein the just shall dwell.

(11.895–901)

Speaking Scripture

If Book 11 begins with visions of man defacing and disfiguring himself, Book 12 begins with a narration of man devoiced that recalls both the "universal hubbub wild ... and voices all confused" of chaos (2.951–52) and the "evil tongues," the "barbarous dissonance," and the "savage clamour [that] drowned / Both harp and voice" of which we heard in the prologue to Book 7. The first story Adam hears is of Nimrod and his followers and of their building of the tower of Babel. We hear how God

in derision sets
Upon their tongues a various spirit to raze
Quite out their native language, and instead
To sow a jangling noise of words unknown:
Forthwith a hideous gabble rises loud
Among the builders; each to other calls
Not understood, till hoarse, and all in rage,
As mocked they storm; great laughter was in heaven
And looking down, to see the hubbub strange
And hear the din; thus was the building left
Ridiculous, and the work Confusion named.

(12.52–62)

Once more, "wearied with [men's] iniquities," God chooses to "withdraw / His presence from among them" (12.107–8), and throughout most of the Old Testament history in Book 12 God's distance from man is stressed. He appears only to a few chosen men of faith. To Abraham he gives a "promise," though in what guise we are not told (12.137). To Moses he is present not in person but "in his angel, who shall go / Before them in a cloud, and pillar of fire" (12.201-2). From Sinai he ordains laws not vocally but "in thunder lightning and loud trumpets' sound" (12.229). By this point in the course of human history, "the voice of God / To mortal ear is dreadful," and to God there is "no access / Without mediator" (12.235–40). Throughout these passages Michael clarifies for Adam the true meaning of the proto-covenant, the promise that Eve's seed shall bruise the serpent's head. But the effect of his very gradual unfolding of that meaning is to emphasize by imitation the all but infinite deferral of the deliverer's final victory.

It is only during a brief passage following the account of Jesus' death and resurrection that Michael gives Adam or the reader any sense of worldly, as opposed to final, eschatological comfort. But Adam, whose ability to understand and judge what Michael tells him has steadily grown, wisely asks:

> But say, if our deliverer up to heaven
> Must reascend, what will betide the few
> His faithful, left among the unfaithful herd,
> The enemies of truth; who then shall guide
> His people, who defend? Will they not deal
> Worse with his followers than with him they dealt?
>
> (12.479–84)

Just as man's self-defacement in the early visions of Book 11 is countered by the appearance of the appeased brow of God that Adam sees in the final vision of the rainbow, so in Book 12 the confusion and destruction of language, the "jangling noise of words unknown" at Babel, are countered, if only temporarily, by Pentecost. To Adam's question Michael replies:

> Be sure they will, . . . but from heaven
> He to his own a Comforter will send,
> The promise of the Father, who shall dwell
> His Spirit within them, and the law of faith
> Working through love, upon their hearts shall write,
> To guide them in all truth. . . .
>   for the Spirit
> Poured first on his apostles, whom he sends
> To evangelize the nations, then on all
> Baptized, shall them with wondrous gifts endue
> To speak all tongues, and do all miracles,
> As did their Lord before them. Thus they win

> Great numbers of each nation to receive
> With joy the tidings brought from heaven: at length
> Their ministry performed, and race well run,
> Their doctrine and their story written left,
> They die.
>
> (12.485–507)

The emphasis here is not only on the gift of tongues, the restoration of speech, but also on the written Word—both the "law of faith" written in the apostles' hearts, and, in turn, their "story written"—not a rainbow, but a New Testament proclaiming a new covenant. The success of the evangelists, however, is short-lived. Just as the brief period of peace that followed the flood soon gave way to tyranny and war, so the purity of the early church will be corrupted:

> Wolves shall succeed for teachers, grievous wolves,
> Who all the sacred mysteries of heaven
> To their own vile advantages shall turn
> Of lucre and ambition, and the truth
> With superstitions and traditions taint,
> Left only in those written records pure,
> Though not but by the Spirit understood.
>
> (12.508–14)

If nature, as it manifests itself in such signs as the rainbow, "the brow of God appeased," is what must suffice for man as the face of God, "those written records pure," the Word of God, must suffice as his voice. What makes Michael's prophecy so bleak, and what so greatly tempers the joy with which Adam had greeted the news of Messiah's birth, is his presentation of history repeating itself in what almost seems a downward cycle. Michael's commentary on the pre-Christian era that the events at Babel inaugurate—"Thus will this latter, as the former world, / Still tend from bad to worse" (12.105–6)—is echoed by his final summary of the course of the Christian era itself: "So shall the world go on, / To good malignant, to bad men benign, / Under her own weight groaning" (12.537–39). Nimrod, with whom Michael's narrative begins, is a figure of secular tyranny. Adam calls him an "execrable son so to aspire / Above his brethren, to himself assuming / Authority usurped, from God not given" (12.64–66). He is, Raphael says, a subduer of "rational liberty"

(12.82), one of those "violent lords" who "enthral [man's] outward freedom" (12.93–94). The Christian church, in parallel fashion, tyrannizes over the spirit, subduing inner freedom, or liberty of conscience. It does so by creating its own linguistic babel through acts of arbitrary self-naming and the substitution of its own laws for those biblical "written records pure" and that "law of faith" which the Spirit had written on the apostles' hearts:

> Then shall they seek to avail themselves of names,
> Places and titles, and with these to join
> Secular power, though feigning still to act
> By spiritual, to themselves appropriating
> The Spirit of God, promised alike and given
> To all believers; and from that pretence,
> Spiritual laws by carnal power shall force
> On every conscience; laws which none shall find
> Left them enrolled, or what the Spirit within
> Shall on the heart engrave. What will they then
> But force the spirit of grace it self, and bind
> His consort liberty; what, but unbuild
> His living temples, built by faith to stand,
> Their own faith not another's.
>
> (12.515–28)

With his impassioned evocation of the Church's tyrannical appropriation of "the sacred mysteries of heaven" and of "the Spirit of God," Michael's language holds out faint hope for truth's survival. The Church will "taint" it with "superstitions and traditions," and it will be left only in the written "doctrine" and "story," the "records," of the evangelists. Michael has given much of that record to Adam orally. Like a catechist, he teaches Adam to read the Bible. The question is whether Adam has the Spirit required to understand. Does he, as Paul would say, have "the word of faith" even in his mouth and in his heart? (Rom. 10:8). I think that Milton wanted us to see Adam as not only hearing the Word but acquiring the ability, prior to his expulsion from Eden and his final severance from the actual presence of God and his angels, to speak it from his heart and on his own.

In that passage in *Christian Doctrine* where Milton is discussing the difficulty of getting at the truth through Scripture he murmurs rather plaintively, "I do not know why God's providence should have committed the contents of the New Testament to such wayward and uncertain guardians, unless it was so that this very fact might convince us that the Spirit which is given to us is a more certain guide than scripture, and that we ought to follow it." "We have," he writes, "particularly under the gospel, a double scripture. There is the external scripture of the written word and the internal scripture of the Holy Spirit which he, according to God's promise, has engraved upon the hearts of believers."[4] In support of that claim he cites Isaiah 59:21, in which Jehovah comes close to identifying his Spirit with his words: "My spirit which is in you, and my words which I have placed in your mouth, shall not leave your mouth or the mouth of your seed or the mouth of your seed's seed . . . from this time forward, for ever." What I wish to suggest is that Milton was at pains to dramatize Adam's possession of that guide which is more certain than Scripture itself, the unwritten, internal scripture. By the time he leaves Paradise, Adam has the words in his mouth.

Adam's progress toward understanding in Book 12 is as faltering, in its way, as it was in Book 11. If he continues to jump to premature conclusions, it is, as Regina Schwartz has observed, not altogether his fault, for Michael's narration is "replete with conclusions that will not finish, moments of revelation that are incomplete, and flashes of insight that turn out to be dim apprehensions."[5] Adam is not daunted, however, either by the unrelenting detail of Michael's discourse or by the speed with which he is carried over mile after mile of biblical turf.

Adam speaks five times during Michael's account. The first four speeches begin with a comment on what Michael has said and end with a question. He feels that he is learning a good deal, but he knows he does not know it all. As he gradually absorbs the significance of what Michael is telling him, his own idiom becomes increasingly biblical. His first two comments are expressed in biblical phrases that he has already heard. In the first he is able to remember and apply the words that God had spoken to him ("Have dominion over the fish of the sea, and over the fowl of the air, and over every living thing that moveth upon the earth" [Gen. 1:28; see also *PL* 8.339–41]) to reach an understanding of the nature of Nimrod's tyranny:

> O execrable son so to aspire
> Above his brethren, to himself assuming

> Authority usurped, from God not given:
> He gave us only over beast, fish, fowl
> Dominion absolute.
>
> (12.64–68)

In the second, after hearing Michael trace Abraham's progeny forward in time, he echoes both the archangel and Genesis when he replies:

> Gracious things
> Thou hast revealed, those chiefly which concern
> Just Abraham and his seed: now first I find
> Mine eyes true opening, and my heart much eased,
> Erewhile perplexed with thoughts what would become
> Of me and all mankind; but now I see
> His *day*, in whom all nations shall be blest.
>
> (12.271–77; my emphasis)

Schwartz points out that Adam appears to be confusing Abraham with Christ.[6] He is nevertheless quoting accurately Michael's assertion that "in [Abraham's] seed / All nations shall be blest" (12.125–26), perhaps conflating it with Michael's later reference to Christ, "whose *day* [Moses] shall foretell" and of whose times the prophets shall sing (12.240–44). He hasn't got it quite straight yet, but he's getting there.

More striking than this, however, is the question to which Michael's references to the imposition of laws have given rise in Adam's mind:

> This yet I apprehend not, why to those
> Among whom God will deign to dwell on earth
> So many and so various laws are given:
> So many laws argue so many sins
> Among them....
>
> (12.280–84)

Adam is puzzled by the need for "so many and so various laws," and senses the existence of a peculiar relationship between law and sin, as if his thoughts were leading him in the direction of passages from Paul's Letter to the Romans, such as "where no law is, there is no transgression" (4:15) or "Nay, I had not known sin, but by the law; for I had not known lust, except the law had said, Thou shalt not covet" (7:7). And it is Paul's treatment of the knotty connection between law and sin that Michael then attempts to untie.

As this passage suggests, Adam is beginning to speak with a biblical authority that is not directly learned. It seems, rather, to come from within. When Michael tells of the savior's birth, Adam responds as if, at first, he were hearing Gabriel's "glad tidings" (Luke 1:19), and then as if he were addressing Mary, with Gabriel's voice speaking through him. As he does so, he puts together two more pieces in the puzzle presented by the curse placed on the serpent:

> O prophet of glad tidings, finisher
> Of utmost hope! Now clear I understand
> What oft my steadiest thoughts have searched in vain,
> Why our great expectation should be called
> The seed of woman: virgin Mother, hail,
> High in the love of heaven, yet from my loins
> Thou shalt proceed, and from thy womb the Son
> Of God most high.
>
> (12.375–82)

And the virgin's name was Mary. And the angel came in unto her, and said, Hail, thou that art highly favoured.... Fear not, Mary: for thou hast found favour with God. And, behold, thou shalt conceive in thy womb, and bring forth a son.... He shall be great, and shall be called the Son of the Highest. (Luke 1:27–32)

Again, when Adam later rejoices to learn that from his sin "much more good thereof shall spring, / To God more glory, more good will to men / From God, and over wrath grace shall abound" (12.476–78), his lines blend words, phrases, and ideas from Luke and, more significantly, from Paul's letters, as if the Spirit were indeed working within him, giving him an abstract understanding of God's plan distinct from, though consistent with, Michael's narrative account of the Son's final triumph and of the last judgment.

For all things are for your sakes that the abundant grace might through the thanksgiving of many redound to the glory of God. (2 Cor. 4:15)

> Where sin abounded, grace did much more abound. (Rom. 5:20)
>
> We shall be saved from wrath through him. (Rom. 5:9)
>
> Good will toward men. (Luke 2:14)

Adam's rejoicing, however, is tempered by his recognition that the resurrection will not put an end to human suffering, and he poses his last question:

> But say, if our deliverer up to heaven
> Must reascend, what will betide the few
> His faithful, left among the unfaithful herd,
> The enemies of truth; who then shall guide
> His people, who defend? Will they not deal
> Worse with his followers than with him they dealt?
>
> (12.479–84)

To turn to, and to dwell upon, the last words Adam speaks in the poem is to realize just how well he has learned the lesson, for they constitute a beautifully compressed summary of the essential scriptural wisdom on how to live in a world such as the one Michael has described:

> Henceforth I learn, that to obey is best,
> And love with fear the only God, to walk
> As in his presence, ever to observe
> His providence, and on him sole depend,
> Merciful over all his works, with good
> Still overcoming evil, and by small
> Accomplishing great things, by things deemed weak
> Subverting worldly strong, and worldly wise
> By simply meek; that suffering for truth's sake
> Is fortitude to highest victory,
> And to the faithful death the gate of life;
> Taught this by his example whom I now
> Acknowledge my redeemer ever blest.
>
> (12.561–73)

Nowhere in the poem, I believe, can we find a more biblical idiom, a language that moves so easily between Old Testament and New.

Adam has been cut loose from his reliance on the heavenly beings who spoke the Word to him. In some instances one can identify an echo of a specific phrase, such as "His tender mercies are over all his works" (Ps. 145:9), or "Overcome evil with good" (Rom. 12:21), or "God hath chosen the foolish things of the world to confound the wise; and God hath chosen the weak things of the world to confound the things which are mighty" (1 Cor. 1:27). But the last five lines seem to blend freely several passages:

If ye suffer for righteousness' sake, happy are ye. (1 Pet. 3:14)

If, when ye do well, and suffer for it, ye take it patiently, this is acceptable with God. For even hereunto were ye called: because Christ also suffered for us, leaving us an example, that ye should follow his steps. (1 Pet. 2:20–21)

Be thou faithful unto death, and I will give thee a crown of life." (Rev. 2:10)

The analogues here are inexact, however, in a way that makes Adam's language both very biblical and very much his own. One also feels, for example, the presence of the notion that "for the suffering of death" Jesus "was crowned with glory" (Heb. 2:9), and of God's having "give[n] us the victory" through Christ's own "victory" over death (1 Cor. 15:57). In the assertion that "to the faithful death [is] the gate of life," the passage from Revelation seems to have been filtered (appropriately, given the subject matter) through the Collect for Easter Day in the Book of Common Prayer: "Almighty God, which through thy only begotten Son Jesus Christ, hast overcome death, and opened unto us the gate of everlasting life."

As for the opening lines of Adam's passage, however, the search for particular passages becomes even more pointless, since the Bible everywhere enjoins us to obey, love, and fear the only God. The fact that Adam is offering what Michael will call the "sum of wisdom" reminds us that in Ecclesiasticus the fear of the Lord is not only "the beginning of wisdom," but "fulness of wisdom," "a crown of wisdom," and "the root of wisdom" (1:14–20). But larger clusters of the ideas of the opening lines can be found in many places, as in Deuteronomy: "The Lord your God proveth you, to know whether ye love the Lord your God with all your heart and with all your soul. Ye shall walk after the Lord your God, and fear him, and keep his commandments, and obey his voice, and ye shall serve him, and cleave unto him" (13:3–4).

Adam's wonderful phrase, "to walk as in his presence," is profoundly biblical, but is nowhere to be found in the Bible. He did not learn from Michael the Hebraic use of walking as a metaphor for spiritual conduct or for living itself. Moses was instructed to teach the people "the way wherein they must walk." It is good, to cite only a few examples, to walk *in the paths* of the Lord, to walk *uprightly,* and *by faith.* It is bad to walk *contrary to* the Lord, or *after other gods,* or *after the flesh.* As for God's presence, the Lord assures Moses, "My presence shall go with thee, and I will give thee rest" (Exod. 33:14). The psalms express faith that "thou wilt shew me the path of life: in thy presence is fulness of joy" (Ps. 16:11) and that "the upright shall dwell in thy presence" (Ps. 140:13). Adam's own experience has taught him what it means to be separated (*cast away,* in biblical terms, or *hidden,* or *departed*) from God's presence. His nonbiblical *as* picks up on Michael's having told him that though God will never again be present to him quite as he had been in Paradise, he must "doubt not" that "God is *as* here" (11.349–50). To "walk as in his presence," then, is to live with a faith in things unseen. It is a succinct and beautifully simple version of Paul's confidence that while we are "absent from the Lord . . . we walk by faith, not by sight. Wherefore we labour, that, whether present or absent, we may be accepted of him" (2 Cor. 5:6–9).

Adam, in short, has so caught the Spirit of what Michael has told him that he can express it, in effect, as Scripture. God had praised Adam's ability to name the beasts as "expressing well the spirit within [him] free" (8.440). If Adam lost the gift of naming things rightly when he fell, he has gained something more necessary, and equally expressive of the Spirit within. Michael assents to Adam almost in the tones of a teacher approving of his pupil, but offering further exhortation, placing in a new perspective not only secret wisdom, but even that knowledge of names and of "all nature's works" which is frequently thought to epitomize Adam's prelapsarian wisdom:

> This having learned, thou hast attained the sum
> Of wisdom; hope no higher, though all the stars
> Thou knew'st by name, and all the ethereal powers,

> All secrets of the deep, all nature's works,
> Or works of God in heaven, air, earth, or sea,
> And all the riches of this world enjoyed'st,
> And all the rule, one empire; only add
> Deeds to thy knowledge answerable, add faith,
> Add virtue, patience, temperance, add love,
> By name to come called Charity, the soul
> Of all the rest: then wilt thou not be loath
> To leave this Paradise, but shalt possess
> A paradise within thee, happier far.
>
> (12.575–87)

Michael casts a new light on the sort of knowledge Adam sought and received from Raphael. Milton knew, of course, as did the Satan of *Paradise Regained,* that Jesus was "wiser far / Than *Solomon,* of more exalted mind," but also that the wisdom of Jesus could embrace much of the wisdom of Solomon.[7] Solomon tells us that God answered his prayer for wisdom by giving him "certain knowledge of the things that are ... the operation of the elements ... the positions of the stars: the natures of living creatures ... and all such things as are either secret or manifest" (Wisd. 7). If Michael does not reject such wisdom, he all but dismisses it as inconsequential when compared to the ethical and spiritual wisdom Adam has attained. Yet in rejecting "all the riches of this world ... and all the rule," he paraphrases Solomon's own comparison: "I preferred her [Wisdom] before scepters and thrones, and esteemed riches nothing in comparison of her." And as Solomon's praise of wisdom continues in chapter 8, it is an ethical wisdom he describes, a wisdom defined by what were to become the four cardinal virtues of the Christian faith: "And if a man love righteousness, [Wisdom's] labours are virtues: for she teacheth temperance and prudence, justice and fortitude: which are such things, as men can have nothing more profitable in their life" (Wisd. 8:7). Michael accepts but supplements this classical formulation, enclosing it in the syntax of the definitive New Testament passage from 2 Peter:

> And beside this, giving all diligence, add to your faith virtue; and to virtue knowledge; and to knowledge temperance; and to temperance patience; and to patience godliness; and to godliness

brotherly kindness; and to brotherly kindness charity. For if these things be in you, and abound, they make you that ye shall neither be barren nor unfruitful in the knowledge of our Lord Jesus Christ. (1:5–8)

The fact that Adam and Eve used the words God spoke to them to recover their faith in his mercy, coupled with the success of Michael's scripture lesson, might suggest that when Milton used the phrases "the sum of wisdom" and "a paradise within" he was referring to something like Bonaventure's garden of scriptural delight: "The soul in which Scripture has been planted is a *paradise,* and it is wonderfully pleasant and agreeable.... This is the garden eternal wisdom loves, and in which she abides.... This garden is watered by the stream flowing from the Holy spirit."[8]

History and the Passions

Seen from Adam's or Michael's point of view, Michael's visions and narrations are prophecy. Seen from Milton's or our own, they are for the most part sacred history. The style of Books 11 and 12, according to Louis Martz, is a "lowered style, so low in places that Milton seems to become almost an ordinary versifier of biblical history."[9] It was, then, for Milton, the right style. Milton was convinced that if historians tell the unembellished truth, that truth alone will produce its appropriate effects. Certainly the style Martz describes accords with Milton's view of how history ought to be written. In his *History of Britain* he described his aim in these simple terms: "to relate well and orderly things worth the noting, so as may best instruct and benefit them that read."[10] And in 1657, responding to a letter from Henry de Brass asking him to set out his views on the writing of history, Milton wrote:

> He who would write of worthy deeds worthily must... relate them distinctly and gravely in pure and chaste speech. That he should do so in ornate style, I do not much care about; for I want a Historian, not an Orator.... If the Historian, in explicating counsels and narrating facts, follows truth most of all, and not his own fancy or conjecture, he fulfils his proper duty.[11]

It is not a bad description of what Michael achieved: a compendium of biblical history and prophecy related "distinctly and gravely in pure and chaste speech." One of Michael's purposes in Books 11 and 12 is to instruct Adam. But there is more to it than that. What God is aiming at is nothing less than the creation of a new state of mind in Adam—a state of feeling based on understanding and faith. Herein lay his mercy. He had told Michael to teach Adam of the future "lest they faint / At the sad sentence rigorously urged." "Dismiss them not disconsolate.... So send them forth, though sorrowing, yet in peace" (11.108–17). And Michael introduces his lesson in future history in similar terms:

> Know I am sent
> To shew thee what shall come in future days
> To thee and to thy offspring . . .
>   thereby to learn
> True patience, and to temper joy with fear
> And pious sorrow, equally inured
> By moderation either state to bear,
> Prosperous or adverse.
>
> (11.356–64)

We are less accustomed than Milton was to thinking of the purpose of the study of history in such affective terms. He saw the genre of history, as Aristotle saw tragedy, as aiming at an exercise in, and education of, the emotions. He introduced *Of Reformation*, his first published tract, and itself a history of sorts, with the following claim:

> Amidst those deepe and retired thoughts, with which every man Christianly instructed, ought to be most frequent, of *God,* and of his miraculous *ways,* and *works,* amongst men, and of our *Religion* and *Worship,* to be perform'd to him; after the story of our Saviour *Christ,* suffering to the lowest bent of weaknesse, in the *Flesh,* and presently triumphing to the highest pitch of *glory,* in the *Spirit,* which drew up his body also, till we in both be united to him in the Revelation of his Kingdome: I do not know of any thing more worthy to take up the whole passion of pitty, on the one side, and joy on the other: then to consider first, the foule and sudden corruption, and then after many a tedious age, the long-deferr'd, but

much more wonderfull and happy reformation of the *Church* in these latter dayes.[12]

In the 1660's Milton would have had scant reason to rejoice at the "happy reformation" of the Church, but God's "miraculous ways, and works, amongst men," do constitute, as French Fogle has pointed out, his definition of the subject matter of history.[13] And we may add that the passions evoked in him by the history of the church, and much more by the history of the suffering and triumph of Christ— the movement from pity at the thought of a past debasement or corruption toward joy at some "long-deferr'd" or still unaccomplished happy event—catch the very rhythms of Adam's emotional education under Michael's tutelage: his response, say, to the story of the Flood ("Far less I now lament for one whole world / Of wicked sons destroyed, than I rejoice / For one man found so perfect and so just" [11.874–76]), or to the good news of Jesus' triumph over Satan ("Full of doubt I stand, / Whether I should repent me now of sin / By me done and occasioned, or rejoice / Much more, that much more good thereof shall spring" [12.473–76]).

This education, this trial of the emotions, begins as Michael forces Adam to relive the torments and despair of his fruitless meditation in Book 10, gradually alleviating them by placing them within a larger framework of understanding. Indeed without Michael's guidance the visions of Cain's murdering of Abel, of the lazar-house, and of the Flood, might well have left Adam once again in a maze, an "abyss of fears / And horrors ... from deep to deeper plunged" (10.842–44), unable to see justice in the death of the pious, devoted Abel, or in the "unsightly sufferings" and "deformities" of the sick and dying. In his meditation Adam had been led to seek his own death as a release from his conviction of his own sinfulness:

> How gladly would I meet
> Mortality my sentence, and be earth
> Insensible, how glad would lay me down
> As in my mother's lap? There I should rest
> And sleep secure; his dreadful voice no more
> Would thunder in my ears, no fear of worse
> To me and to my offspring would torment me
> With cruel expectation.
>
> (10.775–82)

In Book 11, when he sees the "many shapes" of sickness and death he expresses a similar feeling—similar, but universalized, directed not toward "me" but toward "us," mankind, with whom he now fully identifies:

> O miserable mankind, to what fall
> Degraded, to what wretched state reserved!
> Better end here unborn. Why is life given
> To be thus wrested from us? Rather why
> Obtruded on us thus? Who if we knew
> What we receive, would either not accept
> Life offered, or soon beg to lay it down,
> Glad to be so dismissed in peace.
>
> (11.500–507)

The more godlike Adam's knowledge becomes—the more, that is, his mind sees past, present, and future at once—the more unbearable that knowledge becomes. In that respect he is acting out the Preacher's observation that "in much wisdom is much grief: and he that increaseth knowledge increaseth sorrow" (Eccles. 1:18). If he suffers mightily in his meditation when he imagines his cursed offspring, and the curses they will level at him, the actual sight of the evils that shall befall his children and their children's children makes him experience such torment that he wishes for ignorance:

> O visions ill foreseen! Better had I
> Lived ignorant of future, so had borne
> My part of evil only, each day's lot
> Enough to bear; those now, that were dispensed
> The burden of many ages, on me light
> At once, by my foreknowledge gaining birth
> Abortive, to torment me ere their being,
> With thought that they must be.
>
> (11.763–70)

Kathleen Swaim has urged that it is Raphael who is "primarily responsible for supplying Adam with vicarious experience, and Michael with fortifying Adam's faith." Raphael, she says, supplies him with "the equivalent of experience, to give him a past that will allow valid measurement of his present."[14] But if we were to judge from

Adam's emotional responses to what Michael shows and tells him, it would appear that Michael is giving him a truly intense experience of the future. Adam's characteristic response to Raphael is one of wonder and gratitude. Not so with Michael. As the visions of the future continue, Adam is subjected to a harrowing course of upward and downward emotional swings, making him experience, in rapid succession, dismay, compassion and fear, pity and shame, lamentation, grief, joy, fatherly displeasure, abhorrence, ease of heart, a "surcharge" of joy, wonder, and, finally, "peace of thought." It is not necessary to analyze these responses, or Michael's corrective commentaries upon them, in detail; that has been done well by many others.[15] The point is simply Milton's insistence on dramatizing the affective power of historical fact, especially on one who not only believes what he is shown or told but is also seeing or hearing it for the first time. In the light of Adam and Eve's last, and silent, expression of feeling as they leave Paradise—"Some natural tears they dropped, but wiped them soon" (12.645)—it is touching to return to one of Milton's earliest extant writings, an academic exercise in which he mounts an attack on the study of the useless, barren controversies of scholastic philosophy that "certainly have no power to stir up the passions of the soul." In their place he holds up not only "divine Poetry" and "Rhetoric," but also, and climactically, "History," which, "finely and harmoniously ordered, now soothes and composes the restless tumults of the soul, now anoints with joy, the next moment calls forth tears, but tears such as are gentle and agreeable, and bring with them I know not what sort of sorrowful pleasure."[16]

There are few works of literature whose endings are so "finely and harmoniously ordered," so perfectly balanced, as the ending of *Paradise Lost*—balanced, in almost every line, between sorrow and pleasure, nostalgia and expectation. Adam does not leave Paradise possessed of a paradise within him happier far, but only with the knowledge that it lies within his power to create one. The poem achieves a fully satisfying sense of closure not in spite of the open-endedness of the as yet unwritten lives of Adam and Eve, but because of it. As Michael prepares to lead Adam and Eve out of Eden, he passes the tutorial task that God had assigned him on to Adam:

    Go, waken Eve;
. . . .

> Let her with thee partake what thou hast heard,
> Chiefly what may concern her faith to know,
> The great deliverance by her seed to come
> (For by the woman's seed) on all mankind.
> That ye may live, which will be many days,
> Both in one faith unanimous though sad,
> With cause for evils past, yet much more cheered
> With meditation on the happy end.
>
> (12.594–605)

The reader must feel a certain relief at the subsequent picture of Adam, like a schoolboy after classes are over, running on ahead of Michael to rejoin Eve, who greets him with sober yet pleasing words which suggest, as Maureen Quilligan has pointed out,[17] that in fact she has already been instructed, not by Michael but by God himself:

> Whence thou return'st, and whither went'st, I know;
> For God is also in sleep, and dreams advise,
> Which he hath sent propitious, some great good
> Presaging, since with sorrow and heart's distress
> Wearied I fell asleep.
>
> (12.610–14)

If Michael had resolved Adam's earlier doubts and fears about the nature of God's justice and his merciful providence, Eve resolves any lingering doubts about her willingness to leave Paradise with Adam. Her testimonies of her love look back deep into the poem even as they point toward the uncertain future. When she directs Adam, "But now lead on; / In me is no delay" (12.614–15), we sense the change that her experience has wrought in her since Milton's first description of her "sweet reluctant amorous delay" (4.311), and find in that contrast an image of what she has lost and gained. Though she casts herself in the role of follower, she does so with a straightforward, almost imperative sureness of mind, far less submissive, far less passive, than when she had accepted Satan's offer of his conduct to the tree: "Lead then, said Eve" (9.631). At the same time, in the context of their imminent departure from an Eden now "torrid" and "parched," her lines allude to Anchises' words as Aeneas prepares to leave the burning city of Troy: "*Iam iam nulla mora est; sequor et, qua ducitis, adsum*" ("Now, now is no delay: I follow and, where you lead,

I am near").[18] The allusion reminds us that this epic ends, in a sense, at a point where, in the *Aeneid,* the major hardships are yet to come.

The last words that Adam heard Eve speak before going off with Raphael expressed her extreme dismay at the thought of leaving her "native soil, these happy walks and shades," her garden, her nuptial bower (11.268–85). If Adam has any doubts about her willingness to depart, she allays them: "With thee to go, / Is to stay here; without thee here to stay, / Is to go hence unwilling." These lovely lines, which recapture something of her lost lyricism, seem designed to address, and to heal, the hurt pride that was felt in Adam's reluctant granting of his permission to let her work in the garden alone. They return to him what he thought she had taken away: "Go; for thy stay, not free, absents thee more" (9.372). Satan was never able to capitalize on the positive implication of his belief that "the mind is its own place, and in itself / Can make a heaven of hell" (1.254–55). But Eve, now, can do so: "Thou to me / Art all things under heaven, all places thou, / Who for my wilful crime art banished hence." She concludes by expressing her own grateful understanding of that curse upon the serpent whose meaning she had been the first to glimpse, and it is fitting that the last words spoken in the poem should look forward to the annunciation ("thou has found favour with God") even as they recall the poem's opening sentence ("till one greater man restore us"):

> This further consolation yet secure
> I carry hence; though all by me is lost,
> Such favour I unworthy am vouchsafed,
> By me the promised seed shall all restore.
>
> (12.620–23)

To carry hence a consoling thought is also, and necessarily, to keep in mind that fault or grief or loss which created the need for consolation. Consolation thus carries within itself that doubleness, that sense of balance, which characterizes not only Eve's speech but the rest of the episode. The descriptive passage that follows contains images of violent threat—"the brandished sword of God" blazing "fierce as a comet," the "dreadful faces" and "fiery arms"—yet to them, too, Milton provided a counterweight. As Martz points out, Michael does not, as God had directed him to, "drive out the sinful pair" (11.105). He is pictured, rather, as taking their hands and leading them to safety.[19] There is something ominous in the simile which describes the descending cherubim, but something consoling too:

> The cherubim descended; on the ground
> Gliding meteorous, as evening mist
> Risen from a river o'er the marish glides,
> And gathers ground fast at the labourer's heel
> Homeward returning.
>
> (12.628–32)

Even before the Fall, it was Adam's and Eve's labor that declared their "dignity" and "the regard of heaven" on all their ways (4.619–20). And this laborer is "homeward returning." By implication Adam and Eve, too are returning home, partly canceling, in effect, our sense that they are leaving an old place for a new. They are turning to a home scarcely to be distinguished, in its essential features, from the place from whence they fell. Their tears—"Some natural tears they dropped, but wiped them soon"—seem halfway between the careful tears that Eve "let fall" when first she felt remorse and needed cheering and those with which the two, together, "watered the ground" and begged God's pardon with "sorrow unfeigned." As in Eden, they will in the world that is "all before them" be free to wander and to choose. Like the garden, it will be a world in which it is easy to lose one's way. They leave with a new guide, providence, which is the foresight Michael had given them of God's wise governance of the world. The new guide will no more prevent their making wrong choices than Raphael's warning did, should they fail to observe it. As they yielded to temptation, and fell, and suffered, in Eden, so they may yield and fall and suffer when they leave. But perhaps not. The future is in their hands, as it always was, and they, once more, are in each other's hands.

Appendixes

APPENDIX A

The Prologues to Books 3 and 7

In chapter 3 I argued that the prologues to Books 3 and 7 set forth the dominant themes of the four books that follow them: the themes of vision and the reading of nature's works in the first instance, and hearing and obedience to the Word in the second. Roger Sundell has correctly pointed out that in one sense the prologues to Books 1 and 7 are similar in design insofar as they both conclude by posing direct questions to the muse: "Say first... what cause / Moved our grand parents... to fall off from their creator, and transgress his will?" (1.27–31); "Say goddess, what ensued when Raphael... had forewarned / Adam by dire example to beware / Apostasy?" (7.40–43).[1] But it is also clear that the first verse paragraph of the prologue to Book 7 was designed so as to align it very closely with the entire prologue to Book 3.

These two segments are personal in a sense in which the first invocation is not. In the first it is not Milton, but his song, "that with no middle flight intends to soar / Above the Aonian mount, while it pursues / Things unattempted yet in prose or rhyme" (1.14–16). Though one may read "what in me is dark / Illumine, what is low raise and support" (1.22–23) as referring to Milton's condition, one would hardly be able to infer from these universal metaphors for ignorance and humility alone that we are in the hands of a blind poet compassed round with danger.

One can get a sense of the unique importance of the prologues to Books 3 and 7 as structural foci within the poem by noting just how closely the rhythms of the poet's thoughts and feelings parallel each other in ways that distinguish them from the equally powerful but very different prologues to Books 1 and 9. Both begin with uncertain, deferential addresses, the first to Light, the second to Urania, the "voice divine." The deference in each case is expressed through Milton's hesitation over what name or names to use:

> Hail, holy Light, offspring of heaven first-born,
> Or of the eternal co-eternal beam
> May I express thee unblamed? . . .
> Or hear'st thou rather pure ethereal stream,
> Whose fountain who shall tell?
>
> (3.1–8)

> Descend from heaven Urania, by that name
> If rightly thou art called. . . .
> The meaning, not the name I call.
>
> (7.1–5)

In both passages, however, Milton's voice quickly takes on a deeply assured tone, demonstrating a knowledge that reaches back to "the beginnings" and beyond, as if the power or powers addressed had already answered his request and were speaking through him.

> Before the sun,
> Before the heavens thou wert, and at the voice
> Of God, as with a mantle didst invest
> The rising world of waters dark and deep,
> Won from the void and formless infinite.
>
> (3.8–12)

> Before the hills appeared, or fountain flowed,
> Thou with eternal Wisdom didst converse,
> Wisdom thy sister, and with her didst play
> In presence of the almighty Father, pleased
> With thy celestial song.
>
> (7.8–12)

Both prologues then introduce images of divinely guided flight and safe return: the first "through utter and through middle darkness" and back up toward light, which Milton "revisits safe" (3.16–21); the second upward "into the heaven of heavens," followed by the request, "with like safety guided down / Return me to my native element" (7.13–17). From these "revisitings" or "returnings" we move next to brief but powerful descriptions of Milton's own situation:

> But thou
> Revisit'st not these eyes, that roll in vain

> To find thy piercing ray, and find no dawn;
> So thick a drop serene hath quenched their orbs,
> Or dim suffusion veiled.
>
> (3.22–26)

> though fallen on evil days,
> On evil days though fallen, and evil tongues;
> In darkness, and with dangers compassed round,
> And solitude.
>
> (7.25–28)

Then, just as Milton seems to be losing himself to the spirit of complaint, perhaps even of self-pity, he reins his feelings in and counters that mood with his determination, aided by his muse, to continue writing:

> Yet not the more
> Cease I to wander where the Muses haunt
> Clear spring, or shady grove, or sunny hill.
>
> (3.26–28)

> yet not alone, while thou
> Visit'st my slumbers nightly, or when morn
> Purples the east.
>
> (7.28–30)

In Book 3, following his account of his nightly visits to the Muses' haunts, he proceeds to give full play to his sense of loss. Again, however, he counters that movement with a prayer that the "celestial Light / Shine inward," leaving us not with loss but with the poet's positive ambition to "see and tell / Of things invisible to mortal sight." The prologue to Book 7 ends on a less uplifted note, its prayer that "the barbarous dissonance of Bacchus and his revellers" be driven off ending not with an energetic thrust forward, but with a reminder that Calliope could not save Orpheus, and with a rather more urgent plea to Urania: "So fail not thou, who thee implores: / For thou art heavenly, she an empty dream."

In both prologues Milton presents himself as a figure engaged in a struggle to sustain patience and to keep faith both in himself and in the divine inspiration on which he relies. Patience suggests suffering, and the endurance of pain, and indeed the sense of Milton's suffering is strong in both passages. Just below the surface, but well mastered, there is an attitude almost approaching, in the first, resentment, and in the second, fear. It can be heard in lines like "but thou / Revisit'st not these eyes, that roll in vain / To find thy piercing ray, and find no dawn" (3.22–24), which attribute the fault to the light rather than to the eyes, or in the lament in which Milton appears as the object—almost, indeed, the victim—of deprivation:

> Thus with the year
> Seasons return, but not to me returns
> Day, or the sweet approach of even or morn,
> Or sight of vernal bloom, or summer's rose,
> Or flocks, or herds, or human face divine;
> But cloud in stead, and ever-during dark
> Surrounds me, from the cheerful ways of men
> Cut off, and for the book of knowledge fair
> Presented with a universal blank
> Of nature's works to me expunged and razed,
> And wisdom at one entrance quite shut out.
>
> (3.40–50)

"Cut off" and "shut out," each highlighted by its position and followed by a strong stop, express by their very curtness a sense of finality. "Expunged" and "razed" are painfully physical—pricked out, slashed, rasped or scraped away—and though their immediate syntactical application is to nature's works, it is difficult, perhaps because of the earlier description of the poet's eyes seeking the sun's "piercing" ray, not to apply these participles to the eyes as well.

In the invocation to Book 7 the "ever-during dark" of the earlier invocation is still present, but it is largely superseded by solitude, muteness, and dissonance as the chief dangers to be warded off: "evil tongues" without, silence within. The dread of physical violence, of the "wild rout that tore the Thracian bard" and the "savage clamour" that "drowned / Both harp and voice," is keenly felt. Only the mythological vehicle of expression manages to keep these dangers at a distance and hence at bay. But in both passages, as I suggested, the sense of having been hurt, and the threat of being hurt, are offset by humility, determination, gratitude, and prayer. Both passages direct us toward the future, the first toward what remains to be seen, the second, more tentatively, toward what remains to be sung. We are given a sense of the poem in the process of being wrought, and wrought in the face of hardship.

APPENDIX B

Augustine, the Creatures, and the Love of God

The first two paragraphs of the sixth chapter of the tenth book of Augustine's *Confessions* may, I believe, have laid a strong hold on Milton's poetic imagination and inspired two of the passages that have occupied our attention on more than one occasion in the preceding pages. Milton transformed the two paragraphs, I would suggest, into Eve's love poem ("With thee conversing I forget all time" [4.639–68]) and Adam's questioning of the creatures ("tell, / Tell, if ye saw, how came I thus, how here?" [8.257–85]). The first paragraph, in the 1631 translation by William Watts, reads as follows:

> Not out of a doubtful, but with a certain conscience do I love thee, O Lord: thou hast stricken my heart with thy word, and thereupon I loved thee. Yea, also the heaven, and the earth, and all that is in them, behold they bid me on every side that I should love thee.... What now do I love, whenas I love thee? Not the beauty of any corporal thing; not the [splendor of the season], not the brightness of the light which we do behold, so gladsome to our eyes: not the pleasant melodies of songs of all kinds; nor the fragrant smell of flowers, and ointment, and spices: not manna and honey; nor any fair limbs that are so acceptable to fleshly embracements. I love none of these things whenas I love my God: and yet I love a certain kind of light, and a kind of voice, and a kind of fragrance, and a kind of meat, and a kind of embracement, whenas I love my God: who is both the light and the voice, and the sweet smell, and the meat, and the embracement of my inner man: where that light shineth into my soul, which no place can receive; that voice soundeth, which time deprives me not of; and that

fragrancy smelleth, which no wind scatters; and that meat tasteth, which eating devours not; and that embracement clingeth to me, which satiety divorceth not. This it is which I love, whenas I love my God.[1]

The similarities should be relatively apparent. Augustine begins by testifying to the way God's word has stricken his heart, just as Eve testifies to the effect of conversing with Adam. Eve's declaration of love contains two long sentences, and Augustine's three, consisting of phrases designating the beautiful objects of sense experience, with the later sentences repeating the list set forth in the first. In the passage from the *Confessions* the phrases in the first list use the negative, while in Eve's lines the negations come in the second (e.g., "neither breath of morn when she ascends / With charm of earliest birds, nor rising sun . . . nor herb, fruit, flower . . . nor fragrance after showers"). Both passages in effect dismiss the objects of the natural world in favor of the true object of the speaker's love, and yet both succeed wonderfully in foregrounding nature's beauty in ways that render its innocent but very powerful appeal unmistakable.

The first paragraph from the *Confessions* ends with the statement, "This it is which I love, whenas I love my God," and the next paragraph begins with a briefer version of his earlier question, "What now do I love, whenas I love thee?":

And what is this? I asked the earth, and that answered me: I am not it; and whatsoever are in it made the same confession. I asked the sea and the deeps, and the creeping things, and they answered me: We are not thy God, seek above us [cf. Adam's "Straight toward heaven my wondering eyes I turned"]. . . . I asked the heavens, the sun and moon and stars: Nor, say they, are we the God whom thou seekest. And I replied unto all these, which stand so round about these doors of my flesh: Answer me concerning my God, since that you are not he, answer me something of him. And they cried out with a loud voice: He made us. My questioning with them was my thought; and their answer was their beauty. And I turned myself unto myself, and said to myself: Who art thou? And I answered: a Man; for behold here is a soul and a body in me; one without, and the other within. . . . I asked the whole frame of the world concerning my God, and that answered me: I am not he, but he made me.

Milton must have sensed the appropriateness of the childlike simplicity of Augustine's charming story to Adam's first postnatal experience. He echoes the movement from the outer world to the self: "And I turned myself unto myself." "Myself I then perused" (8.267). But the creatures in Adam's story do not, like Augustine's, actually speak. They answer only by smiling, by looking "fair," and remaining silent. The world answers Augustine's question. But Adam answers his own, thus placing the emphasis both on Adam's powers of reasoning, and on his ignorance, at this point, of his "great maker's" name.

Notes

Introduction

1. All quotations from *Paradise Lost* are from Alastair Fowler's edition (London: Longman Group, 1971). Hereafter abbreviated as *PL*. Milton's other poems are quoted from *Complete Poems and Major Prose*, ed. Merritt Y. Hughes (Indianapolis: Odyssey, 1957).
2. I am thinking in particular of John R. Knott, Jr., *The Sword of the Spirit: Puritan Responses to the Bible* (Chicago: University of Chicago Press, 1980); Georgia B. Christopher, *Milton and the Science of the Saints* (Princeton: Princeton University Press, 1982), William G. Madsen, "The Idea of Nature in Milton's Poetry," in *Three Studies in the Renaissance: Sidney, Jonson, Milton*, ed. Richard B. Young, W. Todd Furniss, and William G. Madsen (New Haven: Yale University Press, 1958); Kathleen M. Swaim, *Before and after the Fall: Contrasting Modes in Paradise Lost* (Amherst: University of Massachusetts Press, 1986); and Robert L. Entzminger, *Divine Word: Milton and the Redemption of Language* (Pittsburgh: Duquesne University Press, 1985).
3. Louis L. Martz, *Poet of Exile: A Study of Milton's Poetry* (New Haven: Yale University Press, 1980), 138–39.
4. See Joan S. Bennett, *Reviving Liberty: Radical Christian Humanism in Milton's Great Poems* (Cambridge: Harvard University Press, 1989), especially chapter 1, "Hooker, Milton, and the Radicalization of Christian Humanism."
5. But see Elizabeth Ely Fuller, *Milton's Kinesthetic Vision in Paradise Lost* (Lewisburg, Pa.: Bucknell University Press, 1983), 54–55, 176–81, and Thomas Merrill, *Epic God-Talk: Paradise Lost and the Grammar of Religious Language* (Jefferson, N.C.: McFarland and Co., 1986).
6. See Samuel Johnson's "Life of Milton," *Lives of the English Poets*, ed. George Birkbeck Hill (Oxford: Oxford University Press, 1905), 1:189, and T. S. Eliot, "Milton II" (1947), in *On Poetry and Poets* (New York: Farrar, Straus and Giroux, 1979), 177. For yet another example see Walter Raleigh, *Milton* (New York: G. P. Putnam's Sons, 1900), 153.
7. Virginia R. Mollenkott, "Milton and the Apocrypha" (Ph.D. diss., New York University, 1964), 254–67.

8. David Loewenstein, *Milton and the Drama of History: Historical Vision, Iconoclasm, and the Literary Imagination* (Cambridge: Cambridge University Press, 1990), 108.
9. I disagree with Kathleen Swaim's claim, in the second chapter of *Before and after the Fall*, that Raphael offers lessons only in the book of nature, Michael only in Scripture. Raphael, for example, spends most of Book 7 taking them through the first two chapters of Genesis, and in Book 11 Michael teaches Adam to read the signs of God's presence in nature.

Chapter 1

1. Unless otherwise noted, italics in this chapter are my own.
2. See *Areopagitica* in *Complete Poems and Major Prose*, ed. Hughes, 728–29, and John Dryden, "Preface to the Fables" (1700), in *Essays*, ed. W. P. Ker (1900; reprint, New York: Russell and Russell, 1961), 2:247.
3. Quotations from the "Fowre Hymnes" are from *Edmund Spenser's Poetry*, sel. and ed. Hugh MacLean (New York: W. W. Norton and Co., 1968). The "Hymne of Heavenly Beautie" is hereafter abbreviated as *HHB*, the "Hymne of Heavenly Love" abbreviated *HHL*.
4. Arnold Stein, *The Art of Presence: The Poet and Paradise Lost* (Berkeley and Los Angeles: University of California Press, 1977), 23.
5. Stein, *Art of Presence*, 22.
6. From Baldassare Castiglione, *The Book of the Courtier*, Bk. 4, trans. Sir Thomas Hoby (1561) (London: David Nutt, 1900), 360.
7. In a review of David Spitz's *The Real World of Liberalism* that appeared in *Dissent* (Summer 1984), the late Richard Krouse summarized the "authentic liberal tradition" represented by both Spitz and John Stuart Mill in terms that cannot but remind a Miltonist of *Areopagitica* and *Paradise Lost*:

   The true liberal must . . . esteem liberty above all other values—even, in circumstances where they conflict, equality. . . . Liberty is a necessary condition for the exercise of *choice*. And the exercise of choice in turn is a necessary condition for the development of those powers and capacities—above all, reason and individuality—that define us as human. . . . A liberal can believe confidently in certain objective truths yet still favor tolerance of competing untruths. For if individuals develop their powers and capacities only through the exercise of choice, then no conception of truth, however infallible, can simply be imposed *ex cathedra*; individuals must be free to choose between competing conceptions, through the exercise of autonomous deliberation, if they are to grasp the grounds of truth. (372–74)

   For an argument which would qualify the notion that *Areopagitica* puts forth "a classic liberal vision," see Stanley Fish's "Driving from the Letter: Truth and Indeterminacy in Milton's *Areopagitica*," in *Re-membering Milton: Essays on the Texts and Traditions*, ed. Mary Nyquist and Margaret W. Ferguson (New York: Methuen, 1987), 234–54.

8. As William Kerrigan put it, "The central theological issue of *Paradise Lost* is freedom. The poem argues time after time that its major characters are free to stand or fall. Freedom is the primary concept that vindicates the goodness of the Creator and justifies His ways to man; freedom is the cornerstone of this great argument" (*The Prophetic Milton* [Charlottesville: University of Virginia Press, 1974], 146). See also Dennis Richard Danielson, *Milton's Good God: A Study in Literary Theodicy* (Cambridge: Cambridge University Press, 1982), chapters 4 and 5.
9. *Poet of Exile*, 138–39.

Chapter 2

1. According to Sidney, "[Nature's] world is brazen, the poets only deliver a golden." See Sir Philip Sidney, *The Defense of Poesy*, ed. Albert S. Cook (Boston: Ginn and Co., 1890), 7–8.
2. Richard Hooker, *Of the Laws of Ecclesiastical Polity* 2.1.4 (London: J. M. Dent and Sons, 1907; reprint, New York: Dutton, 1963), 2:237.
3. The woman has been identified as Wisdom by J. van der Meulen. See Engelbert Kirschbaum, *Der Christlichen Ikonographie* (Rome: Herder, 1972), 4.120–21. See also Johannes Zahlten, *Creatio Mundi: Darstellungen der sechs Schöpfungstage und naturwissen schaftliches Weltbild im Mittelalter* (Stuttgart: Ernst Klett, 1979), 56, 117. Given the tendency of the cult of the Virgin Mary and its liturgies to associate her with the Wisdom of Proverbs and Ecclesiasticus, it is sometimes difficult in medieval art to know whether a particular woman represents Wisdom or the Virgin. In an article entitled "The Six Days of Creation in a Twelfth Century Manuscript," Adelheid Heimann wrote that the female figure in question here "must be identified as the Virgin, through whom the work of the Creation was first fully consummated, in that she brought the Son of God into the world, redeemed the sin of Eve, and fulfilled the plan of Salvation." See *Journal of the Warburg Institute* 1 (1937–38): 274. Adelheid fails to identify a tradition in which the Virgin is represented, as the Bible represents Wisdom, as being present with God "before his works of old . . . or ever the earth was" (Prov. 8:22–23). In the light of these and similar biblical passages, several scholars have also identified as Wisdom the adolescent figure within the compass of God's left arm in the Creation of Adam on the ceiling of the Sistine Chapel. See Julian Klaczko, *Rome and the Renaissance: The Pontificate of Julius II*, trans. John Dennie (New York and London: G. P. Putnam's Sons, 1903), 292; and Geoffrey Ashe, *The Virgin* (London: Routledge and Kegan Paul, 1976), 29.
4. Codex 13, folio 155r. See Stylianos M. Pelekanidis, P. C. Christou, Ch. Psioumis, and S. N. Kadas, *The Treasures of Mount Athos: Illuminated Manuscripts* (Athens: Ekdotike Athenon, 1974), 2:272–74, fig. 422. Similar figures of Wisdom as inspiring muse appear in the depictions of Matthew (fol. 9r) and Mark (fol. 98r). See figs. 420 and 421 in Pelekanidis, *Treasures*.
5. See Hugo Buchthal, *The Miniatures of the Paris Psalter* (London: The

Warburg Institute, 1938), 25–27. I am indebted to Christine Kondoleon for directing me to this illumination.

6. See Marina Warner, *Alone of All Her Sex: The Myth and the Cult of the Virgin Mary* (New York: Alfred A. Knopf, 1976), 198.
7. On the history of the two books, see Ernst Robert Curtius, *European Literature and the Latin Middle Ages*, trans. Willard Trask (New York: Harper and Row, 1953), 310–26. On the history of the book of nature broadly conceived, see Ruth Wallerstein, *Studies in Seventeenth-Century Poetic* (Madison: University of Wisconsin Press, 1950), 30–36 and 204–31.
8. *The Advancement of Learning* 1.6.16, in Francis Bacon, *The Advancement of Learning and the New Atlantis*, ed. Arthur Johnston (Oxford: Clarendon, 1974), 42.
9. *Religio Medici* 1.16, in Sir Thomas Browne, *Selected Writings*, ed. Geoffrey Keynes (London: Faber and Faber, 1968), 20–21.
10. *Advancement of Learning*, 42.
11. John Calvin, *Institutes of the Christian Religion*, 1.5.11, 12, and 14, trans. Ford Lewis Battles (Philadelphia: Westminster, 1960), 1:63, 65, 68.
12. John S. Coolidge, *The Pauline Renaissance in England* (Oxford: Clarendon, 1970), 13.
13. Origen, *Contra Celsum*, trans. Henry Chadwick (Cambridge: Cambridge University Press, 1965), 434.
14. See his comment on Psalm 1:4 in *Selecta in Psalmos*, from *Selections from the Commentaries and Homilies of Origen*, trans. R. B. Tolinton (London: SPCK, 1929), 94–95. I am indebted to Steven Knapp for calling this passage to my attention.
15. Hugh of Saint Victor, *Eruditionis didascalicae liber septimus* chapter 4 and *De Arca Noe Morali* 2:12. See Migne, *Patrilogiae cursus completus. Series latina* 176:814, 643.
16. S. Bonaventurae, *Breviloquium* II, c. 5, in *Opera Omnia*, edita studio et cura pp. Colleggii a S. Bonaventura (Florentina, ad Claras Aquas, Quaracchi: 1891), 5:222.
17. From *Quaestio disputata de mysterio Trinitatis*, *Opera Omnia* 5:55.
18. Richard Greenham, *Works* (London: William Welby, 1612), 825.
19. See, for example, *Itinerarii Mentis in Deum*, *Opera Omnia* 5:298.
20. *Itinerarii Mentis in Deum*, *Opera Omnia* 5:302.
21. See Entzminger, *Divine Word*, 33–34, and Christopher, *Milton and the Science of the Saints*, 148–49.
22. *Breviloquium* II, c. 5. The translation is Ewert Cousins' in his *The Soul's Journey into God. The Tree of Life. The Life of St. Francis* (New York: Paulist Press, 1978), 73.
23. From the *Complete Prose Works of John Milton*, ed. Don M. Wolfe et al. (New Haven: Yale University Press, 1953), 6:296. Hereafter abbreviated as *CPW*.
24. G. K. Hunter, *Paradise Lost* (London: George Allen and Unwin, 1980), 65, 182.

25. C. A. Patrides has argued that the distinction between the Father and the Son is maintained in heaven, but beyond its confines Milton for the most part preserved "the unity of the Godhead." For Adam "the 'Presence Divine' is simply 'god'—the 'Author of this Universe,' 'Heav'nly Maker,' 'Creator,' 'Almighty.'" See "The Godhead in *Paradise Lost:* Dogma or Drama?" *JEGP* 64 (1965): 30, 33.
26. Michael Lieb, "Reading God: Milton and the Anthropopathetic Tradition," *Milton Studies* 25 (1989): 235. Lieb presents a powerful argument for the view that "for Milton, the emotional life of God is real and indeed holy" (231).
27. U. Milo Kaufmann, *The Pilgrim's Progress and Traditions in Puritan Meditation* (New Haven: Yale University Press, 1966), 240, 233, 34. On the subject of the priority Puritans gave to the sense of hearing see also Northrop Frye, "Agon and Logos: Revolution and Revelation," in *The Prison and the Pinnacle*, ed. Balachandra Rajan (Toronto: University of Toronto Press, 1973), 145–48, and Entzminger, *Divine Word*, 27–34.
28. John Calvin, *Institutes*, 5.19.340. Arthur E. Barker argued persuasively that after Milton's early high hopes for the Reformation faded, he found the Puritan view of human nature "negative and restrictive," by no means an "ideal integration of the claims of nature and grave [but] a segregation which denied the claims of nature." See *Milton and the Puritan Dilemma 1641–1660* (Toronto: University of Toronto Press, 1942), 17.
29. *CPW* 6:516.
30. *CPW* 2:270, 272; my emphasis.
31. "The First Defense," *CPW* 4.1:422–23.
32. "The readie and easie way to establish a free Commonwealth," *CPW* 8:412–13.
33. *CPW* 6:130.
34. *CPW* 6:132.
35. *CPW* 6:133; my emphasis.
36. *CPW* 6:136.
37. John R. Knott, *The Sword of the Spirit: Puritan Responses to the Bible* (Chicago: University of Chicago Press, 1980), 108–17.
38. *CPW* 6:578–80.
39. *CPW* 6:582–83; my emphasis.
40. *CPW* 6:583–84.
41. *CPW* 6:584.
42. *CPW* 7:242.
43. Herman Rapaport, *Milton and the Postmodern* (Lincoln: University of Nebraska Press, 1983), 210–12.
44. *CPW* 1:246–47, 292. The second passage includes a very Adamesque question about whether the purpose of the rapid motions and "intricate revolutions" of the sun and stars is "merely to serve as a lantern for base and slothful men." See *PL* 8.15–24 and 98–99.
45. *Milton and the Science of the Saints*, 176.
46. *Milton and the Science of the Saints*, 147–48. For a view roughly equidistant

between Christopher's and mine, see Hugh MacCallum, *Milton and the Sons of God: The Divine Image in Milton's Epic Poetry* (Toronto: University of Toronto Press, 1986), 133.

47. "Of True Religion," *CPW* 8:419. In "A Treatise of Civil Power" he wrote that "such things as belong chiefly to the knowledge and service of God" are "above the reach and light of nature without revelation from above" (*CPW* 7:242).

48. *Eikonoklastes, CPW* 3:505, 508.

49. Barbara Kiefer Lewalski, *Paradise Lost and the Rhetoric of Literary Forms* (Princeton: Princeton University Press: 1985), 202. I am taken by Lewalski's notion that in many instances Milton invites the reader to see his characters as devising the perfect prototypes of a variety of literary forms or genres—prototypes that surpass what from one point of view look like Milton's "sources" but from another are the poems of Adam and Eve's fallen progeny. See, for example, 39–43 and 185–202. Her argument is congruent with my own view of Adam and Eve as the creators of a "natural" liturgy that will later, in the hands of the church, become artificially constrained.

50. This prayer can be found in *Private Prayers, Put forth by Authority During the Reign of Queen Elizabeth*, ed. William Keating Clay (Cambridge: Cambridge University Press, 1851), 40. Translated from Ludovices Vives' *Preces et Meditationes Diurnae*, it appeared first in English in 1578 in *A Book of Christian Prayers Collected out of Aunciemt Writers*.

51. The prayers quoted on this and the following pages can be found both in Knox's Liturgy (*The Book of Common Order of the Church of Scotland*, ed. G. W. Sprott [Edinburgh: William Blackwood, 1901], 178–84), and in *Liturgies and Occasional Forms of Prayer set forth in the Reign of Queen Elizabeth*, ed. for the Parker Society (Cambridge: Cambridge University Press, 1847), 258–63.

52. From the Sarum breviary, or *Breviarum ad usum insignis ecclesiae Sarum*, ed. Francis Procter and Christopher Wordsworth (Cambridge: Cambridge University Press, 1879–86), fasc. 2:220.

53. The opening line of the hymn "Somno refectis artubus," Sarum breviary, 2:69.

54. From the hymn "Te lucis ante terminum," Sarum breviary, 2:224–25.

55. "Deus creator omnium," Sarum breviary, 2:220.

56. "Splendor Paternae gloriae," Sarum breviary, 2:88.

57. "Aurora jam spargit polum," Sarum breviary, 2:191.

58. "*Ab omnibus phantasmaticis daemonum illusionibus.*" From the "Ordo ad Facienda Sponsalia" of the Sarum Missal, reprinted in *Monumenta Ritualia Ecclesiae Anglicanae*, ed. William Maskell (Oxford: Clarendon, 1882), 77.

59. This and other quotations from the Elizabethan Prayer Book are from *The Book of Common Prayer, 1559*, ed. John E. Booty (Charlottesville: published for the Folger Shakespeare Library by the University of Virginia Press, 1976).

60. Fowler's note to lines 206–8 cites the hymn "Somno refectis artubus." See Sarum breviary, 2:69.

Chapter 3

1. See, in Book 12, lines 147–51, 232–35, 310–12, 368–71, 386–465.
2. Arthur Barker, "Structural Pattern in *Paradise Lost*," *Philological Quarterly* 28 (1949): 19–21.
3. For other "structures" see Michael Fixler, "Plato's Four Furors and the Real Structure of *Paradise Lost*," *PMLA* 92 (1977): 952–62; Galbraith J. Crump, *The Mystical Design in Paradise Lost*, (Lewisburg, Pa.: Bucknell University Press, 1975); J. R. Watson, "Divine Providence and the Structure of *Paradise Lost*," *Essays in Criticism* 14 (1964): 148–55; Fowler's introduction to his edition of *PL*, 22–25; and John T. Shawcross, *With Mortal Voice: The Creation of Paradise Lost* (Lexington: University Press of Kentucky, 1982), chapters 5 and 6.
4. See Isabel Gamble MacCaffrey, *Paradise Lost and "Myth"* (Cambridge: Harvard University Press, 1959), 56–68; and Shawcross, *With Mortal Voice*, 49–53.
5. See Fowler's note on these and the preceding lines.
6. In "Milton's Hostile Chaos: 'and the sea was no more'," *ELH* 52 (1985): 337–74, Regina Schwartz makes a powerful case for Chaos as the true antagonist of the good in *Paradise Lost:* "In his quest for beginnings...Milton is thrust back again and again to *the* Beginning. And for all its disturbing implications, the chaos he finds there is far more hostile than he would acknowledge in prose" (339).
7. Geoffrey Hartman, "Milton's Counterplot," *ELH* 25 (1958): 1–12.
8. Fuller, *Kinesthetic Vision*, 15–20.
9. See Sanford Budick, *The Dividing Muse: Images of Sacred Disjunction in Milton's Poetry* (New Haven: Yale University Press, 1985), 97.
10. On this theme see Schwartz, "Milton's Hostile Chaos," 340ff. See also, in *Paradise Lost*, 2.134–42 and 11.683–87. Milton relies heavily on this law of nature in the divorce tracts. In *The Doctrine and Disciplines of Divorce*, for example, he asks, "What can be a fouler incongruity, a greater violence to the reverend secret of nature, then to force a mixture of minds that cannot unite, & to sowe the furrow of mans nativity with seed of two incoherent and uncombining dispositions" (*CPW* 2:270).
11. On the relationship between echo and allusion in these passages in Book 2 see John Hollander, *The Figure of Echo: A Mode of Allusion in Milton and After* (Berkeley and Los Angeles: University of California Press, 1981), 41–44.
12. Mary Nyquist, "The Father's Word/Satan's Wrath," *PMLA* 100 (1985): 187–202.

Chapter 4

1. Isabel MacCaffrey, "The Theme of *Paradise Lost,* Book III," in *New Essays on Paradise Lost,* ed. Thomas Kranidas (Berkeley and Los Angeles: University of California Press, 1969), 61.
2. The Father's anger at his children is similar to the divine anger in the prophetic writings. See, for example, the Lord's "I have nourished and brought up children, and they have rebelled against me.... Woe to the rebellious children... that take counsel, but not of me; and that cover with a covering, but not of my spirit, that they may add sin to sin" (Isa. 1:2, 30:1); and "Have I not prayed you as a father his sons, as a mother her daughters, and a nurse her young babes, That ye would be my people, and I should be your God?... I gathered you together, as a hen gathereth her chickens under her wings: but now, what shall I do unto you? I will cast you out from my face" (2 Esd. 1:28–30).
3. See also Psalms 8:3–6, 26:7, 71:17, 72:18, 75:1, 78:32, 86:10, 119:27.
4. See also Ecclus. 18:4–6 and 43:31–32.
5. See Joseph Hall, *The Arte of Divine Meditation* (London, 1607), 15; Lewis Bayly, *The Practise of Pietie Directing a Christian how to walke that he may please God* (1611?), 11th. ed. (London, 1619), 239; Richard Baxter, *The Saint's Everlasting Rest* (1649), (Newcastle upon Tyne, 1819), 278; *Christian Prayers and Holy Meditations as well for private as public exercise* (1566), ed. Henry Bull, reprinted for the Parker Society (London, 1842), 61–72.
6. Thomas Taylor, *Meditations, From the Creatures* (London, 1629), 39.
7. William Riggs, *The Christian Poet in Paradise Lost* (Berkeley and Los Angeles: University of California Press, 1972), 25–26.
8. Stephen Wigler, "The Poet and Satan Before the Light: A Suggestion about Book III and the Opening of Book IV of *Paradise Lost,*" *Milton Quarterly* 22 (1978): 59.
9. *Poet of Exile,* 107–8.
10. Thomas Merrill, *Epic God-Talk: Paradise Lost and the Grammar of Religious Language* (Jefferson, N.C.: McFarland and Co., 1986), 60.
11. *Prophetic Milton,* 152.
12. See, for example:

    > the more I see
    > Pleasures about me, so much more I feel
    > Torment within me, as from the hateful siege
    > Of contraries; all good to me becomes
    > Bane, and in heaven much worse would be my state.
    > But neither here seek I, no nor in heaven
    > To dwell, unless by mastering heaven's supreme;
    > Nor hope to be my self less miserable
    > By what I seek....
    >
    > (9.119–27)

13. For a subtle reading of the soliloquy less trusting than my own, see Stein, *Art of Presence,* 69–77.

14. See Raleigh, *Milton*, 139, and John Carey, "Milton's Satan," in *The Cambridge Companion to Milton*, ed. Dennis Danielson (Cambridge: Cambridge University Press), 139–40.
15. *Epic God-Talk*, 60.
16. Patricia A. Parker, *Inescapable Romance: Studies in the Poetics of a Mode* (Princeton: Princeton University Press, 1979), 134–35.
17. On Milton's refusal to deny freedom of choice to Satan, see Keith W. F. Stavely, "Satan and Arminianism in *Paradise Lost*," *Milton Studies* 25 (1989): 125–39.
18. In his notes on this passage Fowler objects, for example, to Satan's attributing "second thoughts" to God on the grounds that "an omniscient and provident God cannot be said to make mistakes or to correct them." Since the events of the poem are narrated in time, however, the reader is given the *impression* that the Father's plans develop in response to changing circumstances. See 7.150–56. The Son, too, had at least conceived of the possibility of the Father's making a mistake. See 3.150–66. Fowler also finds "contempt" in Satan's use of the word "officious," a "sophistical style," and "confusion of thought." The parallels Fowler cites between Satan's thought and Raphael's, however, seem to me greatly to outweigh the unsubstantiated "charges." See also Budick, *Dividing Muse*, 86: "When he fixes his gaze on the earth, everything else must be diminished to it. . . . All the heavenly bodies must now be seen as pointing to earth, and as existing purposefully for earth, into which they are further and further collapsed, until finally they are concentrated in a focus of dominion that is, for Satan, necessarily a reflection or projection of his all-reflecting self."
19. *Kinesthetic Vision*, 176.
20. A. J. A. Waldock, *Paradise Lost and Its Critics*, (Cambridge: Cambridge University Press, 1947), 81–82.
21. Introduction to *Modern Critical Interpretations: John Milton's Paradise Lost*, ed. Harold Bloom (New York: Chelsea House Publishers, 1987), 7.
22. *Modern Critical Interpretations*, 3.
23. *A Milton Encyclopedia*, ed. William B. Hunter, Jr., et al. (Lewisburg, Pa.: Bucknell University Press, 1979), 7:166–67.
24. See Waldock, *Paradise Lost and Its Critics*, 77; Davis P. Harding, *The Club of Hercules: Studies in the Classical Background of Paradise Lost* (Urbana: University of Illinois Press, 1962), 40–42; Balachandra Rajan, *Paradise Lost and the Seventeenth Century Reader* (London: Chatto and Windus, 1947), 94–96; Douglas Bush, *Paradise Lost in Our Time* (Ithaca: Cornell University Press, 1945), 65; Stanley Fish, *Surprised by Sin: The Reader in Paradise Lost* (Berkeley, Los Angeles, and London: University of California Press, 1967), 1–22; C. S. Lewis, *A Preface to Paradise Lost* (1942) (New York: Oxford University Press, 1965), 95–99; and John M. Steadman, *Milton's Epic Characters: Image and Idol* (Chapel Hill: University of North Carolina Press, 1959), 227–77.
25. See Catherine Belsey, *John Milton: Language, Gender, Power* (Oxford: Basil

Blackwell, 1988), 85–92, and Kenneth Gross, "Satan and the Romantic Satan," in *Re-membering Milton*, 337. Gross writes: "Satan is Milton's picture of what thinking looks like, an image of the mind, of subjectivity, of self-consciousness, a representation of the awkward pressures we put on ourselves to interpret our own situation within the mind's shifting circle of freedom and compulsion."

26. See Johnson's "Life of Milton" in *Lives of the English Poets*, ed. George Birkbeck Hill (Oxford: Clarendon, 1905), 1:189, and Milton's *The Reason of Church-Government Urg'd Against Prelaty*, CPW 1:817.
27. *Surprised by Sin*, 6.
28. Arnold Stein, *Answerable Style: Essays on Paradise Lost* (Minneapolis: University of Minnesota Press, 1953), 124–25.
29. *Paradise Lost in Our Time*, 70.
30. For a similar view of the effects of Milton's similes in Book 1, see Hartman, "Milton's Counterplot," 1–12.
31. *Iliad* 19.371–80, trans. A. T. Murray (London: William Heinemann, 1925).
32. These quotations are from Arnold Stein, "Satan's Metamorphoses: The Internal Speech," *Milton Studies* 1 (1969): 96; Thomas Wheeler, *Paradise Lost and the Modern Reader* (Athens, Georgia: University of Georgia Press, 1974), 99; and Waldock, *Paradise Lost and Its Critics*, 77.
33. Jon S. Lawry, *The Shadow of Heaven: Matter and Stance in Milton's Poetry* (Ithaca: Cornell University Press, 1968), 137.
34. *Answerable Style*, 5.
35. John Peter, *A Critique of Paradise Lost* (New York: Columbia University Press, 1960), 42.
36. See *Of the Laws of Ecclesiastical Polity* 1.7.6,1, 1:172, 169.
37. A. C. Bradley, *Shakespearean Tragedy* (London: St. Martin's, 1903), 28. Helen Gardner reaches a similar conclusion about Satan's tragic stature, comparing him not only to Macbeth but to Dr. Faustus and Beatrice-Joanna. We respond to Satan, she says, with "awe and pity"—awe because of his "heroic and stupendous enterprises," and pity because of his "enormous pain and loss," his progressive degeneration, and his inability to repent. See her *A Reading of Paradise Lost* (Oxford: Oxford University Press, 1965), appendix A.

Chapter 5

1. *On Poetry and Poets*, 178.
2. *On Poetry and Poets*, 178.
3. Northrop Frye, *The Return of Eden: Five Essays on Milton's Epics* (Toronto: University of Toronto Press, 1965), 31.
4. Roy Daniells, "A Happy Rural Seat of Various View," in *Paradise Lost: A Tercentenary Tribute*, ed. Balachandra Rajan (Toronto: University of Toronto Press, 1969), 4.
5. As Anne Ferry has observed, it is the narrator, not Satan, who guides us.

See *Milton's Epic Voice: The Narrator in Paradise Lost* (Cambridge: Harvard University Press, 1963), 51.
6. *A Preface to Paradise Lost,* 49.
7. *On Poetry and Poets,* 178.
8. Helen Gardner, *A Reading of Paradise Lost* (Oxford: Oxford University Press, 1965), 41.
9. See Stein, *Answerable Style,* 65, and Roland Mushat Frye, *Milton's Imagery and the Visual Arts: Iconographic Tradition in the Epic Poems* (Princeton: Princeton University Press, 1978), 224.
10. These adjectives come from Fish, *Surprised by Sin,* 136; Maureen Quilligan, *Milton's Spenser: The Politics of Reading* (Ithaca: Cornell University Press, 1983), 94; Robert Crosman, *Reading Paradise Lost* (Bloomington: Indiana University Press, 1980), 95; and Christopher Ricks, *Milton's Grand Style* (Oxford: Clarendon, 1963), 110.
11. *Reading Paradise Lost,* 92. A. Bartlett Giamatti noted, "if the garden is to be a true reflection of the first couple, it must . . . include that potential for change, change for the better or change for the worse, which is part of their nature." See *The Earthly Paradise and the Renaissance Epic* (Princeton: Princeton University Press, 1966), 299.
12. John R. Knott, *Milton's Pastoral Vision: An Approach to Paradise Lost* (Chicago: University of Chicago Press, 1971), 42–43.
13. Paul Alpers, "The Milton Controversy," in *Twentieth Century Literature in Retrospect,* ed. Reuben A. Brower, Harvard English Studies 2 (Cambridge: 1971), 276.
14. Joseph Addison, Papers 412 and 417 of *The Spectator,* ed. Donald F. Bond (Oxford: Clarendon, 1965), 3:541, 542, 566.
15. See, for example, Fish, *Surprised by Sin,* 92–93, and Crosman, *Reading Paradise Lost,* 101–2.
16. William Kerrigan and Gordon Braden, "Milton's Coy Eve: *Paradise Lost* and Renaissance Love Poetry," in *Modern Critical Interpretations,* ed. Bloom, 149.
17. This point is made forcefully by Anne Ferry, *Milton and the Miltonic Dryden* (Cambridge: Harvard University Press, 1968), 106–7.
18. Christine Froula, "When Eve Reads Milton: Undoing the Canonical Economy," *Critical Inquiry* 10 (1983): 326–29.
19. Ferry, *Milton's Epic Voice,* 171, 169, 173.
20. *Paradise Lost,* 181.
21. For a development of this idea along different but parallel lines see Diane McColley, "Subsequent or Precedent? Eve as Milton's Defense of Poesie," *Milton Quarterly* 20 (1986): 132–36. See also her "Eve and the Arts of Eden," in *Milton and the Idea of Woman,* ed. Julia M. Walker (Urbana: University of Illinois Press, 1988), 107–8.
22. If we are concerned with the question of whether there are seasons in our sense of the word before the Fall, we should keep in mind that birds such as the "prudent crane" were created "intelligent of seasons," and migrate annually. See 7.425–31.

23. *Milton's Epic Voice*, 32.
24. *Selected Writings*, 19–20.
25. On the importance of moments of transition in *Paradise Lost*, and of evening in particular, see Parker, *Inescapable Romance*, 114ff.
26. Leland Ryken, *The Apocalyptic Vision in Paradise Lost* (Ithaca: Cornell University Press, 1970), 3–4.
27. For a detailed study of Milton's use of various translations of Genesis and his departures from them, see Ernst Haublein, "Milton's Paraphrase of Genesis: A Stylistic Reading of *Paradise Lost*, Book VII," *Milton Studies* 7 (1975): 101–25.
28. The King James translation reads, "All things were made by him; and without him was not any thing made that was made. In him was life; and the life was the light of men" (John 1:3–4). The Latin text (Jerome) reads "3.omnia per ipsum facta sunt et sine ipso factum est nihil *quod factum est* 4.in ipso vita erat et vita erat lux hominem." It makes considerable difference, however, if the italicized clause is seen as ending the preceding sentence or beginning the following one. In the latter case one might translate the passage as follows: "All things were made by him; and without him nothing was made. Whatever was made, in it was life, and the life was the light of men." Both ways of punctuating *quod factum est* exist in early Latin translations, including some editions of Junius-Tremellius, as well as in Greek manuscripts, where the equivalent phrase is ὃ γέγονεν. Reading the clause with the following sentence emphasizes the life that was in all things, as does the NEB translation: "all that came to be was alive with his life."

Chapter 6

1. Like the epigraph to chapter 6, this passage is from "The Form of Marriage" in *The Book of Common Order of the Church of Scotland*, ed. G. W. Sprott (Edinburgh: William Blackwood, 1901). The instruction is based on 1 Cor. 7:5.
2. Arnold Stein, *Answerable Style*, 102; Beverly Sherry, "Speech in *Paradise Lost*," *Milton Studies* 8 (1975): 260.
3. *Surprised by Sin*, 231, 238.
4. Mary Nyquist, "Reading the Fall: Discourse and Drama in *Paradise Lost*," *English Literary Renaissance* 14 (1984): 199–229.
5. Dennis Burden, *The Logical Epic: A Study of the Argument of Paradise Lost* (Cambridge: Harvard University Press, 1967), 88.
6. *The City of God* 14.10, trans. Philip Levine, Loeb Classical Library (Cambridge: Harvard University Press, 1966), 4:321.
7. As Fish says, "The decision to separate is unfortunate, but not fatal. Separation no more assures the Fall than staying together would *certainly* have prevented it" (*Surprised by Sin*, 231).
8. *CPW* 2:514–15.
9. See, for example, John S. Dieckhoff, "Eve, the Devil, and the *Are-*

opagitica," *Modern Language Quarterly* 5 (1944): 429–34; Burden, *The Logical Epic,* 88–89; and Leopold Damrosch, Jr., *God's Plot and Man's Stories: Studies in the Fictional Imagination from Milton to Fielding* (Chicago: University of Chicago Press, 1985), 108.

10. In Adam's dream (8.295–314) it is not specified that the fruit which "hung to the eye / Tempting, [and] stirred in [him] sudden appetite /To pluck and eat" is the forbidden fruit. But the phrase recalls the "he plucked, he tasted" of Eve's dream, and anticipates the serpent's "to pluck and eat my fill / I spared not," and the narrator's description of Eve's act: "she plucked, she eat." We are apparently invited to think of Adam's dream as embodying an instructive temptation to sinful indulgence, instigated by God, analogous to Eve's. Both dreamers awake to be set straight by a guide. God immediately informs Adam about the presence, among the trees of Paradise, of the one tree whose fruit he is not to taste.

11. *Surprised by Sin,* 238.
12. *Answerable Style,* 102.
13. *The Logical Epic,* 89.
14. Joseph H. Summers, *The Muse's Method: An Introduction to Paradise Lost* (Cambridge: Harvard University Press, 1962), 174.
15. For a superb account of Eve's syllogistic and Adam's axiomatic logic in their conversation see Joan S. Bennett's chapter on "Milton's Antinomianism and the Separation Scene in *Paradise Lost*" in her *Reviving Liberty: Radical Christian Humanism in Milton's Great Poems* (Cambridge: Harvard University Press, 1989). She treats the scene as "a concentrated exploration of the antinomian experience" in which Milton addresses the question, "How do genuinely righteous persons fall?" (109). Adam lacks the patience, she argues, to enable Eve to develop an understanding of "the whole picture." His command to "go" "allows Eve to reduce 'obedience' to its merely logical, or legalistic, meaning" (114–17).

Three other excellent studies of the scene are Thomas H. Blackburn, "'Uncloister'd Virtue': Adam and Eve in Milton's Paradise," *Milton Studies* 3 (1971): 119–37; Diane McColley, "Free Will and Obedience in the Separation Scene of *Paradise Lost*" *SEL* 12 (1972): 103–20; and Mary Nyquist, "Reading the Fall," 199–229.

16. *Reviving Liberty,* 111.
17. *Milton and the Science of the Saints,* 160, 159.
18. "Reading the Fall," 219.
19. I owe this observation to Nyquist, "Reading the Fall," 221.
20. Diane Kelsey McColley, *Milton's Eve* (Urbana: University of Illinois Press, 1983), 198.
21. "Reading the Fall," 221.
22. See the serpentine questions in Francis Quarles' *Emblems, Divine and Moral* (Halifax, 1851), book 1, emblem 1.
23. Fowler translates "author unsuspect" as "informant not subject to suspicion." The word "author" may simply mean "authority," i.e., the source

of authoritative information. But in a poem where, in each of its other fourteen uses, "author" clearly refers to the creator or originator of something, I doubt that any reader would suppress that meaning in this case. When Eve calls the serpent "author unsuspect," I suspect that she simply means that she hadn't suspected (i.e., imagined) it to be the author or giver of good.

24. *CPW* 6:394–95.
25. *Answerable Style,* 102.
26. *Surprised by Sin,* 229.
27. On an abstract level, Eve's plea to Adam resembles Lady Macbeth's arguments to her husband. Lady Macbeth tries to confuse Macbeth's sense of "what may become a man" by telling him that he was a man when he dared to do the deed, and that "to be more than what you were, you would / Be so much more the man." Eve thinks of the serpent as having attained a sort of manhood, and of herself as "growing up to Godhead." Both, that is, pervert the hierarchical order which is portrayed as natural in the worlds they inhabit. What is masterful in both scenes is the refusal to dramatize either husband's decision as the product of his wife's arguments. The relationship between the woman's logic and the man's decision is indeterminate and hence mysterious (in sharp contrast, say, with Iago's elaborate, step-by-step deceptions of Othello), even though both Macbeth and Adam enact their wives' intentions.
28. See, for example, Ferry, *Milton's Epic Voice,* 60: "His speech is moving, passionate, romantic, but it is never deceived. . . . His choice is to die *with* Eve, not *for* her, and already his passion is a kind of beautiful self-concern."
29. *Surprised by Sin,* 262.
30. *The Doctrine and Discipline of Divorce, CPW* 2:245–46.
31. *The Logical Epic,* 165.
32. *Surprised by Sin,* 263.
33. Helen Gardner puts the matter well in *A Reading of Paradise Lost,* 91: "Having insisted that the mutual love of man and woman is the highest earthly good, that to be 'imparadis'd in one another's arms' is the 'happier Eden,' and that in our fallen world the source of 'Relations dear and all the Charities' is to be found in wedded love, Milton gives to Adam a motive it impossible not to sympathize with, and that sets in the clearest possible light the meaning of the ancient story."
34. *Milton's Epic Voice,* 62.
35. *Milton's Epic Voice,* 62.
36. *Answerable Style,* 110. See also Summers, *The Muse's Method,* 181; Burden, *The Logical Epic,* 172; J. M. Evans, *Paradise Lost and the Genesis Tradition* (Oxford: Clarendon, 1968), 286; Burton Jasper Weber, *The Construction of Paradise Lost* (Carbondale: Southern Illinois University Press, 1971), 225; and Thomas Wheeler, *Paradise Lost and the Modern Reader* (Athens: University of Georgia Press, 1974), 82–83.
37. Numbers 14:13–18. See also Genesis 18:23–25 and Exodus 32:11–13.

On the relevance of these passages to the Son's speech, see John E. Parish, "Milton and an Anthropomorphic God," *Studies in Philology* 56 (1959): 619–25, and Michael Lieb, "*Paradise Lost*, Book III: The Dialogue in Heaven Reconsidered," *Renaissance Papers* (1974): 39–50.

38. Based on the claim that Adam "assert[s] that no price will have to be paid for man's disobedience," and on the fact that, whereas the Son offered his life to save Man, Adam lacked "the imagination to offer his life for Eve," John Leonard calls his lines "a demonic parody." But I find no such assertion in Adam's lines. And it was the Father, not the Son, who "imagined" the idea of "some other" paying "the rigid satisfaction, death for death" (3.211–12). See *Naming in Paradise: Milton and the Language of Adam and Eve* (Oxford: Clarendon, 1990), 226–27, 220.
39. *Answerable Style*, 113–14.
40. *CPW* 2:602–3.
41. *The Logical Epic*, 163. See also 151–52, 166–67.
42. *Tetrachordon, CPW* 6:379.
43. *CPW* 6:379.
44. *The Laws of Ecclesiastical Polity* 5.73.3, 2:391.
45. "The Idea of Nature in Milton's Poetry," 250.
46. "On the Good of Marriage," trans. C. L. Cornish, *Nicene and Post-Nicene Fathers*, ed. Philip Schaff (Buffalo: Christian Literature Company, 1887), 3:399. For the Latin text, see Migne, *Patrilogiae cursus completus. Series latina*, 40:373.
47. *The City of God*, 14.1, 4: 247. My translation.
48. *The City of God*, 12.12, trans. Levine, 4:111.
49. On this point see Waldock, *Paradise Lost and Its Critics*, 47.
50. *The City of God*, 14.11, trans. Levine, 4:331. On the relevance of this passage to Milton's view of the Fall see A. B. Chambers, "The Falls of Adam and Eve in *Paradise Lost*," in *New Essays on Paradise Lost*, ed. Thomas Kranidas (Berkeley and Los Angeles: University of California Press, 1969), 118–30.

Chapter 7

1. *CPW* 6:383–84.
2. *CPW* 6:396, 394.
3. *The Works of John Milton*, ed. Frank Allen Patterson et al., (New York: Columbia University Press, 1931–38), 15:358; hereafter cited as Columbia *Works*.
4. See, for example, Martin Luther, *Lectures on Romans*, trans. Walter G. Tillmanns, in Luther's *Works*, ed. Hilton C. Oswald (St. Louis: Concordia Publishing House, 1972), 25:20, and Giovanni Diodati, *Pious and learned annotations upon the Holy Bible* (London, 1648).
5. See, for example, *PL* 8.499, 604; 9.958–59, 967; 12.603.

6. C. S. Lewis, *Mere Christianity* (London: Fontana Books, 1970), 16.
7. *CPW* 6:453, 466, 471, 457, 462, 463.
8. Dennis Richard Danielson, *Milton's Good God: A Study in Literary Theodicy* (Cambridge: Cambridge University Press, 1982), 71.
9. C. A. Patrides, *Milton and the Christian Tradition* (Oxford: Clarendon, 1966), 213.
10. John Spencer Hill, *John Milton: Poet, Priest, and Prophet* (London: MacMillan, 1979), 131.
11. *Milton and the Christian Tradition*, 205.
12. Hill, *Poet, Priest, and Prophet*, 131.
13. See *PL* 3.330–80, 11.61–66, 12.458–65.
14. *CPW* 6:397.
15. *Surprised by Sin*, 19, 272. See also Anne Ferry's *Milton and the Miltonic Dryden*, 103: "Because he postpones this repetition of the doctrinal explanation until after Eve's redemptive gesture and Adam's conversion, Milton encourages us to conceive of the turning point of the drama in human terms."
16. See William Haller, *The Rise of Puritanism* (New York: Columbia University Press, 1938), chapter 2. The writers cited on the following pages who were affiliated with Christ's College are William Ames (1576–1633), Arthur Hildersam (1563–1632), William Perkins (1558–1602), Richard Rogers (1550?–1618). Other Cantabridgensians are Thomas Gataker (1574–1654), Richard Greenham (1535?–1594?), Thomas Hooker (1586?–1647), Richard Sibbes (1577–1635).
17. William Perkins, *The Workes of that Famous and Worthy Minister of Christ... Mr. Williams Perkins* (London: John Leggatt, 1612–13), 2:178.
18. Richard Sibbes, *The Soules Conflict with it selfe, and victory over it selfe by Faith*, 3d. ed. (London, 1636), 51.
19. Edmund S. Morgan, *Visible Saints: The History of a Puritan Idea* (Ithaca: Cornell University Press, 1963), 68–69.
20. On the "preparationist" theology in England and America, see Norman Pettit, *The Heart Prepared: Grace and Conversion in Puritan Spiritual Life* (New Haven: Yale University Press, 1966). On Protestant meditation see also Louis Martz, *The Paradise Within: Studies in Vaughan, Traherne, and Milton* (New Haven: Yale University Press, 1964), 23, and Barbara Kiefer Lewalski, *Protestant Poetics and the Seventeenth-Century Religious Lyric* (Princeton: Princeton University Press, 1979), 149. I am greatly indebted to Lewalski's chapter on Protestant meditation, and to Frank Livingston Huntley's introduction to his *Bishop Joseph Hall and Protestant Meditation in Seventeenth-Century England* (Binghamton, N.Y.: Center for Medieval and Early Renaissance Studies, 1981).
21. *Protestant Poetics*, 150.
22. Thomas Hooker, *The Soules Implantation* (1637), 11.
23. Hooker, *The Soules Preparation for Christ. Or. A Treatise of Contrition. Wherein is discovered How God breakes the heart, and wounds the Soul, in the Conversion of a Sinner to Himselfe*, 6th. ed. (London, 1643), 126, 130.

24. *Works*, 1:462.
25. William Ames, *Conscience withe the Power and Cases Thereof* (1639), book 2, chapter 4, and book 1, chapter 11.
26. *Works*, 1:408.
27. Arthur Hildersam, *The Doctrine of Fasting and Praier, and Humiliation for Sinne* (London: E. Brewster, 1633), 113, 119.
28. Richard Rogers, *Seven Treatises* (London, 1616), 263–64.
29. *CPW* 6:392.
30. See also Job 33:6 and Isa. 45:9.
31. On this point see *Surprised by Sin*, 273.
32. *Seaven Treatises Containing Such direction as is Gathered out of the Holie Scriptures, Leading and Guiding to true happinesse* (London, 1610), 12. The phrase "endless woes" is commonplace in this context both before and after Milton. There is a folk carol dating back at least to the first half of the nineteenth century that includes the following verses:

> Then after this, 'twas God's own choice
> To place them both in Paradise,
> There to remain from evil free
> Except they ate of such a tree.

> But they did eat, which was a sin,
> And thus their ruin did begin;
> Ruined themselves, both you and me,
> And all of their posterity.

> Thus were we heirs to endless woes,
> Till God the Lord did interpose....

See "The Truth Sent from Above" in *English Folk Carols*, ed. Cecil J. Sharp (London: Novello and Co., 1911), 47.
33. *CPW* 6:400–403.
34. *Doctrine of Fasting*, 126.
35. In verse 15 of Psalm 38 the psalmist writes, "For in thee, O Lord, do I hope: thou wilt hear, O Lord my God." See also Psalms 46:1, 7, 11; 48:3; 57:1; 59:16; 62:7, 8.
36. Richard Greenham, *Works* (London: William Welby, 1612), 704.
37. *Works*, 164.
38. Milton, *Doctrine and Discipline of Divorce*, *CPW* 2:251.
39. *The Faerie Queene* 1.9.52–53, ed. A. C. Hamilton (London: Longman, 1980).
40. Greenham, *Works*, 175.
41. Thomas Gataker, *The Spiritual Watch, Or Christs Generall Watch-word. A Meditation on Mark. 13. 37* (1619), 48.
42. Sibbes, *The Soules Conflict with it selfe*, 49.
43. Joan Mallory Webber, *Milton and His Epic Tradition* (Seattle: University of Washington Press, 1979), 136–37.
44. The precise phrase "strength and stay" does not occur in the King James

Version, but it does occur in the Sternhold and Hopkins metrical translation of the first verse of Psalm 81.
45. Summers, *The Muse's Method*, chapter 7. Patrides, referring to this episode, went so far as to say that "it is not Adam but Eve to whom God's grace is initially 'put forth'" (*Milton and the Christian Tradition*, 211).
46. *Seaven Treatises*, 235.
47. See Luke 1:42, 44 and John 16:21.
48. Greenham, *Works*, 825.
49. My emphasis. I am indebted to Ilona Bell for pointing out the relevance of Herbert's sonnet.
50. *Doctrine of Fasting*, 127.
51. *Surprised by Sin*, 145–46.
52. *Art of Presence*, 136.
53. This view is forcefully expressed by Edward M. Tayler in his *Milton's Poetry: Its Development in Time* (Pittsburgh: Duquesne University Press, 1979), 84.

Chapter 8

1. Quoted in Fowler's edition, 3–4.
2. Two helpful and systematic treatments of knowledge and wisdom in *Paradise Lost* are Howard Schultz's *Milton and Forbidden Knowledge* (New York: Modern Language Association, 1955), 157–83, and John M. Steadman, *Milton and the Renaissance Hero* (Oxford: Clarendon, 1967), 43–77. Neither Schultz nor Steadman, however, notes Milton's heavy reliance on Scripture. For an excellent survey of the classical, Christian, and Renaissance treatments of wisdom see Eugene F. Rice, Jr., *The Renaissance Idea of Wisdom* (Cambridge: Harvard University Press, 1958).
3. For Milton's reluctance to identify the Holy Spirit, see *Christian Doctrine*, *CPW* 7:281–98. In *Christian Doctrine* Milton discusses wisdom and prudence as the two general virtues which belong to the understanding, a traditional pairing which may be traced back at least as far as Proverbs 8:12: "I wisdom dwell with prudence." Milton defines wisdom as "the virtue by which we earnestly search out God's will, cling to it with all diligence once we have undertood it, and govern all our actions by its rule" (*CPW* 7:647).
4. I am indebted to James H. Sims, *The Bible in Milton's Epics* (Gainesville: University of Florida Press, 1962), with its helpful index of biblical references; to Mollenkott's New York University dissertation, "Milton and the Apocrypha"; and to Fowler's useful and learned footnotes in his edition of *Paradise Lost*. For a helpful summary of Milton's attitude toward and use of the Apocrypha see Mollenkott's article "Apocrypha and Pseudepigrapha" in *A Milton Encyclopedia*.
5. See, for example, Proverbs 1:2–5, 4:1, 13; Wisdom 6:17; Ecclesiasticus 1:27.
6. *Before and after the Fall.*

7. *Of the Laws of Ecclesiastical Polity* 2.1.4, 1:236.
8. Cicero, *De Officiis* 1.4, 6, trans. Walter Miller (London: William Heinemann, 1913), and *Tusculan Disputations*, trans. J. E. King (London: William Heinemann, 1927) 5.4.10–11.
9. Augustine, *Enchiridion*, trans. Ernest Evans (London: SPCK, 1953) V, 16.
10. *Milton and Forbidden Knowledge*, 177.
11. This tradition has been traced by J. M. Evans in *Paradise Lost and the Genesis Tradition* (Oxford: Clarendon, 1968), 69–77. Evans quotes (28–29) a pertinent passage from the Ethiopic Book of Enoch, where "the tree of wisdom" has a "goodly fragrance" that "penetrates afar." Raphael points it out to the narrator, saying, "This is the tree of wisdom, of which thy father old [in years] and thy aged mother, who were before thee, have eaten, and they learnt wisdom and their eyes were opened, and they knew they were naked and they were driven out of the garden."
12. "Textual Overlapping and Dalilah's Harlot-Lap," in *Literary Theory/Renaissance Texts*, ed. Patricia Parker and David Quint (Baltimore: Johns Hopkins University Press, 1986), 343.
13. Du Bartas, Guillaume de Salluste, "Urania: or the Heavenly Muse," in *Bartas: His Devine Weekes and Works*, trans. Joshua Sylvester (Gainesville: Scholars' Facsimiles and Reprints, 1965), 530.
14. 1.43, 157.
15. Wisdom's "lovable and humanitarian character" in The Wisdom of Solomon is also stressed by William B. Hunter and Stevie Davies in "Milton's Urania: 'The Meaning, Not the Name I Call,'" in Hunter's *The Descent of Urania: Studies in Milton, 1946–1988* (Lewisburg, Pa.: Bucknell University Press, 1989), 31–45.
16. On the comedy in Book 8 see Robert H. Bell, "'Blushing like the morn': Milton's Human Comedy," *Milton Quarterly* 15 (1981): 47–54.
17. *The Spectator* (no. 345), ed. Donald F. Bond (Oxford: Clarendon, 1965) 3:287.
18. Du Bartas, 276.
19. *Milton and the Miltonic Dryden*, 99ff.

Chapter 9

1. Louis Martz has suggested that Michael's forward look into human history was intended as an ironic contrast to "the history of the rise of Rome that Ovid presents in the closing books of the *Metamorphoses*" and to the last book of Camoens' *Lusiad*, with its delineation of "the past and future glories of the Portuguese empire." *Poet of Exile*, 156. But Virginia R. Mollenkott has pointed out that "Milton had a great deal of Apocryphal precedent for his birds'-eye view of history in order to bring hope." She cites II Esdras 1–2; Judith 5:6–21; Wisd. 10–12; and Ecclus. 44–50. See her *Milton and the Apocrypha*, 214ff.
2. Michael's brief diatribe against "idol-worship" ["O that men / (Canst thou believe?) should be so stupid grown . . . As to forsake the living God, and

fall / To worship their own work in wood and stone / For gods!" (12.115–20)] may owe something to the thirteenth and fourteenth chapters of *The Wisdom of Solomon*, which treat of the origins of idol-worship, including the carving of piece of wood into "the image of a man" or of "some vile beast" and praying to it, and the ascribing "unto stones and stocks the incommunicable name." Michael's comment on Cain's descendants—"Studious they appear / Of arts that polish life, inventors rare, /Unmindful of their maker, though his Spirit / Taught them" (11.609–12)—is reminiscent of Solomon's comment on the potter who "striveth to excel goldsmiths and silversmiths ... and counteth it his glory to make counterfeit things.... He knew not his Maker, and him that inspired into him an active soul, and breathed in a living spirit" (Wisd. 15:9–11).

3. See Crosman, *Reading Paradise Lost*, 216–48; Summers, *The Muse's Method*, 196–222; Mary Ann Radzinowicz, "'Man as a Probationer of Immortality': *Paradise Lost* XI-XII," in *Approaches to Paradise Lost*, ed. C. A. Patrides (Toronto: University of Toronto Press, 1968), 37–51; H. R. MacCallum, "Milton and Sacred History: Books XI and XII of *Paradise Lost*," in *Essays in English Literature from the Renaissance to the Victorian Age Presented to A. S. P. Woodhouse*, ed. Millar MacLure and F. W. Watt (Toronto: University of Toronto Press, 1964), 160–68; Wittreich, *Visionary Poetics*, 188ff.; Fuller, *Kinesthetic Vision*, 229–42; Swaim, *Before and after the Fall*, chapters 1 and 2; and Marshall Grossman, *"Authors to Themselves": Milton and the Revelation of History* (Cambridge: Cambridge University Press, 1987), 161–76.
4. *CPW* 6:589, 587.
5. Regina Schwartz, "From Shadowy Types to Shadowy Types: The Unendings of *Paradise Lost*," *Milton Studies* 24 (1988): 124.
6. "Shadowy Types," 125.
7. *Paradise Regained* 2.205–6; see also Matt. 12:42.
8. Collatio 15, para. 3, from *Collationes in Hexaemeron, Opera Omnia* 5:409.
9. *Poet of Exile*, 155.
10. *CPW* 5.1:4.
11. Columbia *Works*, 12:93–95.
12. *CPW* 1:519.
13. *CPW* 5.1:xxvii.
14. *Before and after the Fall*, 13.
15. See note 3 above.
16. Columbia *Works*, 12:164; my translation.
17. *Milton's Spenser*, 240–41.
18. The *Aeneid* 2.701., Virgil's *Opera*, ed. R. A. B. Mynors (Oxford: Clarendon, 1969). Anchises speaks these words to the gods of his fathers, then, three lines later, turns to Aeneas and says, "*Cedo equidem nec, nate, tibi comes ire recuso*"—I yield, and do not, my son, refuse to go in your company.
19. *Poet of Exile*, 186.

Appendix A

1. "The Singer and His Song in the Prologues of *Paradise Lost*," in J. Max Patrick and Roger H. Sundell, eds., *Milton and the Art of Sacred Song* (Madison: University of Wisconsin Press, 1979), 68–69.

Appendix B

1. Augustine, *Confessions*, 10.6, trans. William Watts (1631) and corrected for the Loeb Library edition (London: William Heinemann, 1912), 2:87. I have included in brackets the more literal rendering of Augustine's *decus temporis* to emphasize the similarity not apparent in Watts' "the order of times."

Index

Adam: "better knowledge" of, and the Fall, 151–54; 159–68; compared to Macbeth, 154; effect of Fall on, 227–30; effect of Michael's history on, 250–54; Eve's effect on, 13–14, 152–54; fall of, 154–59; friendship of, with Raphael, 223–26; and the interpretation of nature's works, 13–15, 119–21, 210–13, 236–39; soliloquy of, as Protestant meditation, 180–90; speaking Scripture, 242–50. *See also* Adam and Eve; Divine Wisdom

Adam and Eve: condition of, before and after the Fall, 139, 176–80; contrasted, 109–14, 118–21; conversion of, 181, 190–203; fall of, and Paul's Letter to the Romans, 169–76; separation of, 133–43. *See also* God's Word, Book of; Liturgy

Addison, Joseph, 109, 226
Alpers, Paul, 108
Ames, William, 183, 190
Aristotle, 251
Arminius and Arminianism, 34, 177–81
Augustine, Saint, 137, 165–67, 213, 216, 267–69

Bacon, Sir Francis, 21, 24
Barker, Arthur E., 54
Baxter, Richard, 76
Bayly, Lewis, 76

Belsey, Catherine, 85
Bennett, Joan S., 142, 283n.15
Bloom, Harold, 84
Bonaventure, Saint, 27–29, 40, 250
Braden, Gordon, 111
Bradley, A. C., 97–98
Browne, Sir Thomas, 21, 120
Budick, Sanford, 279n.18
Bull, Henry, 76
Burden, Dennis, 137, 140, 157, 164
Bush, Douglas, 85, 87

Calvin, John, and Calvinism, 19, 24, 34, 40, 177, 181
Castiglione, Count Baldassare, 14
Christopher, Georgia B., 40–42, 143
Cicero, 213, 222
Coolidge, John S., 25
Creatures, the: Adam's and Eve's appreciation of, contrasted, 112–13, 118–23; Adam's reading of, after the Fall, 236–39; idolatry as worship of, 27, 58–59, 149, 170–71, 217; reader's difficulty visualizing, 99–109; Satan's wonder at, 69–84. *See also* Adam; Nature's works, Book of; Satan
Crosman, Robert, 107

Daniells, Roy Harvey, 100
Danielson, Dennis, 177
Divine Wisdom: and Adam's fall, 217–220; attributes of, 19–21, 206–7; Cicero and Augustine on,

294 / INDEX

213; compared with Spenser's Sapience, 15; and the creation, 19–20; and Eve's fall, 214–17; and forbidden knowledge, 207–14; and friendship with the gods, 221–23; in Milton's drafts for a tragedy, 205; Raphael and Michael as embodiments of, 123–26, 152–55, 208–14, 231–50; and Urania, 220–22; and the Word, 20–21
Du Bartas, 222, 226–27

Eden: fallen world's likeness to, 3, 16, 31, 119, 178–80, 257; heaven's likeness to, 16–17, 30–32, 123–25; increasingly sensuous descriptions of, 117–24; losing one's way in, 99–111, 114–16; meaning of loss of, 227–30; temptations of, as a virtue, 100, 107, 116
Eliot, T. S., 5, 99, 100, 103
Eve: and her conversion of Adam, 191–96; her dream, 121–23; lyricism and artistry of, 111–13, 118–19; and Narcissus, 113–14; Satan and the fall of, 142–50; wisdom of, in separation scene, 136–39. *See also* Adam and Eve

Fall: Augustine's account of, 167; effects of the, 28, 149–50, 169–76, 227–30; as a failure to listen, 33, 143; reasons for, 133, 140–49, 155–68
Ferry, Anne Davidson, 115, 119, 159, 160
Fish, Stanley, 85, 134, 140, 152–53, 156, 157, 180, 201–2
Fogle, French, 252
Fowler, Alastair, 50, 83, 119, 146, 279n.18, 284n.23
Froula, Christine, 114
Frye, Northrop, 100
Frye, Roland Mushat, 84–85, 107
Fuller, Elizabeth, 57, 83

Gardner, Helen, 106, 280n.37
Gataker, Thomas, 191
God's Word, Book of: Adam and Eve's collaborative interpretation of, 190–203; Adam's meditation on, 181–90; Bonaventure on, 27–28; as focus of Books 7–10, 52, 128–31, 143–49, 181–200; as focus of Book 12, 53, 239–50; as focus of Book 2, 59–67; Hugh of Saint Victor on, 27; Milton's ambivalence toward, 35–39; as motivating Satan's rebellion, 62–67; Origen on, 26; and Satan's deception of Eve, 144–49; sixteenth- and seventeenth-century attitudes toward, 19, 21–24, 33–42, 181–90; as supplementing nature's works, 28–30, 34; Wisdom and, 20–21
Greenham, Richard, 28, 189, 190, 191, 198
Gross, Kenneth, 279n.25

Hall, Bishop Joseph, 76
Harding, Davis P. 85
Hartman, Geoffrey, 56
Heaven: earth's and Eden's likeness to, 16–17, 30–32, 124–28; war in, and destruction of nature's works, 123–28
Heimann, Adelheid, 273n.3
Herbert, George, "The Holy Scriptures," 199–200
Hildersam, Arthur, 183, 189, 200
Hill, John Spencer, 178, 180
Homer, *The Iliad*, 93
Hooker, Richard, 19, 24, 97, 165, 208
Hooker, Thomas, 182
Hugh, of Saint Victor, 27
Hughes, Merritt, 119
Hunter, G. K., 30, 116

Johnson, Samuel, 5, 85

Kaufmann, U. Milo, 33–34

Kerrigan, William, 79–80, 111, 273n.8
Knott, John, 36, 108
Knox, John, 43, 44, 133

Leonard, John, 285n.38
Lewalski, Barbara Kiefer, 43, 182
Lewis, C. S., 85, 102, 176
Lieb, Michael, 32
Liturgy: Adam and Eve's construction of a, 42–50, 200–203; *Book of Common Order of the Church of Scotland*, 43, 44, 133; *Book of Common Prayer*, 42–43, 50, 202; "Occasional Forms of Prayer," 43; *Private Prayers, Put forth by Authority During the Reign of Queen Elizabeth*, 44; *Sarum Breviary*, 46–50
Loewenstein, David, 7
Luther, Martin, 40

MacCaffrey, Isabel, 70
McColley, Diane, 146
Madsen, William, 165
Martz, Louis, 4, 17, 77–78, 250, 256
Merrill, Thomas, 79, 81
Michael, as mediator and instructor in Wisdom, 208, 231–50
Milton, John: and Arminianism, 34, 177–80; biblical hermeneutics of, 35–39; in prologues to Books 3 and 7, 4, 117–18, 261–65; and the purpose and style of the genre of history, 250–54; and relationships among freedom, grace, merit, and good works, 177–81. Works: *Areopagitica*, 138; *Of Christian Doctrine*, 30, 35, 36, 37, 151, 165, 171, 173, 177, 180, 185, 188, 242–43; *Doctrine and Discipline of Divorce*, 35; 277n.10; *Of Education*, 1–2; *Eikonoklastes*, 43; *The First Defense*, 35; *History of Britain*, 250; *Paradise Regained*, 66, 77, 249; *Prolusions 3 and 7*, 39; *The Ready and Easy Way to Establish a Free Commonwealth*, 35; *Of Reformation*, 251; *Tetrachordon*, 164–65; *A Treatise of Civil Power*, 38; *Of True Religion*, 42
Mollenkott, Virginia M., 6
Morgan, Edmund S., 181

Nature and Scripture: compared, 19–30; and the structure of *Paradise Lost*, 51–68. *See also* God's Word, Book of; Nature's works, Book of
Nature's works, Book of: Adam's reading of signs in, 235–39; Bonaventure's metaphors for, 28–30; Calvin on, 24; destruction of, in heaven, 125–28; as focus of Book 11, 13, 52–53, 236–39; as focus of Book 1, 55–59; as focus of Books 3–6, 51–52, 69–84, 99–128; Hugh of Saint Victor on, 27; Milton's attitude toward, 34–35, 39–42; and *Of Education*, 1–2; Origen on, 25–26; Saint Paul on, 25; and Satan's deception of Eve, 144–46; sixteenth- and seventeenth-century accounts of, 24–29; as source of liturgy, 42–50; Spenser's rejection of, 11–15; and the third and seventh Prolusions, 39; Wisdom and, 19–20; and The Wisdom of Solomon, 26–27. *See also* Creatures, the
Nyquist, Mary, 62, 134, 145, 146, 219

Origen, 25–26
Ovid, 113–14

Paradise Lost, structure of, 4, 51–68, 128–29, 236–41, 261–65
Parker, Patricia, 82
Patrides, C. A., 177, 178
Perkins, William, 181, 182, 183
Peter, John, 96

Quilligan, Maureen, 255

Rajan, Balachandra, 85
Rapaport, Herman, 39
Raphael: as friend to Adam, 223–27; as mediator and instructor in Wisdom, 152–55, 208–14, 217–20
Riggs, William G., 77
Rogers, Richard, 184, 187, 197
Ryken, Leland, 125

Satan: compared to Macbeth, 97–98; and deception of Eve, 144–49; effect of creatures on, 16–17, 75–84; humanity of, in Book 1, 84–98; meditations of, on the creatures, 69–84, 126–27; rebellion of, against the Word; 62–66; as Spenserian platonist, 10–11; as testifying to God's goodness and justice, 77–79, 83, 86, 88–89
Schultz, Howard, 214
Schwartz, Regina, 243, 244, 277n.6
Shakespeare, William: *Macbeth*, 97, 154; "Venus and Adonis," 48
Sherry, Beverly, 133, 135
Sibbes, Richard, 181, 191–92
Sims, James H., 206
Son, The: and Adam's prelapsarian foreknowledge, 159–63; exaltation and begetting of, as provoking Satan's rebellion, 61–63; as image and Word of God, 30–32

Spenser, Edmund: *The Fairie Queene*, 191; "Fowre Hymnes," 3, 9–14
Steadman, John, 85
Stein, Arnold, 12, 13, 86, 87, 94, 106–7, 133, 140, 152, 160, 163–64, 201–2
Summers, Joseph, 140, 194
Sundell, Roger, 261
Swaim, Kathleen, 208, 253, 272n.9
Sylvester, Joshua, 277

Taylor, Thomas, 76

Urania, and Divine Wisdom, 15, 220–22, 226–27

Virgil, *Aeneid*, 255–56

Waldock, A. J. A., 84–85
Webber, Joan Mallory, 193
Wigler, Stephen, 77
Wisdom. *See* Divine Wisdom
Wisdom Literature, Biblical: Ecclesiastes, 191, 234, 253; Ecclesiasticus, 20, 74, 75, 208, 210, 214, 216–18, 225, 232, 247; Job, 74, 185, 188, 234; Proverbs, 206–8, 216, 218–22; Psalms, 20, 73, 74, 76; The Wisdom of Solomon, 20, 26–27, 74, 206–10, 212, 217, 222, 231–33, 249